Cambridge Studies in Social Anthropology

General Editor: Jack Goody

57

AGE CLASS SYSTEMS

D1524544

For other titles in this series turn to page 189.

Age class systems

Social institutions and polities based on age

BERNARDO BERNARDI

Translated from the Italian by David I. Kertzer

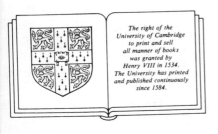

The right of the
University of Cambridge
to print and sell
all manner of books
was granted by
Henry VIII in 1534.
The University has printed
and published continuously
since 1584.

CAMBRIDGE UNIVERSITY PRESS

Cambridge
London   New York   New Rochelle
Melbourne   Sydney

Published by the Press Syndicate of the University of Cambridge
The Pitt Building, Trumpington Street, Cambridge CB2 1RP
32 East 57th Street, New York, NY 10022, USA
10 Stamford Road, Oakleigh, Melbourne 3166, Australia

First published in 1985

Printed in the United States of America

Library of Congress Cataloging in Publication Data
Bernardi, Bernardo.
Age class systems.
(Cambridge studies in social anthropology ; v. 57)
Bibliography: p.
Includes index.
1. Age groups.   2. Ethnology – Africa, Sub-Saharan.
3. Social structure.   I. Title.   II. Series: Cambridge
studies in social anthropology ; no. 57.
GN490.5.B46   1985   305.2′0967   84–29394
ISBN 0 521 30747 3 hard covers
ISBN 0 521 31482 8 paperback

For Lilly,
another flower

Contents

Contents

Contents

Contents

x

Translator's preface

Bernardo Bernardi is one of the pioneers of the anthropological study of formal age group systems. His dissertation work, under Isaac Schapera, in the early 1950s and his article "The age systems of the Nilo-Hamitic peoples," appearing in the journal *Africa* in 1952, helped catalyze research on this fascinating topic. This book represents a culmination of a lifetime of work, including many years spent among the peoples of southern and eastern Africa.

Although the nature of age group systems has become one of the classic issues in modern social anthropology, it has proved to be a complex and often elusive topic. There are a large number of individual case studies of African societies with formalized age groupings, but surprisingly few full-scale comparative analyses of such systems. The result is that substantial confusion is evident in discussion of these systems, as reflected in the treatment anthropologists give the subject in introductory textbooks (Kertzer 1978). Yet, paradoxically, despite the lack of suitable comparative and general materials on age group systems, an increasingly wide range of social scientists are citing such systems in connection with the expansion of scholarly interest in the process of aging. The fact that sociologists, for example, so often refer to Eisenstadt's (1956) secondary analysis of age group systems, although a tribute to the enduring value of that work, bespeaks the dearth of more up-to-date and accessible materials on the subject, despite the outpouring of individual ethnographic accounts of age group systems over the past three decades.

In this book, Bernardi helps us to make sense of the diversity of formal age group systems, to better appreciate their common features and the pattern of their differences. In so doing, he goes beyond the other recent overview of such systems, Stewart's (1977) *Fundamentals of Age-Group Systems*, which concentrates largely on the formal, structural properties of these systems. Bernardi is above all concerned with the role age groups play in different societies. In this, he takes issue with the major recent statement of African age group systems offered by Baxter and Almagor (1978). According to these prominent anthropologists, age group systems serve primarily ritual purposes and have but limited significance for people's social, political, and economic lives. Bernardi, developing the thesis he has been identified with since the early 1950s, and making use of the ethnographic evidence that has accumulated since then, rejects this argument and shows just how socially far-reaching age group systems are.

Bernardi currently heads the new department of anthropology at the University of Rome and is one of Italy's most prominent anthropologists. In addition to the international reputation achieved by his scholarly work, he has done a great deal to build bridges between Italian anthropology and the rest of the international scholarly community. The breadth of sources used in writing this book reflects in a small way the internationalization of anthropology toward which he has long worked.

Bernardi wrote this book in Italian (an Italian edition was published in 1984 by Loescher) and asked me if I would be interested in translating it. I suppose the combination of my interest in African age group systems and my knowledge of Italian made me a logical candidate, though I hardly consider myself expert enough in the Italian language to qualify as a professional translator. If this text is clear and the prose cogent, it is largely due to the help I received from Bernardi in the translation. He carefully read through all parts of the translation, answered my queries, and suggested revisions. It was a pleasure to collaborate with him in this process.

I worked on the translation during 1982–3, a year I spent as a fellow at the Center for Advanced Study in the Behavioral Sciences in Stanford, California. I would like to thank the staff at the center for its support of this project and especially note the assistance of Rosemary Martin in typing the manuscript. I would also like to thank the John D. and Catherine T. MacArthur Foundation for helping support my year at the center.

Since the translation of this book was a project I reserved for evenings and weekends, I owe a special thanks to my family for the time taken away from them. Without the support and understanding provided by Susan, Molly, and Seth, this translation could not have been undertaken or completed.

Bowdoin College   David I. Kertzer
Brunswick, Maine

Preface

My goal in these pages is to clarify the nature of age class systems and to identify their basic characteristics. The social and political organization set in motion by such systems is of a peculiar type: Through the classification of coevals into formal social groupings – that is, into age classes – it provides for the promotion of all members of a society along a scale of social gradation. Classes and grades within such systems have an institutional character. Those who become members of the same class are not necessarily coevals in the sense of their physiological age; rather, their grouping is based on the structural value attached to the idea of age, so that the recruits of the same period of time who form a single class are conceived of as if they were of the same age. Clearly, structural age is a species of relative and social age. (A glossary of terminology related to age class systems is found at the end of this book.)

By their institutional character, age classes and grades are distinguished from *informal age grades* – which are found in all societies as indicative categories (such as infancy, adolescence, etc.) – and from occasional *age groups* that, for various reasons, may be formed by coevals on the basis of their physiological age or on any other interpretation of the idea of age. The identifying characteristic of age class systems is the institutional relationship that exists between classes and grades: Once a class is formed, it proceeds through the grades of social promotion as a corporate body. As recruitment into an age class is generally restricted to males, I shall normally use masculine pronouns throughout the text.

My definition of age class systems is the result of a wide comparative analysis of the ethnographic evidence. This book, however, does not intend to be an exhaustive review of the entire literature; rather, it aims to demonstrate the social and political significance of age class systems. I have not attempted to describe the entire range of age class systems. References have been deliberately restricted to those systems deemed most useful in developing a series of models according to which age class systems might be distinguished. This series of models is not exhaustive. There is no doubt that more discussion and comparison will help to develop further the theoretical issues they raise.

In this context, it has been necessary to define better such basic concepts as

xiii

age, class, and grade, concepts normally used in a generic and often contradictory way. In the process of describing and comparing the models, the distribution and rotation of power have emerged as the main social and political characteristics of age class systems. Within these systems, the concept of power cannot be identified with mere political power, as this appears to be just one of the various forms in which power is distributed and exercised; rather, power must be seen as a more general and comprehensive concept. The apparent ethnographic relationship between acephalous societies and age class systems must also be explained. Indeed, this link is not coincidental; the relationship is due to the fact that the distribution and rotation of power, caused by age class systems, may not coexist with any political system where power is personally accumulated and centralized.

This book is organized in three parts. The first, Chapters 1 through 3, deals with preliminary concepts, the geographical distribution of age class systems, and the anthropological approach to their study. The second part, Chapters 4 through 11, describes the ethnographic models of these systems and examines the problem of the position of women. The third part, Chapters 12 and 13, attempts to portray the ethnemic relationship between these systems and the other elements of social structure and, finally, to approach the problem of contacts and transformations through which age class systems have been forced to pass.

My interest in the study of age class systems goes back to the now distant time when, in Cape Town, South Africa, I wrote my doctoral dissertation on the age systems of the Nilo-Hamitic Peoples under the direction of Isaac Schapera. I am delighted to express, once again, my esteem for him, my teacher and friend. Later, in Kenya, from 1953 through 1959 and on occasional return visits, I had the opportunity to observe and study the surviving aspects of age class systems among the Meru, the Embu, the Kikuyu and, on occasion, among the Masai, the Samburu, and the Rendille. I only briefly visited the Oromo Boran of Kenya.

In the past decade, stimulated by the publication of new ethnographic material, I took up once again my study of these systems in both my teaching activities and in various seminar presentations. I am grateful to those friends and colleagues who invited me to discuss this subject at their institutions. I would like to thank in particular Jack Goody, who, through the British Academy, provided me with the opportunity for a study trip to Cambridge in May 1978; Emrys C. Peters, Paul Baxter, and David Turton of the Department of Social Anthropology at Manchester University, where, as Simon Fellow, I conducted two seminars in March 1979; and David I. Kertzer, chairman of the Department of Sociology and Anthropology at Bowdoin College in Maine, where I spent 1979–80 on leave from the University of Bologna as Tallman Visiting Professor. In May 1980, I gave seminars on the concept of power in age class systems at the Department of Anthropology of the University of Chicago and at the University of California at Santa Barbara. For these two seminars, I would like to thank

Preface

Terence Turner and Valerio Valeri of Chicago and David Brokensha of Santa Barbara. After I had completed the draft of this book, I was invited to conduct a seminar on the "models of age class systems" at the Ecole des Hautes Etudes en Sciences Sociale in Paris. I would like to thank Isac Chiva, who was responsible for my invitation, as well as all my other French friends and colleagues for their contribution to the discussion, especially Claude Tardits, Marc Augé, and Pierre Bonte. It is difficult to say how much I owe to all these encounters; certainly, through the discussions we had, I was able to form a more "systematic" vision of the entire problem; various parts of this book were originally drafted on these occasions.

A warm thanks to my Italian colleagues and good friends, Italo Signorini, Antonio Colajanni, and Francesco Remotti, with whom I have had frequent occasions to discuss the issue of age class systems through the various phases of writing and revision of this book. Finally, I would like to thank in a very special way my friend David Kertzer, whom I have already mentioned, for the trouble he has so generously taken and so furbishly accomplished in translating into English my original Italian, thus allowing the possibility of a contemporary publication of my book in two languages.

University of Rome "La Sapienza"   Bernardo Bernardi
Rome, Italy

1

Characteristics of age class systems

The relativity of the age concept

To examine age class systems, we must evaluate a concept of age that is alien to our Western social tradition. In Western societies, we do not find such groupings of age mates, designed to govern the participation of individuals in social and political life. Age is employed conceptually to define certain categories of persons, but it is not used as a basis for constructing the societal structure. Groups of conscripts may, perhaps, exhibit some similarity, but here we are dealing with voluntary associations that are more or less temporary and are, in any case, used almost exclusively for recreational purposes.

In both current usage and in historical tradition, the Western concept of age seems ambiguous and fluid. At one time, for example, medieval medicine distinguished the physiological development of human beings into "climacterics," or seven periods of seven years each. Today, no one views the life course in these terms. We celebrate birthdays, with happiness in childhood and with sadness in old age, but there are those who prefer to ignore them, or, indeed, to conceal their date of birth. We speak very broadly of a first, second, and third age, and we distinguish a series of grades that signal the passage from the one to the other, but without giving them too much weight. As a matter of necessity, we endorse the legal establishment of the "age of majority," as we think it just that all adults are guaranteed certain inalienable rights of individual autonomy. We also approve of a law that fixes the obligation of school attendance on the basis of age and, similarly, an age-based selection for military service. Yet once these milestones have been passed, transitions that anthropologists list as being aspects of enculturation and socialization, we do not give much weight to age. Rather than age, we now uphold the principle of "merit" as we put up with the ambiguities of fortune. The retirement system, signaling the passage from the second to the third age, is more closely linked to the number of years in the work force than to age of physiological development, and the results are therefore extremely varied and even contradictory. Nor are we greatly interested in the kinds of age groupings of the population found in censuses, other than for their statistical value. In fact, our social and political system runs largely on other principles, not on that of age.

The variety of conceptual interpretations of age for social purposes, as shown by anthropological research, is very large indeed: Age class systems, the subject of our analysis, are one conspicuous example. This polysemic pliability of the concept of age may be a cause, however, of conceptual ambiguity and confusion. As it is, we look for the age of everything and of everybody: of the cosmos and the earth, of things and beings. We try to discover their origin and calculate their end. These two terms, origin and end, birth and death, serve as the two poles for measuring age. The criteria of measurement, however, may change according to the different nature of the subject under measurement.

We normally distinguish between physiological and cultural criteria, taking the first to be more objective because we base them on natural indices. However, it is only through our cultural consciousness that we are able to evaluate them. In other words, the very idea of age, as we use it, is a cultural product. It is just because age is a cultural concept that it is apt to be assigned a relative value and used for social purposes.

Age class systems afford a very special instance of relative age. Within such systems, age assumes a preeminent role as a principle of social structure. Members of society come to be classified into special groupings by being assigned a common age and, thus, by forming a collective body of age mates with special prerogatives and specific tasks. It is for this reason that age classes have acquired, in the anthropological literature, the precise reference to institutionalized groupings. Thus, age classes, where they exist, are not informal groupings; rather, they are essential parts of the social structure.

Age grades within age class systems

Age class systems are distinguished from any other age system by the special relationship between age classes and age grades. Such a relationship is the basis for the special structure of age class systems. The two concepts, classes and grades, may not be disconnected within the context of age class systems, though, however intimately connected, they must be distinguished to clarify their significance. To this end, it is also useful to distinguish between formal and informal grades. It is only formal grades that are institutionalized in relationship with age classes, thus becoming one of the determining factors of the age class systems. In ordinary language, we don't normally make such a distinction, and we are inclined to describe any grouping of coevals in terms of age grades or age classes indifferently. It is a way of speaking that needs rectification if we wish to clarify the specific character of age class systems.

Informal grades possess only an approximate and indicative value: childhood, adolescence, youth, etc. Normally, no precise term is used to signal the passage from one informal grade to another. The indications may vary from culture to culture, and they may change according to new situations. In Italy, for example, the English word *teenagers* has recently become part of current usage to indicate a certain attitude in the behavior of adolescents. Only a few cases of informal grades are fixed by law in all Western systems: Examples are the age of majority and the age of pension, when the law makes the attainment of such a grade somehow compulsory. It happens thus that informal grades are superimposed by institutionalized grades.

It is such superimposition that has been a cause of great confusion in ethnographic writings, hindering the understanding of age class systems. We find a typical example of this in the first ethnographies of the Masai. Though those early writers perceived the importance of age grades, they did not realize the differences between formal and informal characteristics. A comparison of their reports provides sufficient evidence. Johnston (1902:827) distinguished three grades: young boys, warriors, and old men. Merker (1910:66) listed five:

1. *ol aijioni* pl. *ol aijiok* – up to circumcision;
2. *os siboli* pl. *es sibolo* – up to the time of the healing of the circumcision;
3. *ol barnoti* pl. *el barnot* – during the time of induction into the life of a warrior;
4. *ol morani* pl. *el moran* – fully organized warriors;
5. *ol moruo* pl. *el moruak* – married men until death.

Hollis (1905:28), in the glossary of his work, entered four grades:

1. *engeru* pl. *in-gera* – child
2. *o-sipolioi* pl. *i-sipolio* – the recluse;
3. *ol-barnoti* pl. *il-barnot* – the saved ones;
4. *ol-murani* pl. *il-muran* – the warriors.

These series have almost nothing in common with the age class system of the Masai (see Chapter 4).

The formation of class and promotion in terms of grades are two aspects of the same phenomenon of formal institutionalization: The recruitment of candidates to a class implies, in fact, their promotion to an initial age grade. Thus the relationship that is set in motion by recruitment and promotion not only brings about the structure of a special grouping; it also implies the chronological succession of classes in the grades, so that the emerging structure is rightly called an "age class system."

Every grade corresponds to a social position, that is, a status with special prerogatives acquired by a class as a right, which, in any case, is only a temporary right. In fact, after a definite period a class is expected to abandon the grade and leave it for the following class. The series of grades is thus conceived as a potential acquisition of rights by all the classes, and its very conception serves as a propeller to the succession of classes in the grades.

Class formation and grade promotion imply a differentiation beween succeeding classes, and such a differentiation is brought to bear on continuous classes in terms of antagonism aimed at catalyzing the normal succession from the younger to the senior grade. Thus, the interrelationship between classes and grades is what we call an age class system. In every such system, there is found: (1) the formal institution of classes; (2) the configuration of promotional grades; and (3) the succession of the classes in the grades. It is thus evident that, when we refer to grades as one of the fundamental factors of age class systems, the reference is to institutionalized age grades and not to informal ones.

Where age class systems are at work, the attainment of a grade and its relative status confer the juridical right that regulates participation in social life. Promotion to a grade, therefore, is not simply a nominal passage; it also implies the legitimation to take certain social actions. Even where grades are only informal, there may exist some relationship between grades and social rights. But in such cases, except where a special law is applied (as in the case of majority age or pensionable age), the relationship is not compulsory but a very loose one. Besides, social recognition of the status that accrues to one by informal grades is normally attained individually, whereas, in the case of institutionalized grades the attainment is formal, ritual, and corporate: It is the class as such that is promoted to the grade and, consequently, all its members obtain the rights connected with its relative status.

The corporate promotion of a class does not mean that the transition involves the physical presence of all members of that class. A gathering of all members of a class is not only a rare event; often enough, it is not even possible, especially among sparsely settled pastoral populations living among their far-flung herds, covering a vast territory. In any case, the ritual celebration of promotional passages takes up a symbolic value and involves all members in a corporate way even if they are not physically present.

Rites of promotion and principles of recruitment

The formal institutionalization of age classes takes place through the celebration of rites of passage of the candidates on the basis of two principles: either the public recognition of the candidates' physiological maturation with the celebration of postpubertal initiation, or the determination of the generational distance between each candidate and his father. These are the two principal rules of recruitment into age classes. It is important to note that recruitment into a class also represents a social promotion because it is connected to the assignment of an age grade and, with it, of a certain status with accompanying rights. In this way, the succession of age classes through the grades, the age class system itself, becomes the mechanism of social promotion.

The principle of recruitment is thus a good criterion for distinguishing among age class systems. The variety of forms in which that principle is expressed may also be seen in the rites of recruitment. We distinguished between promotional rites and initiation rites, both of which are part of the larger category of rites of passage. Initiation rites normally have an individualistic character, in the sense that each candidate must undergo them. Promotional rites, on the other hand, even though they may be carried out by official representatives of the class, alter the status of all class members and, for this reason, can be called corporate rites.

Undergoing the prescribed rites during the same period makes the candidates involved coevals. They become age mates. Evidently, what ties them together is not physiological age, but rather relative age as determined by their having participated in the rites of passage in the same period. Relative age thus becomes social age, based on membership in the same class and expressed in the status proper to the grade acquired by the class.

Celebration of rites of passage connected to age class systems takes place according to established norms of time. The celebration of postpubertal rites, in particular, is scheduled in such a way as to allow all candidates to undergo them, for these must be performed by each and everyone. There are times in which such initiation ceremonies are permissible and periods in which they are not. The successive performance through time of these ceremonies forms the basis of particular groupings of age mates – or initiation units – that are incorporated, in varying degrees of salience and permanence, within each class. What is important to note is that the rites of passage thus constitute the mechanism of recruitment of the members into a class and the factor determining their common social age.

Initiation and generation, as I have just hinted, are the two basic principles of class recruitment. Initiation (and I mean by this here postpubertal initiation) involves the public recognition of a physiological fact that makes an adult out of an adolescent. Generation stresses the relationship that is formed at birth between an individual and his or her parents. Despite their apparent diversity, there are certain similarities between the two concepts, as shown by the fact that both serve to create similar social groupings – age classes – albeit in systems having different characteristics. To better flesh out these similarities, let us examine the two concepts in terms of birth.

As with all rites of passage, postpubertal initiation may be considered a birth: Before the initiation, the individual does not have any social recognition; he is not even considered a full person. Afterward, not only is he recognized as a responsible person, but he becomes a full part of the society and acts autonomously. In those age class systems that use initiation as the basis of recruitment, the social birth of the individual takes place with his entrance into an age class, among his age mates, and his attaining of the first grade that marks his social promotion. Classes formed in this way can appropriately be termed *initiation classes*.

The generational principle establishes a relationship between parents and their children based on genealogical birth. This relationship is normally expressed in terms of descendance. It is not descendance that interests us in age class systems, but rather the structural distance beween the father and his children. The distance between mother and children is not considered because, as we shall see, age class systems are largely patrilineal and masculine.

5

Age class systems

The recognition of the generational relationship between father and son is a sufficient basis for the social recognition of the son and his entrance into the age class system: It is through this entrance that the son participates in social activities with full rights. The generational relationship between father and son is expressed in the structural distance that separates and distinguishes them. Structural distance implies a chronological distance expressed with reference to the years that separate the father from the son within the system of classes, or simply with reference to the names of the classes involved. For example, among the Oromo of southern Ethiopia, the official distance between father and son is forty years, or five classes, with each class being promoted from one grade to another every eight years (the name of the class coincides with the name of the grade). Thus, the determination of generational distance is not a generic index (or nominal index), but it is ruled by a precise criterion dictated by the series of grades. In fact, the systems based on *generation classes* are always complex, just because of this rigidity.

The succession of the classes in the grades gives rise to the creation of a social stratification, represented by the classes existing at any one time and occupying the various social grades. It could be said, schematically, that the framework of gradations, formed by the totality of grades in each system, represents the ideal model of the social structure; the classes, on the other hand, represent the legitimate though temporary incumbents of each grade.

It is in the dynamic relationship of grades and classes that age class systems provide a framework for social organization. It is this feature that, although demonstrating the institutional value of age class systems, distinguishes them from all other kinds of age systems and from any other type of aggregation occasionally based on age. In addition to their mode of recruitment, age class systems differ among themselves by the way in which they create and maintain the social order. In the most typical cases, it is age class systems themselves that form the principal element of the social structure. In other cases, their value is secondary in the sense that they constitute just a structural element that is complementary and alternative, as happens, for example, among the Nuer, where the most important structural element is the kinship system.

However, it is important to note that age class systems do not operate in a cultural vacuum, nor are they dissociated from other elements of structural systems. On the contrary, they are bound in various ways, ritually and structurally, to territorial divisions, to kinship systems, and to the cosmological beliefs that almost always underlie associated rites of passage. One of the most important aspects of age as a structural principle is its efficiency in bringing about unity; in situations where other social elements produce division, age can produce unity. When age is employed for structural ends, it does not know territorial boundaries nor divisions based on kinship. Indeed, paradoxically, because its ultimate end is death, age is mystically placed beyond all age, as when it creates a link to the ancestors beyond time.

6

Characteristics

The anthropemic value of age

The process by which the elements of nature are transformed into elements of culture is very complex. It is fundamentally brought about by choices from among possible alternatives of cultural evaluation. The same element of nature, such as age, may be used, as we have just said, in formal and informal ways. Such choices are normally made by single individuals or by groups of individuals, but they are always somehow influenced by the natural environment and by the time when they are made. They are also influenced by the reciprocity that relates individuals and groups among themselves. Individuals and groups, however, are the ones responsible for the choices; environment and time are mere points of reference for the choices. To describe such a process with a single word, we use the term *anthropeme*. By anthropemic value, I mean any conceptual evaluation of an element of nature in order to make use of it as a principle of cultural elaboration or of social structure. The bond between anthropemic choices and individuals, who always succeed themselves in time expressing new needs, explains the extraordinary variety by which the same natural elements are valued by all the peoples in the world in the countless forms of social organizations and cultural expressions.

The cultural evaluation of the idea of age characterizes all age systems generally and age class systems in a very special way. The same distinction of generic age systems and special age class systems is based on a cultural interpretation that affects the idea of age in the same way that occurs to any other element of nature when it is culturally evaluated. Age class systems differ among themselves by the way they apply the principles of recruitment and by the forms of their respective structures and functions. In the following pages, I shall distinguish, for such reasons, a series of models of age class systems.

All this is a typical reflex of the cultural complexity of the idea of age. It may be useful now to look deeper into the relationship introduced by the idea of age between "individual beings" and "time succession." The identification of an individual through time is only possible if we observe all changes and modifications he or she undergoes in maturing. Such an observation makes it possible to locate those points of reference – the before and the after – that afford the necessary poles for defining the chronological boundaries of the idea of age. Age, therefore, while serving to identify an individual as self, may also be used to mark his or her differentiation and the changes that may alter his or her being. It appears, thus, that movement and change are intrinsic to the chronological aspect of the idea of age. Indeed, age implies flowing and changing. As such, it differs from the idea of sex, which normally implies permanence: either male or female.

Age also implies succession: New individuals, by maturing, replace their elders: *Les enfants poussent.* The impulse to individual autonomy, brought about by maturation, is a physical as well as cultural and social necessity. The process

7

is not realized without tensions and conflicts. On reaching personal autonomy, individuals dissociate themselves from their parents and elders and tend to associate with their equals. Whenever tensions and conflicts arise, the matter of contention is the attainment of new positions for the youngsters so that they may be assured of their autonomy. It is in such a context that we may better realize the function of age class systems as instruments of social organization. They are devised to control and regulate the entire process by which individuals attain autonomy and take part in communal life, in the same way as kinship systems are devised to regulate the orderly descendance of offsprings and matrimonial alliances.

The peculiarity of age class systems consists in using age as a principle of social organization: On that basis, individuals are classified, the relationships between the classes and their particular functions are defined, and the norms for keeping tensions in check and curbing conflicts are passed and applied.

Some definition of time is a basic requirement for any age classification. All age class systems respond to this requirement, although they differ in the way they apply it. By being classified together, class members are equated as coevals, and this chronological equation means they share the same social status. In this way, every age class takes up its own identity as a class and is thus distinguished from any other class that has existed before or will follow it. Identification and succession of classes are normally expressed in terms of age grades, which define their specific functions at a particular time.

It is important to note that the concept of class, as an aggregation of age mates, does not coincide with the concept of generation. The overlapping of the two concepts is apt to occur whenever we speak in terms of "class of the fathers" and "class of the sons." In fact, the very concept of generation is rather fluid, and even in the context of age class systems it may take on different meanings. We have already seen how one of the two main principles of recruitment in those systems is the idea of generation (in the sense of the structural distance between fathers and son). In such systems, it would be logical to expect a perfect coincidence between the concept of class and generation. But that is not exactly what happens, because, as we shall see, the rigidity of generational systems makes recruitment into a class a rather complicated business. In the other systems, the generational relationship between father and son is not structurally applied, and it may only affect indirectly the interested persons through the relationship that binds their respective classes.

Lastly, it is worth stressing one final aspect of the anthropemic value of age, that regarding the possibility of expressing the promotional push, intrinsic to the age concept, in terms of right and of power. A maturing youth wants to affirm himself and his own personality. He aspires to taking on his own social life, whether by getting married and establishing his own home, or owning the means of production necessary to support himself and his family. He is eager, in the same way, to take part in communal decisions and in all social activities.

Characteristics

Age class systems are unique, for not only do they regulate the attainment of individual maturity or autonomy, but they regulate the distribution and rotation of all forms of power.

Physiological age and structural age

The anthropemic choices regarding age bring up the distinction found, in ethnographic reality, between physiological age and structural age. These two are but aspects of relative age and social age.

Physiological age is responsive to the measurement of the physiological development of an individual, or the calculation of the time passed from his or her birth to the present. In Western systems, this calculation no longer depends on the simple observation of the person's physiological development, but on the application of an autonomous method of measuring time, namely, the calendar, with the years calculated on the basis of the recurrence of a certain day in a certain month. In these cases, the birthday is accompanied by traditional observances. Yet, regardless of how solemn and communal such birthday celebrations may be, their significance is simply personal and individual. It is only in the event that the person in question occupies an institutional position of authority, as in the case of a king, that these celebrations take on greater structural and social significance.

Structural age is characterized by its institutional impact. It is evaluated in relationship to the degree of integration into social life and the grades of successive promotion in society. This concept is analogous to the "structural time" analyzed by Evans-Pritchard. He maintains that the Nuer "think much more easily in terms of activities and of successions of activities and in terms of social structure and of structural differences than in pure units of time" (1940a:104).

A similar phenomenon is found in the concept of structural age. The age of an individual is not measured in relation to the stages of his or her physiological development, but in relation to the social activities that are consigned to the individual. It could be said that structural age measures the juridical capacity of the individual to perform certain social activities.

In every age system, the concept of structural age has its distinguishing connotations. For example, in Western systems, the attainment of the right to vote is an index of the structural age of a person. In age class systems, structural age is reached with the individual's entrance into the class structure and is measured with his progressive advance along the line of social gradation.

In societies having age class systems, it is only structural age that is important; physiological age is ignored. There are age class systems in which the person enters at the moment of birth, but here it is not the physiological aspect that is the determining element, but rather the existing structural situation that allows the immediate assignment to the newborn of a structural position within the age class system. An illustration of this point is provided by the system of the Oromo

9

Boran of southern Ethiopia. There the rule is that the son's entry into the age class system, known as *gada*, can take place only at five grades distance from the grade of his father. Because each of the grades has a span of eight years, the rule is that entrance into the system can take place only forty years after that of the father. If this distance already exists at the time of the son's birth, the son can be immediately entered into the system and, from that moment, his age will be calculated on the basis of the activities consigned to him by the position he occupies in the succession of grades.

In age class systems, structural age can also be defined as the relationship existing between class and grade. The person enters the system with his recruitment into a class; he progresses through the system by traveling, together with all fellow members of his class, through the grades of social promotion.

The articulation between class and grade, the dynamic characteristic of age class systems, brings with it something of a semantic equivalence between the two concepts; indeed, they seem to be almost synonymous. To say that someone "belongs to a certain class" can mean that he has the right to take part in certain activities because his class occupies the grade responsible for such activities. To say that the same person "belongs to a certain grade" can mean the same thing because that grade, in that moment, is occupied by the class to which the individual in question belongs. Such equivalence of the two concepts is the cause of a great deal of confusion in the ethnographic literature, which can be avoided by keeping their basic distinction in mind.

2

The anthropological study of age class systems

Before attempting the comparative analysis of the various age class systems and their models, it may be useful to sketch the systems' geographical distribution and briefly review the anthropological approach to their study.

I must first admit that even today we do not have an exhaustive ethnographic picture of societies with age class systems. In describing the development of the anthropological studies of such systems, I do not intend to evaluate critically all that has been written on the subject. Rather, my intent is to identify the major issues raised in the study of age class systems.

The geographical distribution of age class systems

The kind of social organization represented by age class systems is not very widely distributed ethnographically, but it is not rare by any means. In reality, recognition of the specific structure and significance of these systems was slow in coming.

Although the first news of an age class system goes back to the end of the seventeenth century and involved one of the most interesting and complex systems, the *gada* system of the Oromo Galla, the institutional nature of the system was not appreciated. Difficulty in interpretation was augmented by the fact that age class systems were always found together with an acephalous society, with these acephalous societies only being understood and studied rather late in the day. The most recent research projects and analyses have painted a composite ethnographic picture that has been extended to all continents. We here provide some indication of our current knowledge of the geographical distribution of these age class systems. The list should be considered as a basis or orientation for the reader rather than as an exhaustive listing.

We begin with Africa, which has always been considered the part of the world richest in age class systems. These are found, above all, in the vast territory of East Africa that includes the Sudan, Ethiopia, Uganda, Kenya, and Tanzania.

11

Age class systems

In the Sudan are found various Nilotic and Nilo-Hamitic* populations, such as the Nuer, the Dinka, the Bari, and the Latuka. In southern Ethiopia, aside from the numerous groups of Oromo (often better known by the name of Galla), are the Konso, who are sedentary horticulturalists, and the numerous ethnic groups that form small cultural enclaves that gravitate around the Oromo, such as the Dassenetch and the Mursi. In northern Kenya, where the Oromo Boran extend, there are other small groups found in the same territory, including the Gabbra and the Rendille. Between Kenya and Uganda live a number of related Nilo-Hamitic people, primarily engaged in herding, where age classes have, or had, full-scale development. These include the Turkana, the Karimojong, the Jie, the Dodoth, and the Topotha. In Uganda, forms of age class systems are also found among the Labwor and the Lango.

Lewis (1961: 25) reports of the Somali that "the Digil and Rahanwiin tribes . . . from the Galla temporarily copied their system of military age-grades. In much the same way the trans-Juban Daarood briefly adopted the Galla age-set system and like the Rahanwiin later relinquished it."

In the borderlands of Kenya and Tanzania, an age class system is found among the Masai, who are pure pastoralists. In northern Kenya, it is found among the Samburu, themselves pastoralists related to the Masai. In northern Tanzania, an age class system is even today organized by the Arusha, a pastoral Masai people who became sendentary agriculturalists. Similarly, the Parakuyo of the Western Bagamoyo District of Tanzania, who are predominantly but not exclusively pastoral, hold strongly to their age class system, which is of the same model as that of all other Maa-speaking peoples.

Before the colonial period, age classes were fully followed among the Kalenjin peoples of western Kenya: the Pokot (Suk), the Kipsigis, and the Nandi. They were also fully practiced among the Bantu-Hamitic agriculturalists of Kenya and, particularly, among the Kikuyu, the Embu, the Mbeere, the Meru, and the Kamba. Among all these peoples, the system was progressively abandoned during colonial rule; today it is virtually extinct.

An age class system was also found in Kenya among the riverine Bantu of the Tana, and among the Pokomo and the Giriama, not to mention the Bantu of Lake Victoria, the Gusii, the Kuria, and the Zanake.

In southern Tanzania, the case of the Nyakyusa has become famous due to their so-called age villages. The Nyakyusa are Bantu agriculturalists of the mountains around Lake Malawi.

In central Africa, various forms of residence based on generational age have been recorded for the Ndembu of Zambia and the Lele of Kasai in Zaire. Among

* Though Nilo-Hamites and Bantu-Hamites are old terms (see Baumann 1940: 201–12, 222) they are still meaningful and as satisfactory as their possible substitutes, Nilo-Cushites and Bantu-Cushites (see Ehret 1974: 151). The latter have never been used as such in the current literature.

12

the other peoples of this region, almost all matrilineal, the age system presents none of the institutional forms that characterize age classes.

In southern Africa, age class systems were extraordinarily well developed among the Nguni in the period of large-scale migration at the beginning of the past century. They served to reinforce the military organization found within the various Nguni groups and account for the surprising military efficiency of these populations. With the coming of colonial occupation, the Nguni separated, forming various ethnic groups scattered around southern Africa. The principal groups, besides the Xhosa, are the Zulu of South Africa, the Swazi of Swaziland, the Ndebele of Zimbabwe, and the Ngoni of Malawi.

In West Africa, age class forms are found, above all, among the Malinke (Mandingo) of the ancient Mande stock, currently scattered in a number of countries. In eastern Senegal, similar forms are found among the Bassari and the Bedik; in Upper Volta among the Bobo and the Bwa Pesya; in Benin (Dahomey and Togo) among the Nawdeba and the Somba; in the Ivory Coast among the Lagoon Peoples that include, among others, the Ebrie, the Mbato, the Atie, and the Adjoukrou; and in Nigeria among the Igbo and, in particular, among the Afikpo. One of the major characteristics of the age class system in these West African societies is their relationship with the residential organization of the village.

Among the Bantu of West Africa, age class systems are found among the Dwala and the Bamileke of Cameroon.

Certain forms of age classes are also found in Asia. Stewart, who has made note of this ethnographic fact, observes, however, that the available documentation is rather skimpy. He notes that the village organization of the aboriginal inhabitants of Taiwan was based on an age system. Stewart compares this with the age class systems of East Africa, but this is a general comparison that has yet to be verified through any rigorous field study (Stewart 1977: 16, 22).

Similarly general are the descriptions we have of age classes among the Ao Nagas of India, the Tanimbar Islanders of Indonesia, and the Pukapuka of the Cook Islands. The same can be said of the system of age grades and classes in ancient Japan, of which little is known. Stewart (1977: 339–40) also cites a document that tells of the existence of an age class system among the Uzbek of Klorezm in central Asia.

In all, the picture we have of age class systems in Asia consists entirely of scattered and general references. The need for a careful analytical and comparative study is evident if we are to learn the details of such systems and evaluate them in relationship to our knowledge of other systems.

In the case of the Americans, we must first distinguish clearly between northern and southern American Indians. Among the former, although age class systems were once found, they now are only of historical significance. The literature on these comes from the reports of the first explorers, the only ones who actually provided direct evidence on the functioning of these systems. Stewart (1977) has reviewed the entire ethnographic evidence available and, in a careful and intelligent way, has provided a clear comparative reconstruction. This involves five Indian groups of the prairie: the Mandan, the Blackfoot, the Arapaho, the Hidatsa, and the Gros Ventres.

In South America, although age class systems are virtually extinct among the Gẽ-speaking peoples of Central Brazil, like the Kayapò and the Apinayé, they were still found among the Akwẽ-Shavante. Among other peoples, like the Bororo, the Karajá (Carajá), and the Tapirapé, age classification is by informal grades.

Stewart also includes Europe in his survey. In his appendix, he reports some documentation that attests to the existence of a formal system of age organization among the Swiss of Winterthur in the canton of Zurich – Jahrgängenverhein – and among the Albanians of Elbasan (1977: 333–58). Upon closer inspection, however, these appear to be voluntary types of age association that, though institutionalized, have no significance for social organization outside of leisure time. Similar associations include the organizations of conscripts found among the Alpine peoples of Switzerland and Italy, including the Ladins. We lack analytical and comparative studies of any of these cases that might shed light on their history and current social function.

Indicating some constants

To provide a comparative conclusion that raises some issues for study on the basis of this survey, I think it worthwhile to note some of the constants that emerge from this simple listing of age class systems.

The ethnic groups that have been noted are almost all included in Murdock's "Ethnographic Atlas" (1967: 109–236). The comparative sample found in the "Atlas" includes 862 societies, to which must be added the supplements (Murdock 1967: 481–7 and 1968: 106–12, 218–28). Following the codes used by Murdock, I have examined the relationship between the presence of age classes and the presence of various types of kinship and political systems.

The first constant to emerge is the correlation between patrilineal descent and age class systems. This relationship is found in the great majority of cases, so much so that it must be considered characteristic of age class systems. On the other hand, the correlation with matrilineal systems is virtually absent; in the few cases in which it does appear, it is never clear. Either it is a bilineal system or a system of moieties. This sort of constant seems especially significant in analyzing the position of women in age class systems, an analysis that we will turn to after having put forth the various ethnographic models.

The second constant involves the presence of age class systems in acephalous societies. According to Murdock's code, political systems are placed under the rubric of the *jurisdictional hierarchy* (1967: 160). Analysis of this rubric in the columns of the "Atlas" shows the great prevalence of societies at the minimum levels of political organization – that is, having acephalous forms of authority (code 0) or *petty chiefdoms* (code 1). Thus it seems that there is a structural connection between age class systems and societies in which political organization is minimal or acephalous. This is indeed a connection of great interest, and by analyzing it we may be in a position to better understand the nature of age class systems as unique institutions of social organization.

The anthropological approach: formulating the problem

The scarcity and vague quality of available ethnographic evidence have been the principal reasons for the long time it has taken scholars to recognize the complex set of problems connected with age class systems. It was only the accumulation of new and more detailed ethnographic material that led to a deeper comparative analysis of those systems and the development of new theoretical perspectives.

The first interpretive scheme for the cultural and social significance of age dates from the work of Schurtz (1902) and is based on the evolutionary theory of human society. In their study of the origins of culture and, in particular, of social organization, scholars had proposed an evolutionary line that included a first stage of sexual promiscuity, followed by a stage of matriarchy, during which power belonged to the women, and then a stage of patriarchy when men acquired the power. According to this evolutionary conception, the passage from matriarchy to patriarchy represented a true revolution because the men seized power from the women by hatching a conspiracy through "secret societies" open only to men.

Schurtz's study of "age classes" and "men's leagues" sprang from these premises. Women, according to Schurtz, remained tied to their kinship groups, whereas men were organized in age groups that separated children from youths and youths from adults. In Schurtz's view, this threefold distinction represents the first organizational form of human society, corresponding to the social distinction among the noninitiates, the bachelors and married men.

At the same time, and working independently from Schurtz, Webster (1932) focused on "secret societies" and interpreted the tribal initiations of youths as a form of recruitment into these societies. Only males could belong to the secret societies because the societies were dedicated to the cult of esoteric mysteries that had to be kept hidden from uninitiated males and women. In fact, according to Webster, the men used the cult of the mysteries as a means to conquer and maintain power. "Even where the rites are of the simplest character, it is possible to find the germs of that terrorism exercised over the women and the uninitiated men which forms perhaps the most striking characteristic of the secret societies in their complete development" (1932: 99).

However, Webster does grasp the social significance of postpubertal initiations: "The initiation ceremonies of puberty serve to complete this transfer to the child from mother-right to father- and tribal-right" (1932: 21). He considers the de-

15

velopment of the grades to be a sign of social development: "With the fuller development of secret society characteristics, these degrees become more numerous, and passage through them more costly" (1932: 83).

The work of Schurtz and Webster represents the point of departure for anthropological study of age class systems, but it was Schurtz in particular who deserves the credit for emphasizing the social significance of age. Webster himself declared: "Had I learned of Dr. Schurtz's book at the beginning of my studies instead of at their conclusion, I should have gained a greater profit from this first effort to summarize the evidence for the puberty institution and the secret society" (1932: viii).

Robert Lowie fully recognized the importance of Schurtz's work, even though Lowie offered a devastating criticism of Schurtz's theses. Lowie (1920: 257–8) wrote: "To Schurtz above all others belongs the glory of having saved ethnologists from absorption in the sib organization . . . his insistence on the theoretical significance of associations must rank as one of the most important points of departure in the study of primitive sociology" (1920: 257–8). According to Lowie, the opposition between younger men and elders is to be seen as the primary cause of age associations, but he considers Schurtz's tripartite division too simplistic: "Where he errs is in taking it for granted that this inveterate tendency [opposition between young men and elders] must always be *formally* organized, that where it is so recognised it invariably goes back to a tripartite organization of society into boys, bachelors, and married men, and that this scheme represents the oldest form of association" (1920: 315).

Lowie backed up his criticism with data on "age societies" that he gathered during his research among the Prairie Indians. Unfortunately, the cultural situation of the Indians had already been greatly altered. There was thus no longer any possibility of directly observing the "age societies," although there were still some elderly informants alive who could provide Lowie with their own experience and testimony. But perhaps Lowie's greatest contribution consists in his having inserted the problem of age classes into the larger context of a comparative, theoretical study of the characteristic elements of "primitive society." In this work, which remains a classic of its genre, Lowie summarizes his critical and interpretive conclusions in a few general points: (a) The threefold division (proposed by Schurtz) is one thing, whereas the age classes of the Prairie Indians are another; (b) the same term of "class" is used to refer to quite different social phenomena in different societies; (c) age is a factor in people's instinct for sociability, and this is manifested in the tendency to form secondary and even primary groups on the basis of age; (d) however, generalizations of this kind have a sociological, not historical, value.

Out of the great ethnographic variety, Lowie recognizes the multiple sociological meanings of age classes. However, he limits his analysis by placing age classes in the general category of "associations." Under this rubric, he includes "the social units not based on the kinship factor" (1920: 256), but he does not

16

analyze the distinction between class and grade. Nor does he bother to distinguish the concepts and the terms that the variet, of age class systems suggests (cf. Lowie 1920: 297–337).

Refining the tools

The conceptual vagueness with which theoretical problems related to age classes were addressed began to be rectified with Radcliffe-Brown's letter to the journal *Man* in 1929. In what superficially appeared to be a rather unimportant matter, Radcliffe-Brown tried to "draw attention to the need of somewhat more exact terminology in the sociological description of age-organization." Toward this end, he suggested, first of all, that the term *age class* be abandoned because he considered the word *class* to be "ambiguous and otherwise objectionable" due to the common use made of it in sociology to refer to "social class." Instead, he proposed to adopt two terms. The first term was *age set*, to indicate "a recognized and sometimes organised group consisting of persons (often male persons only) who are of the same age . . . Once a person enters a given age-set, whether at birth or by initiation, he remains a member of the same set for the remainder of his life." The second term he proposed was *age grade*, to be used to indicate "recognized divisions of life of an individual as he passes from infancy to old age . . . infant, boy, youth, young married men, elder, or whatever it may be" (Radcliffe-Brown 1929: 21).

It is thus evident that Radcliffe-Brown did not make a definite distinction between informal and formal or institutionalized age grades and did not sufficiently stress the interrelationship between classes (or sets) and grades. As a consequence, his suggestions were not so innovative or useful. Indeed, the word *set* is among the most generic of English terms, though the modifier of *age* has proved useful to indicate a new, distinct concept for discrete groupings within age class systems. It should be noted, however, that although the term age set is now generally, though not always consistently, used in the Anglo-American literature, it has never been widely adopted among non-English-speaking anthropologists, who have continued to use such terms as *classe d'età*, *classe d'âge*, or *Altersklasse*. In any case, even more than as a result of Radcliffe-Brown's weighty influence, the term age set has been spread by Evans-Pritchard's use in his work on the Nuer. In addressing the question of age sets, just as in so many other aspects of anthropological analysis, Evans-Pritchard was a pioneer. Indeed, he opened the way for placing age class systems in the context of political systems. Beyond the fundamental value of the lineage system in the structure of Nuer society and its political system, he indicated the "integrating" and complementary value of age class systems. As he states: "Whereas the political system and the lineage system of dominant clans are interdependent, the political system and the age-set system are only a combination, in Nuer society" (Evans-Pritchard 1940a: 260).

Age class systems

In examining age sets, Evans-Pritchard notes the peculiarity of the Nuer system. We find what is basically an initiation model (the incision of three cuts across the forehead substitutes for the circumcision found in other, similar systems). The naming of the classes is of the linear type, and Evans-Pritchard maintains that the class names are "irrelevant to an understanding of the system" (1940a: 251). For the Nuer, there are only two age grades: the youths (noninitiates) and the adults (initiates). There are no warrior grades, nor any elders' grade, nor are there any periods of residential segregation or any related marriage norms. The functions of the system are not administrative, nor juridical, nor military, "though war and raids are often spoken of as the actions of a certain set because they took place during the initiation period of this set and its members took the most prominent part in them" (1940a: 254).

Class membership affects the behavior of the Nuer, but only in the local context of kinship and domestic relations. The structure of the age set system, like that of the lineage system, is segmentary, and each and every set constitutes a group within a special hierarchy. An individual's relation to others is always one of either superior age (and, thus, he treats the others as inferiors), or of the same age (hence, there is equality among age mates), or of inferior age (hence, respect is due to the elders). These relations conform to the norms governing kinship:

It is this action of the age-set system, in establishing ties between members of local communities and in giving them a kinship value, that we chiefly stress in a political context rather than its indication of leadership, for outside small kinship and domestic groups the authority derived from seniority is negligible, and the sets lack leadership and administrative and judicial functions. (1940a: 26)

Evans-Pritchard never had to face a situation in which the age class system was the only or the predominant basis of the political system. However, with his analysis of age classes, to which he devoted the concluding chapter of his monograph on the Nuer, age classes came to be a prominent topic in the study of social organization. As a consequence, there was an intensification of field research and a broadened interest in theoretical discussion of age class systems.

In the same year that *The Nuer* was published, Fortes and Evans-Pritchard (1940) published their edited volume *African Political Systems*. In his chapter, Evans-Pritchard confirms the analysis he offered in his monograph:

The age-set system may be regarded as a political institution, since it is, to a large extent, segmented tribally and since it divides a tribe – as far as its male members are concerned – into groups, based on age, which stand in a definite relation to each other. We do not consider, however, that it has any direct accord with the tribal structure, based on territorial segmentation, which we have recorded. The politico-territorial system and the age-set system are both consistent in themselves and to some extent overlap, but they are not interdependent. (Evans-Pritchard 1940a: 290–1)

The historical importance of this book on African political systems, buttressed by the quality of the various chapters it contained, consists in having demonstrated to a scientific world that was still incredulous and ethnocentric with respect to "primitive" societies, the relevance of the traditional political systems of Africa. The volume provided the first systematic approaches to the theoretical interpretation of these systems, an interpretation that would be of great significance to political science. The introduction to the book, written by the two editors (Fortes and Evans-Pritchard 1940: 1–23), was a seminal contribution that represented an important theoretical development. The editors divided traditional societies into two categories: one with state and the other with stateless systems. It was the first time that the uniqueness and structural consistency of stateless political systems were recognized. More explicitly, they were also to be called acephalous systems, for not only did they not have state organization, they were marked by the absence of any centralization of power and the absence of chiefs.

It is to the second category that the age class systems belong, with the exception of the case of the regimental model. The case studies of this second category that are illustrated in *African Political Systems* involve acephalous systems where the dominant structural element is kinship, as in the case of the Tallensi, studied by Fortes, and that of the Nuer. In the case of the Nuer, the age classes constitute an element, albeit minor though significant, of the political system. It is for this reason that the age class systems have not been examined in this pioneering review of stateless political systems. This lacuna is not due to oversight, but rather reflects the limited knowledge about such systems then available. Thus, the monograph on the Nuer and the volume on African political systems, both issued at the beginning of the Second World War, signal a watershed in the history of studies of age class systems.

Field research on age class systems

In the postwar period, with the rapid extension of anthropological studies, age class systems came to be the subject of broad and continual interest in both field research and comparative analysis. These were the years in which social anthropology became an established academic profession. The phase of dilettantism in field work was outgrown and with it the close ties to humanistically inclined colonial and missionary work. In the past, this type of work often went no further than the simple collection of facts, yet it would be unfair and inaccurate not to recognize the precious material provided to us by their writings, which have become valuable historical sources. However, the fact remains that age class systems were among the social elements least amenable to study by nonprofessionals. East Africa, understandably, provided the most propitious ground for the study of age classes. Among the recommendations to the Kenyan government on the most urgent topics for anthropological research, which he published in the series of *Memoranda* of the International African Institute of London, Schapera (1949) included the study of age class systems.

In 1939, Peristiany devoted an important chapter of his monograph on Kipsigis social institutions (1939) to their age classes. In his introduction to the monograph, Evans-Pritchard made special note of the significance of "age-sets." It is interesting to consider his declaration:

It is clear that the age-set system of the Kipsigis has very great political importance. It cuts across provincial boundaries giving common groups for all the major territorial divisions of Kipsigisland and even the whole Nandi-speaking aggregate of peoples, for a Kipsigis who enters Nandiland at once fits into the set which corresponds to his own and is accepted as a member of it . . . We shall not be surprised to find that the dispersed Kipsigis clans have little political significance. (Evans-Pritchard 1939: xxxi)

In 1951, Peristiany published an analysis of the class system of the Pokot (Suk), based on detailed material he had gathered on the rites of passage and on the functions of the system, leading to the following synthesis: "Pastoral society, without a territorial or lineage structure, is thus divided into an age class hierarchy, which serves as a political platform" (Peristiany 1951: 301).

In Kenya, the situation of the Kikuyu may be taken as typical of the Bantu-Hamites. The Kikuyu have, of course, been the center of world attention because of their struggle over land and related conflicts, including the violent Mau Mau uprisings. Kenyatta's (1938) book on the Kikuyu, extremely popular in the wake of his extraordinary political career, is highly emotional; in particular, his description of the age class system does not do justice to the complexity of this typically generational system. But this same observation may be repeated for Lambert's book on Kikuyu social and political institutions (1956). (In speaking of the Kikuyu, he also includes the Embu, along with the Mbeere and the Meru.) In his data analysis, Lambert draws attention to the multiple functions of the system and devotes individual chapters to the ritual, social, military, and political aspects of the age classes, but he does not evaluate the interrelationship between class formation and social promotion through the grades. Unfortunately, a thoroughgoing study of the Kikuyu age class system has never been made, and one may question whether it is any longer possible to do it. This gap is even more lamentable because it is clear that the historical study of certain events – including the early organization of the Mau Mau guerrillas – will never be satisfactory without an adequate understanding of the traditional structure and importance of the Kikuyu age class system (Bernardi, 1973: 374–5).

Among the professional scholars who have studied age class systems, Gulliver is notable for the contributions he has made based on his field studies among the Turkana of Kenya and the Jie of Uganda in the period between 1948 and 1951, and among the Arusha of Tanzania between 1956 and 1958, the period in which he occupied the position of "government anthropologist" of Tanganyika. His studies have done much to clarify the uncertainties that have surrounded these populations, all belonging to Nilo-Hamitic stock. In an item published in the *International Encyclopedia of the Social Sciences*, Gulliver (1968) proposed a conceptual systematization of age differentiation. There he presented "age classes" as a "non-corporate" grouping of age mates, contrasting these with

The anthropological study

"age groups," defined as "corporate" groupings "based on the criterion of coevality." (The absence of any mention of the concept of age set in Gulliver's scheme, given the popularity of this term in the English-language literature, is rather surprising.) Gulliver also suggested an interesting distinction between "transitory age-group systems," in which the efficiency of the groups declines along with the decline in the physical strength of their members, and "comprehensive age-group systems," in which the people remain members of their groups for their entire lives. Yet Gulliver's proposed systematization was not taken up by other scholars; it was not subsequently applied empirically, nor did it give rise to any comparative discussion.

Knowledge of the Nilo-Hamitic peoples, who have constituted the classic case of East African age class systems, was further enriched by the research of Dyson-Hudson (1963) on the Karimojong of Uganda, a people from the same general ethnic group as the Jie. Dyson-Hudson makes clear the multiple functions of the Karimojong age class system. The *gasapaneta* (or *ngasapanisia*), "corporate" initiation units (called age sets by Dyson-Hudson), and the *anyamet*, "corporate" age classes (called generation sets by Dyson-Hudson because they aggregate a number of initiation units from the same twenty-five- to thirty-year period) have functions that affect kin relations, economic activities, and political activities. Indeed, it is just their fundamental value in coordinating the entire social organization that caused Dyson-Hudson (1963: 394) to conclude that "the age system is the source of political authority and the age organization the main field for the exercise of that authority in Karimojong society." Maconi (1973) has added to our knowledge by his field research on the female age class system of the Karimojong.

Comparative analysis

Beyond those studies already mentioned, the years immediately preceding and after the Second World War saw an increasing number of ethnographic reports dealing with many other East African populations and, in particular, those of southern Ethiopia (Cerulli, Jensen, Pecci, Haberland). These studies reflected an ever-increasing interest in comparative analysis and theoretical inquiry.

In the first half of the 1950s, three studies, all independently undertaken, reopened the theoretical discussion that had remained unchanged from the time of Lowie's work and the terminological proposals offered by Radcliffe-Brown. In the first of these three studies, Bernardi (1952), through the comparative analysis of ethnographic reports on the Nilo-Hamites, shows how age class systems, although bringing about a structural aggregation of groups (the age classes), perform a function of power distribution (through age grades), and thus he argues that the age class system served as the basis of the Nilo-Hamitic political system.

In the second of these studies, Prins (1953) compares three very different

21

systems that permitted him, with considerable acuity, to clarify the essential elements of the age class systems: the distinction between formal and informal grades, the interrelation between age classes and age grades, and, finally, the multiplicity of functions of the system resulting from this interrelation. The societies analyzed by Prins are the Galla of southern Ethiopia and the Kipsigis and the Kikuyu, both of Kenya. He warns us "we must not interpret the species 'age grades' in terms of the genus 'organization of adolescence' but in terms of 'organization of social order' " (1953: 123). He considers an age class to be "an institutionalized group"; an age set is, for Prins, "the sum total of the persons, the man-power thus, of the institutionalized group called 'class,' or to be the number of people initiated together, but without reference to any specific task." He defines age grades in relation to the position temporarily occupied by a class with rights and duties connected with it (1953: 10–11), so that, together, age classes and age grades form "a multipurposive institution" (1953: 23).

The third of these studies is a wide-ranging inquiry undertaken by Eisenstadt (1956) with strictly sociological methods and purposes. A careful reader of ethnographic sources, Eisenstadt places the phenomenon of age classes in a comparative perspective where his interest is not so much focused on the specific structure and significance of the age class systems as on the use of age in the process of social maturation. He proceeds by two preformulated hypotheses. In hypothesis A, he states that "the criterion of age as a principle of role allocation is most important in those societies in which the basic value orientations are harmonious with those of human image of age i.e., particularistic, diffuse and ascriptive. In such societies . . . age-homogeneous relations are only of secondary importance." In hypothesis B, he states that "age-homogeneous groups . . . tend to arise in societies in which the family or kinship unity cannot ensure, or even impedes, the attainment of full social status by its members" (1956: 54–5). Eisenstadt constantly uses the concept and term age group, which he employs as an analytical instrument. Indeed, the generality of this concept, as he uses it, does not represent an impediment to his analysis, which is entirely dedicated to proving the validity of his preestablished hypotheses. These hypotheses have, despite – or perhaps just because of – their sweeping generality, identified a certain theoretical concern that has made them a recurring point of reference in both sociological and anthropological studies of age.

In the past decade, the study of age class systems has responded both to attempts at ethnographic verification and theoretical progress. Further research has been conducted in the classic sites of age class systems: among the Nilo-Hamitic populations of the Maa language (Hurskainen 1984, Jacobs 1965, Spencer 1965) and among the Oromo-speaking peoples (Baxter 1954, Haberland 1963, Legesse 1973), whereas similar studies have been undertaken in several West African populations (cf. Paulme 1971a), and even in South America (Maybury-Lewis 1974, 1984). Indeed, the Harvard Central Brazil Research Project,

The anthropological study

directed by Maybury-Lewis, has produced insight into the processes of change and virtual disappearance of age class systems in Central Brazil.

The growth in this ethnographic patrimony has stimulated important analytical studies of both monographic and comparative kinds (Balandier 1974; Baxter and Almagor 1978; Bonte 1974; La Fontaine 1978; Paulme 1971a; Ritter 1980; Stewart 1977). In this way, the theoretical importance of age class systems has finally been recognized. Through the different perspectives found in the various analyses, age class systems have been recognized to foster a basic cognitive value and to serve, as well, various functions for the distribution of power. In synthesis, we have come to realize the seminal (or anthropemic) capacity of the concept of age for social organization as a whole.

3

Legitimation and power in age class systems

Stateless societies

Acephalous societies are distinguished from other stateless societies by their low level of centralization. The realization of the political significance of such societies did not come easily, for it was difficult to comprehend that there could be a political system in which authority was neither centralized nor delegated through administrative channels. Indeed, before the issue was posed on a theoretical level it had to be addressed in the practical terms of administration. The conquering nations, at the moment of territorial occupation, needed local leaders to serve as brokers in their rule over the populations. In the case of centralized kingdoms, this was simply a matter of forcing the king and the other leaders to follow the orders of the conquerors or to substitute them with others, maintaining the ancient structure. However, where there were no heads, the conquerors were faced with an enigma. In any case, they imposed a solution. The lack of leaders was viewed, conceptually, as a lack of civility; leaders were created and imposed administratively, selected by the government. It is interesting to follow the origins of these solutions in the historical documents dating back to the early days of the colonies. An apt example is provided by the remarks of C. Dundas regarding the Bantu-Hamites of Kenya, written in the second decade of this century:

After the most careful enquiry and consideration of what is still in evidence, I feel convinced that the tribes had no head or leaders who could be dignified with the name of chief.
... The conception of a chief as a functionary essential to the welfare of the tribe had not become familiar to the people, and therefore the office of such an authority formed no part of the tribal organization.
... The lack of authority vested in individuals may lead us to the assumption that the state of society before us is wholly disorganized and uncontrolled, yet it is not entirely so, though its actual foundation is difficult to discover, and it is possibly inadequate to provide for more advanced conditions. (C. Dundas 1915: 238–9)

The history of the naming of paramount chiefs, chiefs, and headmen offers a significant chapter in colonial history, the study of which is far from being completed.

Slowly, with the development of a less biased and more intimate view of the local institutions, the colonial governments realized that, even where authority was not centralized and there were no chiefs, there existed structures that underlay an efficient social order.

It was through a series of comparative studies that stateless societies were placed in a rigorous anthropological and political perspective, and it was only in the later stages of this process that the age class systems were included in the same perspective. Fortes and Evans-Pritchard, in their preface to *African Political Systems*, were the first to introduce the category of "stateless societies" as against what they called "primitive states." Within stateless societies, they proposed to distinguish three types of political systems: (1) ones where "the political structure and kinship organization are completely fused"; (2) ones where "a lineage structure is the framework of the political systems"; and (3) ones where "an administrative organization is the framework of the political structure" (Fortes and Evans-Pritchard 1940: 5–7). However, it was soon evident that this typology was incomplete (see Bernardi 1952: 331–2). In fact, stressing the uncentralized authority that marked all types of stateless societies, Middleton and Tait (1958: 3) added three other types to the above list, including the age class systems.

This, then, is the typology of political systems in stateless societies that has finally emerged: (1) Systems where the political structure is fused with kinship, exemplified by very small societies such as the Bushmen; (2) ones where the political system is based on a lineage structure, typified by the Nuer of Southern Sudan; (3) ones where the political system is based on administrative organization, illustrated by West African societies such as the Igbo and the Lagoon Peoples of the Ivory Coast; (4) ones where the political structure is based on villages of cognatic kin, with the villages related to chiefs and headmen who are vested with political authority; and (5) ones where the political system is based on the framework of age class systems.

In the following analysis, I propose to examine the way in which the age class systems are structured and to see how they constitute a multifunctional framework for political systems as well as for other aspects of society. In this connection, it is important to elaborate further on the notion of stateless societies as types of uncentralized and acephalous systems of political power.

Primary polities

In approaching the analysis of political power in age class systems, I shall make use of the definition of stateless societies proposed by Southall (1968). He shows how stateless societies, in spite of their variety, can be recognized by five formal and consistent characteristics. I shall try to summarize them briefly.

Stressing the fact that stateless societies afford more than one level at which political activity can be performed, he indicates the first characteristic as *mul-*

tipolity. Political activity takes place at the level of tribe, clan, lineage, and so forth. The real meaning of these units is frequently left undefined, but in spite of their semantic relativity, the multiplicity of such levels is to be considered essential, not exceptional, in connection with stateless societies.

The second trait, *ritual superintegration*, emphasizes the communal aspects of rituals, when people of different social units join together for the same purpose and "the community emerges," as Fortes states of the Tallensi (Fortes and Evans-Pritchard 1940: 263). *Complementary opposition*, the third trait, is evidenced by the segmentary nature of the lineage system, analyzed by Evans-Pritchard among the Nuer. Segments are opposed to segments of the same level, and they unite in opposition to wider segments, thus offering different levels at which tensions and conflicts can be worked out. Complementary opposition is also realized in situations where cognatic ties are at work; thus Southall refers to these situations as the fourth characteristic, referred to as *intersecting kinship*. Finally, the fifth trait, *distributive legitimacy*, follows logically from the former traits as premises of political action.

In his analysis, Southall takes into consideration only the type of stateless society based on kinship systems. He does not include age class systems, though the traits he indicates can be applied to those systems and may be useful in analyzing how power and political community emerge in them. There is no doubt, in fact, that age class systems, just as kinship systems, provide a framework for political activity in stateless societies and should be analyzed in themselves. In this regard, I entirely agree and support the recommendation that Kertzer and Madison express at the end of their study of the Latuka age class system: "Age-set systems constitute a distinctive mode of social and political organization. They provide an alternative answer to the problem of maintaining social order in a noncentralized polity. It is time that more systematic attention be given to this system and toward its explanation" (Kertzer and Madison 1980: 105).

The problem should be approached in a positive way. Rather than stressing what stateless societies lack, pointing out the fact that they have no state or any centralized authority nor chiefs, we should endeavor to discover how they are structured, how they work, how they allow members to perform their activities and develop their abilities, how they face and overcome tensions and conflicts.

Let us consider stateless societies as polities in order to stress their positive aspects. "The polity of a given society," wrote Parsons (1967: 300), "is composed of the ways in which the relevant components of the total system are organized with reference to one of its fundamental functions, namely effective collective action in the attainment of the goals of collectivity." We need not follow Parsons's definition in all its implications. Both societies with a state and those without one can be considered as polities; I shall refer to the latter kind as *primary polities*.

Primary polities are, in fact, as Southall has indicated, multipolities. They

26

constitute a peculiar mechanism for constructing a political system: "A political system, tribal or Western, is a system both of roles and offices," writes Mackenzie (1967: 203). Roles and offices are actually defined within the age class system and are distributed according to recruitment into a class and its promotion in the scale of grades. It should be evident that whatever roles and offices exist in the age class system should be understood with reference to the peculiar structure of the same system. This observation applies also to the idea of power connected with roles and offices, as we shall see in the following section.

Power in the age class system

In trying to define the idea of power in the age class system, it is helpful to first ask: Is power within such a system actually identified with political power? We can also pose an alternative question: What ambitions of power do the members of the age classes have?

If we assume, as I have done, that the age class system is a polity and provides a framework for political activity, it seems logical to conclude that political power is the form of power within the system. In fact, however, things are not so simple. Whatever the ambitions of age class members, they are regulated and limited by the norms related to the forming of the classes and their promotion in the grades. Members' ambitions are bound to be graduated according to the scale of grades and the relationship of the latter to the classes, a relationship that forms the essence of the age class system. All social activity, including political activity, is somehow conditioned to membership in the age class system. But what is political activity? Normally, "by political we mean that aspect of social activity which is primarily concerned with power – with getting certain things done, with making decisions and getting them carried out, or preventing things from being done, by and on behalf of some collectivity of persons" (Southall 1968: 157). Such a meaning corresponds to Weber's idea of power as the possibility of forcing the other's attitude to one own's will.

The definition of power propounded by Weber and Southall does not readily apply to the peculiarities of the age class system as a system of classes in a scale of grades. Getting things done, for a member of the age classes, is only possible through membership in the age class system. Baxter and Almagor (1978: 14) state: "An individual's position in a set, and the position of his set in a system of sets, may influence his access to one or several of the following: social privileges, marginal economic resources, choice of wives and hence of affines, political office and authority and general access to ritual benefits (especially blessings) which can affect his whole well-being."

In the age class system, it is the position in the grades that regulates access to those forms of social activity bearing on the emergence of a political community. Thus, a political community does not simply result from ritual integration, but derives rather from whatever activity is carried out on a corporate class basis, within the limits of each grade. We can thus see how and why the resulting community is structured on the basis of the interconnection between classes and grades. This is often reflected in communal meetings, where the ordering of the participants reflects their class membership and the position of each class in the grade system: The elders are found at the center, the middle classes are second in line, and the young men and youths are on the periphery.

Distribution and differentiation of power among the classes are a peculiarity of the system. No form of power is suddenly achieved, nor can it be obtained simultaneously with other forms; rather, it is gradually distributed in turn through succession. It is also important to note that power, whatever its form, is never kept for life, but has to be surrendered to successors according to the order of classes in the line of grades.

In defining power in relation to the age class system, we must thus take a broader view. Rather than the idea of forcing others to one's own will, power should be viewed as one's own *capacity to perform social acts*, a capacity regulated and constrained by the limits established by membership in the age class system. Of course, individuals in a class enjoying the privileges associated with the grade occupied may be reluctant to surrender these rights to their juniors. Hence, transitions are often a time of tension and conflict.

This leads us to distinguish two aspects or moments in the idea of power as we have defined it: one potential, the other effective. The potential capacity to perform social acts provides an individual with the fundamental right to act socially. This is acquired at the time of recruitment to the age class system, and it is a right that is never taken away from a member. Recruitment in the system endows a member with the basic legitimation for his social action as defined by the norms of the age class system. Potential capacity, however, being potential, remains such until the individual is actually entitled to perform certain actions by his class promotion in the proper grade. This is what we call effective capacity, or effective power.

Political power, in the age class system, is just one form of effective power: the power to make decisions in councils, decisions that bind an entire community. Other forms of effective power include the right to bear arms and be a warrior; the rights to get married, bear children, and own property; the right to sit in council; and the right to perform certain rituals. These are the positions that age class members long for. They cannot be obtained at one time, for effective power is graduated and achieved following class promotion along the line of age grades.

The distribution of power

Membership in a class affects members both as a body and as individuals. It is the position of their class in the grades that defines the nature and extension of social action performed by members: Every member, as an individual, is entitled to perform the same type of social action as his mates, within the limits of the

28

established norms. This premise is reflected in the social maturation of individuals. If we take, for example, a young Masai: He is recruited into a class after having been circumcised; at this time he becomes an adult and ceases socially to be a nonperson. On being recognized as an adult and a member of a class, he acquires the potential capacity to act socially, but the effective capacity to perform certain actions legitimately is graduated: He is entitled to bear arms and take part in military activity, but he is not entitled to get married. Only at the end of his military period, when his class is promoted to a second age grade, is he allowed to marry, bear children, and own property; at the next stage, when at least one of his sons has been recruited into a class, and his own class has been promoted to the third grade, he achieves political power in the sense that his word in council may be decisive and affect the policy of the entire community. Finally, when he "retires" as an old man, he will be entitled to perform special rituals for the entire community.

Each of these passages marks a definite growth of the structural age of a class and of each of its members, bringing about a change in their social position. Thus, the interconnection between classes and grades works as a mechanism for the distribution of power in the general social context.

It is thus evident that the series of grades and the promotion of the classes through these grades constitute the dynamic mechanism for the distribution of rights and duties in the general context of the society. In such a manner, the age class system emerges as a unique primary polity. Its uniqueness is that it gives all the members of the society, according to a graduated series of stages, the right to participate in all social activities. To the extent that this mechanism functions and participation is distributed equally to all, it can be seen that, not only is the presence of centralized leaders superfluous, but their existence is not possible. Centralization of authority would contrast with the nature and the structure of the system and would be a sign of its demise.

The tie that we have noted between acephalous society and the age class system is no longer to be seen as posing a problem, for it can be explained as a necessary outcome of the distributive nature of age class systems. This connection, in other words, is one of its distinctive characteristics.

Baxter and Almagor (1978: 5) state that "age-systems attempt to create cognitive and structural order within and for a population," but I would add that they also attempt to create order for legitimizing and distributing power, both potentially and effectively.

The distributive order, one of the most significant characteristics of age class systems, stresses the differences caused by classifying people in structural age groups. Such a classification, by assigning a common age to class members, reduces the possibilities of tensions and conflicts that set individuals against individuals and groups against groups. By the order established by the system, every class member is invested with a definite capacity to act socially and enters the line of class promotion. Every class member is aware of what his status and capacity are at a definite moment and is conscious of the rights of his class in relation to other classes. Members will act accordingly, performing what is expected of them, but claiming what they expect from others.

Age, and structural age at that, is at the root of the system, and elderhood is indeed the highlight of the entire system. However, to make of the age class system a gerontocracy, as it is so frequently described, is to stress uncritically the nature of the system. Elders do not hold the entire block of power, and what they hold, they hold temporarily, for they are expected to hand it over to their successors. Tensions and conflicts may arise at the time when the right of a class to a successive stage is to be fulfilled. This is a phenomenon that should be regarded as normal, implicit in the nature of social classification. This does not in any way contradict the distributive aspect of the system, which in fact is a means to counteract tensions and conflicts.

It is hardly necessary to point out that, as in any dynamic process, not all social systems correspond to the ideal. In actual historical reality, the social mechanisms and the political order become entangled and thereby altered. But this is a problem that will be examined in Chapters 5 through 10 when we turn to our ethnographic models.

In assuring everyone the same rights of participation, the distributive character of age class systems guarantees the social equality of all members of the society. This represents, quite clearly, a lofty ideal. Nevertheless, it should be seen in relation to the diversity implicit in the structure of the grades and in the succession of classes through grades. I have said that the dynamic relationship between grades and classes is a basic characteristic of age class systems. I must now clarify this statement by saying that the equality of rights, obtained through class membership, depends on the grade. It is from the contrast between equality and differentiation, from the dynamic relationship between grade and class, that tensions and conflicts can and do arise.

The interpretation of age class systems in terms of gerontocracy, uncritically accepted by so many observers, including scholars, derives from the view that presupposes that the elders, as natural leaders, exercise the authority. In fact, as we shall see, this is not the case. The elders, just as the youths, are members of the system of classes; they have an *equal* potential right, although they exercise *different* effective rights. It is normal that, in the execution of authority, particularly in periods of succession from grade to grade, conflicts arise; often, the elders tend to prevail. Nonetheless, the existence of situations of conflict and tension should not distract us from the proper perception of the structure and the ideal functioning of the system. It is only through such an understanding that the meaning of these conflicts and tensions can be accurately interpreted.

Military activity as one of the functions of age grades

Age class systems have been often described as bearing such a close relationship with military activity as to be entirely identified with the organization of warriors.

The only case in which such an identification could be accepted as corresponding, at least in part, to ethnographic reality is the Nguni system. However, this system, as we know it, was the result of the reform actions taken by Shaka for purposes of conquest. The Nguni system, therefore, should not be seen as typical of age class systems and should be considered in light of its own peculiarities. Otherwise, the attribution of an exclusively military nature to age class systems is a distortion. In its best sense, it can be taken as a synecdoche by which military activity is extended to signify the whole system. However, in this case semantic emphasis misrepresents the real nature of the system. Only by acquiring a perspective on the entire structure involving the interconnection of classes and grades can we understand the true significance of age class systems.

There is no doubt that, in the past, warriors and military activity connected with age class systems have been most prominent, and the first visitors from the West were certainly much impressed by them. In those days, people like the Masai were commonly described as a republic of young warriors, the term republic being used as tantamount to anarchy. Indeed, they were anarchic in the sense of being acephalous societies, but they proved to be an ordered anarchy; the problem for the researcher was to discover how order was produced and maintained.

Another reason for distortion was caused by a superficial comparison between warriors in age class systems and conscripts in Western societies. Both were equally obliged to spend a period of military service in segregation from their family of origin, which normally delayed marital and career arrangements. But the analogy does not go beyond that. In Western systems, military conscription normally is a temporary obligation to train citizens for the possibility of a call to arms, and it does not represent an essential preliminary stage for social promotion. But in age set systems, recruitment to an age class gives its members a capacity for legitimate action and introduces them into the process of social promotion. Systems, of course, do not all follow the same principle of recruitment, but in spite of that the social outcome for members is similar.

Seen in the whole perspective of age class systems, military service is just one of the activities – or effective powers – that a class member is entitled to perform. We should not be deceived by the prominence that warriors were given in the old structure, nor by the readiness of elderly warriors (or ex-warriors) to recount their deeds and past glories. Every researcher among peoples having an age class system has probably recorded similar memories and heroic narrations. It was through a similar experience among the Meru of Kenya that I came to realize how the scope of age class systems went deeper and wider than the mere organization of warriors and military activity.

The "class in power"

Frequently used in reference to age class systems, the expression "the class in power" is one whose meaning is left uncertain. There are at least two possible references conveyed by the same expression. One is related to the position reached by a class when it is promoted to the grade of political power. As a consequence of that promotion, members sitting in council have the power to say the final word and make decisions on current matters that bind the entire community. The other meaning is connected with the position reached by a class at a different or wider level, for instance, as an alternating moiety or as a "generation," implying the same decision-making power.

As I have said, "political power" is just one form of effective power reached within the age class system. Therefore, the expression "the class in power" should not be left unspecified. We should not think of this in terms of a concentration of power in the hands of a single class or that this same class, as is often said, controlled the "government."

The ambiguity that expressions and terms of this sort lead to can only be dispelled by recalling, first, the distinction made between potential capacity and effective power, and, second, the many forms that effective power takes along the line of succession of the age grades. Besides, to avoid further confusion, it should be recalled that age classes are not centralized units and their members are dispersed in their local community. It is within this community that class members normally perform their social activity, and it is in their local councils that their deciding power is exerted. If, therefore, this type of power may be described in terms of government, we are clearly dealing with a type of "diffused government," as has been discussed by Mair (1964: 78–106). Such a government is a typical outcome of the distributive aspect of age class systems.

A similar problem may be raised by certain figures who seem to take unto themselves the power of their class while they emerge as leaders with special functions. This is particularly true of those who are invested with a ritual office that is a component part of the age class system and of those dignitaries whose function of pronouncing blessing is marginal to the system. A typical example of the first is the *Abba Gada* of the Boran, while an example of the second is provided by *laibon* of the Masai. In Chapters 5 and 7, I shall discuss their special position with relation to their own system. Here I simply note that normally their authority constitutes a focus of attraction and respect for the entire society. As for the *Abba Gada*, he is one of a number of officers who are elected to represent their own class, and his authority reaches its climax when his class is promoted to the grade that entails decision-making political power. At this stage, the amount of power in his hands, both natural and political, would seem to contradict the uncentralized aspect of the system, were it not for the fact that his position is temporary to the same extent that the position of his class in that very grade is temporary; his power ceases when his class moves up to the next grade. As for the *laibon* and other similar dignitaries, they retain a ritual power that is checked by its very marginality and is counterbalanced by the entire structure and functioning of age class systems.

The emergence of individuals as leaders, both at the level of the entire class or of its internal units, constitutes a current element of age systems, but the nature of the office is tied to the ups and downs of class movements in the line of grades.

A class that claims promotion to the next grade will not stay put and allow itself to be delayed and deprived of its right to achieve the effective power that inheres in the grade to which the class is entitled. The opposition that may, thus, occur between two succeeding classes is one of the expressions that tensions and conflicts may take, but these very tensions and conflicts serve as an effective check against any possible abuse of the position held by leaders and their supporters.

It should also be added that the leaders and officers of a class, however exalted their position may be, as in the case of the *Abba Gada*, are always considered peers by their age mates. The respect they are shown is entirely based on their capacity to take effective action to resolve problems. If a leader's ability declines or fails, or if he abuses his power, he will be deserted, and revenge may be taken against him. This may also apply to ritual dignitaries marginal to age class systems. There are some well-known cases, such as among the Nandi of Kenya, where defeated warriors took revenge on their *orkoyot* for the humiliation they suffered, killing him because he had predicted and guaranteed victory (Huntingford 1953: 2, 40). In this sense, Tignor's observation is pertinent: "Scholars must examine more carefully how military defeat affected societies, how it altered institutions, killed respected leaders and produced reactions" (1972: 275).

We may conclude this section by observing that the concept of power in the context of age class systems should be understood in a polivalent sense. We have defined it as a potential capacity that establishes the right of class members to act socially, as well as an effective capacity expressed by different forms of action, according to the various grades every class reaches in chronological turn, following the rhythms of social promotion.

Ritualization in age class systems

The formal institutionalization of a class, at the time of its formation, and the later transitions that follow, are always solemnized by rites and ceremonies. The ritual celebrations validate the groups that have been formed and legitimize them in the eyes of the community. In this way, age class systems are connected to the symbolic system, as well as the structure, of every society. Thus, Baxter and Almagor's (1978: 5) observation appears to be justified, in which they maintained that age class systems "tend to create a cognitive and structural order."

I have already noted that the age class system does more than this; it also allocates social status and power. Thus, age class systems provide evidence of the relationship between rites and power. As Cohen points out, rites, being symbolic, are not simply "expressive," but also instrumental; "only when the

relations between the two domains are studied can significant analysis be made''
(1974: 13).

There are two ways in which symbols are used as a means of defining power
relations within the context of age class systems. One is by reference to the
fundamental symbolic conceptions through which the relationship between human beings and mystical reality developed; the other finds expression in the
more specific phenomenon of ritualization. Both ways are expressed differently
and to a different extent in the various systems, but together they represent one
of the abiding characteristics of age class systems.

There are systems that explicitly reflect the fundamental conceptions of a
particular society, whereas in others the relationship is less direct. Sometimes
this diversity may be derived from the different sensibilities of the ethnographer,
more or less attentive to and accurate in describing the presence of symbolic
values internal to the various ceremonial and ritual celebrations. For this reason,
we may not always be convinced when we come across generic ethnographic
descriptions of the various systems in terms that are entirely secular or profane.
In any case, I repeat, although the reference to symbolic values is a constant,
the scale with which this is found and its importance differ from society to
society.

An example of this diversity of scale, in the sense just mentioned, may be
found in the general contrast between the system of the Masai and that of the
Oromo. In the former, all the passages from grade to grade as well as the divisions
of structural time are signaled by rites, but as a whole the symbolic references
that they contain are not nearly so numerous and obvious as they are in the
Oromo system. The ritual characteristic of the Oromo system has been emphasized in all ethnographic accounts. However, even among the Oromo there are
noteworthy differences. Thus, for example, the Guji are distinct from the other
groups because their unique variant of the system ''is rooted in religion and the
symbolic dichotomies which are related to it'' (Hinnant 1978: 209). At one end
of Guji ideology, two basic concepts are expressed by *Waka*, the high god, and
kayyo, ''which may be loosely translated as destiny, or perhaps providence,''
subsuming ''the entire philosophy of interaction between man and God.'' At the
other end, we find concepts related to the idea of virility and humanity (Hinnant
1978: 210).

The ''age societies'' of the Prairie Indians furnish another significant example.
Stewart (1977) defines them as ''secular,'' but in reality their relationship with
dances and singing cannot be understood without taking into account the underlying symbolic conceptions that give the dancing and the singing their own
ritual value.

The phenomenon of ritualization of social relations has been analyzed by
Gluckman in his comments on Van Gennep's classic work on rites of passages.
Gluckman is led to formulate two generalizations, the second of which may be
of interest for our present purpose. He states that ''the greater the multiplicity

of undifferentiated and overlapping roles, the more the ritual to separate them''
(1962: 34). Gluckman is uncertain whether his proposition may be applied to
age class systems. If we consider the essential nature of age class systems as
primary polities, I think that the proposition holds true for them as well. Essentially, as we have seen, the interconnection of classes and grades creates a
mechanism for the distribution of power. This mechanism is the main avenue
for status and power in societies where authority is not invested in chiefs nor in
any centralized agency. Recruitment in a class provides members with a status
that remains undifferentiated and somehow egalitarian within the same class. It
is only by promotion through grades that the status of class members will change,
but the change will not affect the internal relations of members, for it relates
only to the external relations with other classes. Recruitment in a class and
promotion through grades is always brought about and solemnized by rituals. It
is thus that individuals as well as groups are made to be and are recognized as
members of a class and that they acquire the same status as other members of
the same class entitled to perform the same type of social action. At the same
times that rituals mark the equality of status of class members, they also create
a differentiation of status among the classes. The result is a typical social stratification that coincides with the structure of age class systems. Thus, the ritualization of social relations is to be considered as a common mark of age class
systems, though the extent of ritualization may differ from system to system.
Indeed, the *gada* system of the Oromo seems to present a maximum degree of
this phenomenon, as has been emphasized by Baxter and Almagor (1978: 27).
They write that ''age-set rituals exaggerate the differences between age-groups
and generations and, in one sense, it can be argued that it is the very volume
and richness of *gada* ritual which differentiate men who are very alike and only
slightly different in their social roles.''

The whole phenomenon, however, is to be considered as a consequence of
the very nature of age class systems as primary polities and mechanisms for the
distribution of power.

The same phenomenon of ritualization of social relations gives rise in age
class systems to a number of unusual traits. Of special interest is the liminal
value ascribed to certain age grades expressing a kind of sacred ambiguity. This
may be seen in the position of the so-called retired elders, who are normally
assigned a symbolic value as if they represented a link between the living and
the dead. It is also best seen in the value attributed to the first and last grades
of the *gada* system of the Oromo, wherein class members of the first grade,
''the infants,'' are considered pure and sacred in the very same way as class
members of the last grade, ''the old elders,'' and both are viewed as mediators
between God and men.

We should finally add that ritualization of social relations in age class systems
is also performed by those ritual dignitaries marginal to the system, to whom
we have referred earlier in this section. The so-called prophets are the most

prominent among these. Their divinatory and blessing functions allow them to be consulted in every important matter, so that they are apt to appear at the center of all social life and sometimes exercise a deciding influence that contrasts with their normal marginality. Among such figures, we should list the *kallu* of the Oromo, the *laibon* of the Masai, the *orkoyot* of the Nandi, and the *mugwe* of the Meru.

Chronology and age class systems

The use of the age concept for the construction of the social structure represents the primary characteristic of age class systems. Age comes to be employed not so much as a chronological measure but as a principle of social organization. Yet, despite this, and despite its social-symbolic usage, the concept of age does not lose its intrinsic meaning as a measure of time. As a result, age classes may be referred to as temporal points in order to recall the past and to set historical events in a chronological order. Historical chronology is not, however, a direct or essential scope of the system, but it represents one of its most significant secondary effects. Each age class may, thus, be used for dating the past. The determination of dates, however, can only be approximated by reference to the period encompassing the formation of a class between the opening and closing rituals of its recruitment. A class period differs from system to system. In the initiation model of the Masai, for instance, a class period covers about fifteen years, whereas in the Boran generation model, it covers eight years. The entire phenomenon of age classification assigns a social value to time. Thus, one is reminded of Durkheim and Mauss (1903: 8) when they state, in relationship to the marriage classes of the Australian aborigines, that "the classification of things reproduces the classification of men." In this sense, it is certainly true that age classification creates a cognitive system, as Baxter and Almagor emphasize (1978: 5). It works on the idea of age and time, and by the interconnection of classes and grades it provides a symbolic representation of time itself. The phenomenon is brought about by rituals defining the period of class recruitment and by the assignment of names to every class, thus providing members with a social means of identification.

Class naming follows two different systems, linear and cyclical. In the linear systems, class names are freely chosen, and each class is given a unique name by which it will always be identified and referred to. In cyclical systems, names are assigned from a fixed sequence, systematically repeated; the choice of names is necessarily limited and automatic. Each naming system allows itself to be illustrated by an imaginative representation of time flux. Thus, the linear system is compared by Baxter and Almagor to a movement of an arrow ever stretching onward, whereas the cyclical system is represented by a helical movement "careening like a winged chariot" (1978: 25). One has to admit, however, that whatever the system, they do not supply a very valuable instrument for historical reference. The linear systems based on a series of unrepeated class names lend themselves to a richer specification of time in order to set a number of relatively reliable points of reference. Cyclical systems are not so suitable for chronological measurement, as the same class names are repeated, depriving them of much of their mnemonic value. The availability of age class naming systems is certainly much more useful if they can be associated with calendric computations. The distinction of months, weeks, and days in systematic calendars provides better-defined points of reference, but in societies that have no writing, their use lacks that kind of consolidation that would make of them a much more reliable source than the lists of age class names. All in all, in spite of their apparent chronological value, the reliability of age class names, (as of other analogous categories such as unwritten calendars or genealogies) has been called into question by some historians, who see them as merely a chimera (see Henige 1974).

4

The choice of ethnographic models

Having clarified the basic concepts related to age class systems, we need to take an objective overview of the ethnographic situation before any further discussion. This is no easy matter. We must somehow establish an adequate method for using the extremely uneven documentary material relevant to the question. The reports by the first ethnographers, describing rituals and activities they had actually seen, are certainly most valuable, but they are often the least satisfactory since the observations are often lacking in detail or not to the point. In contrast, more recent reports, normally undertaken by professional scholars, do not always refer to firsthand data and frequently are inconsistent in their use of concepts and terms regarding age class systems.

To overcome such difficulties, it may be useful to devise a typology that permits us to distinguish among the systems on the basis of certain specific characteristics and to examine the resulting varieties comparatively. In analyzing the basic concepts, I have already identified some of the structural principles that underlie the working of age class systems. I have also pointed out the dynamic relationship that exists between classes and grades forming the basic structure of the system and the mechanism for the distribution of power. The structure and functions of age class systems can thus be employed as our first two criteria for the choice of ethnographic models. These must be based on aspects that are distinguishing features of the main systems. Another criterion, which I shall call *ethnemic*, refers to the relationship between age class systems and the other elements of society, such as kinship, territory, and ritual.

Structural criteria

The construction of the structure of age class systems takes place with the recruitment of candidates into a single class, which will be connected, as a whole, to other classes through the process of promotion along the ladder of grades. I have noted two principles of recruitment: initiation and generation. Using these, I distinguish two main models: an initiation model and a generational model. In addition, I must recognize a third type, one that is something more

38

than simply a variant of the initiation model; I refer to this as the initiation-transition model.

The *initiation model* includes all those systems in which initiation provides the propelling impulse for the formation of an age class and for its progression through the age grades. Of course, the type of initiation referred to is that form of passage that permits a youth to be socially recognized as an adult. All types of postpubertal initiation imply social recognition of the youth's physiological maturation. The youth is marked as being socially autonomous and therefore capable of acting responsibly in his community's social activities. What is peculiar to the initiation model of age class systems is the structural outcome of youth initiation, which is not simply and not only the social recognition of the youth's physical maturation, but also its structural consequence – by which the same youth, on being recognized as an adult, is made a member of an age class, assigned the same social age as his mates in the same class, and assigned a social grade. Normally, too, youth initiation has a dual facet, individual and collective. Initiation, as such, operates on the individual candidates in that each of them is expected to undergo those trials that are part of the initiation process, and each of them will experience the social effects that are brought about by initiation. At the same time, initiation constitutes a collective event, both in its ritual performance and in the social effects, which together imply recognition of the newly proclaimed adults by the entire community.

This dual aspect is made particularly evident in the initiation model of the age class systems by the fact that individuals are recruited as members of a class system: The individual is proclaimed an adult while he is made a member of a collective body. In this model, the initiation thus represents the very moment when the interconnection of the age classes with the age grades is established and set in motion. The model is represented in East Africa by the Masai and other Nilotic peoples.

The *initiation-transition model* might be considered a variant of the initiation model. In fact, it is more than that, because it is marked by a unique and distinguishing characteristic: the transition of the age classes from collective bodies of members to mere categories of social reference. In fact, after having been formed into a collective body on coming out of initiation, and being thus promoted to the first grades of the social scale, class members seek its higher social positions individually, relying on other types of social resources than their age class. Class membership is not abandoned, but remains at a nominal level, ceasing to represent the collective basis for social promotion through grades. The most significant examples of the model may be found in the age class system of the Akwẽ-Shavante of the Mato Grosso in Brazil.

The *generational model* is characterized by a rule governing the recruitment of members into the age class system, a rule that defines the structural distance between a father's position in the scale of grades and the position of his sons. This implies that the recruitment of a candidate into a class is determined by his physiological birth, rather than by his social birth through initiation. The distance between father and son is structural because it affects the capacity of the individual to act socially, both potentially and effectively, by permitting or preventing him from being recruited into a class and being promoted through the grades. Indeed, the distance between father and son must remain fixed and must always be maintained through time. As a consequence, a son's position in the age class system and, by reflection, in society, is entirely dependent on the position of his father, one might add for better or for worse. In fact, the rigidity of the norms derived from the basic rule may bear some paradoxical consequences. One son may be recruited into the age class system while an infant, because he is at the right distance from his father's position in the grades; another boy, due to the timing of his birth, is not at the right distance and must wait a long time to enter an age class, thereby never reaching the higher grades and thus never attaining the power to perform the social acts that are the prerogative of those grades.

It is also possible to see the rule dictating the structural distance between father and son in a perspective of parental succession. In fact, father and son are necessarily set at regular chronological points in age class systems, forming a generational line of their own. We shall discuss the problem as it arises in examining the typical systems of the model. What I want to stress now is the complex character of the generational model, primarily derived from the rigidity of its basic rules and secondarily caused by some of the devices that are applied to mitigate its negative social effects.

A typical example of the generational model is found in the *gada* system of the Oromo of southern Ethiopia.

Functional criteria

Whereas the structural criteria, by employing the basic principles of class recruitment, place the accent on the position acquired by candidates as class members, the functional criteria emphasize the types of framework within which age class systems build their own structure: Age classes are formed and promoted through grades so as to define the social status of their members and their effective capacity to act socially. Thus, on this basis, we distinguish three types of models: residential, regimental, and choreographic.

The distinctive characteristic of the *residential model* is the use of age class systems to organize the communal settlement. The ways in which this takes place may differ, but two of them can be cited as most typical. The first is exemplified by the so-called age villages of the Nyakyusa of southern Tanzania. The second is relatively widely spread throughout West Africa, but we select the most typical examples from the Afikpo of southern Nigeria and the Lagoon Peoples of the Ivory Coast.

The "age villages" begin with the segregation of adolescents at the time of

40

The choice of ethnographic models

their puberty, for social and ideological reasons. Even in initiation systems, residential segregation is imposed on initiates during their convalescence after circumcision and while they are expected to live as warriors and remain celibate. In these cases, however, segregation is only temporary. At the time of class promotion, members settle in their former village or that of some relative. By contrast, segregation related to age villages is permanent and actually provides the starting point for building a new village.

In the West African variety of the model, age class systems may afford a basis for the distribution of people within the quarters or wards of a village and may also define their status and functions in village activity.

The *regimental model* is best exemplified by the age class system of the old Nguni of South Africa. Their case is in many respects unique. Though it is a long time since it was in use, its historical significance is great. Having issued from the reform of Shaka, it shows, on the one hand, how the military potential of the system may be so emphasized as to make it virtually the entire functioning of the age class system; on the other hand, it shows how a strong personality may be able to take hold of the system and bend it to his own will, to the advantage of his own kin and his own political power. As a consequence of such manipulation, the age class system no longer works as a mechanism for the distribution of power, but, on the contrary, is monopolized by the chief and used as the framework of his monarchic ambition.

The *choreographic model* is marked by the regulation of dances and songs. The word choreographic is thus taken in its etymological sense as dance (choreo) describing (graphic). The model is typified by the so-called age societies of the Prairie Indians based on the age of candidates, but it involved payment for acquiring the privilege to perform certain dances and songs. Accession to dances and songs was a reflection of members' social age and status and was thus a form of social grading. Indeed, rights over a series of dances did not simply imply the privilege to perform a special type of dancing, but also involved the right to perform other activities, each reflecting the status of members, such as keeping order within the community or performing certain rituals.

The models and their variables

It should be obvious that the proposed models are ideal schemes. Their value is essentially heuristic. They serve as a guide through the complexities of ethnographic reports. By defining some ideal models, we are better able to identify the structural forms of age class systems and to base our effort for sound conceptualization on ethnographic reality. It is only through the evidence of such ethnographic reality that we shall be able to discover the structural features of age class systems. As we have seen, the concept of age is such that it can be used and applied in multitudinous ways, typical of the dynamic process of cultural and social phenomena.

41

Age class systems

The ethnographic models here proposed are by themselves a variety of the general category of age, that defined by the expression "age class system." I have taken this to mean the structural interconnection between age classes and age grades. As such, the age class system is to be distinguished from an even more general category, the age system. The characteristics of each age class system are unique, but they are also marked by a fundamental similarity derived from the fact that the systems are all based on a certain manipulation of the principle of social age for the definition and distribution of social status and power among the members of a society. By testing each system against the ideal models, we shall be able to understand better their peculiarities and to evaluate the process of their structural forms, making possible the comparative analysis of the ethnographic variables of the systems.

Primary and secondary models

The perspective that I have adopted in studying age class systems has led me to place special emphasis on the systems that are notable for being essential elements of the polity. However, not all age class systems can be viewed in this way. Some constitute merely secondary and complementary elements of the polity. For this reason, I distinguish between primary and secondary models.

I term *primary* those models in which the age set system constitutes one of the essential components – if not the most essential component of the polity. I consider *secondary* those models in which the age class system plays a secondary and complementary role. As can be seen, the defining characteristic is entirely ethnemic. It refers less to the structural and functional aspects of the systems and more to their relationship with the other elements of social organization.

In the course of our analysis, I will pay particular attention to the primary models. My goal is to emphasize the specificity of age class systems as social institutions and their structural and functional characteristics in relation to the polity. This is the case only for the primary models. I will not deal explicitly with the secondary models, in part because their structural meaning and functioning have already been made clear in other studies that have become classics of anthropological theory. I refer here, in particular, to Evans-Pritchard's analysis of the Nuer system.

In fact, the Nuer system represents a typical secondary model. Evans-Pritchard clearly explains that, for the Nuer, "the state is an acephalous kinship state and it is only by a study of the kinship system that it can be well understood how order is maintained and social relations over wide areas are established and kept up" (1940a: 181). Later, he clarifies the secondary value of age classes, maintaining that "it is in more general social relations, chiefly of a domestic and kinship order, and not in political relations that behaviour is specifically determined by the position of persons in the age-set structure" (1940: 245).

The primary models obviously represent substantially different ethnographic systems. It is only in these systems that the use of structural age sees its full development, in the sense suggested by Balandier's perspicacious comment that "the organizing principles based on age are capable of providing the global control of society" (1974: 109).

Stewart's models

Stewart, in his work on age group systems, has elaborated two theoretical models, one regarding age classes (1977: 28–30), the other age grades (1977: 130–1). He provides a precise definition of what an age class is by listing a series of characteristics considered essential to identify an age class. Similarly, he lists a series of norms regulating the scale of grades, from first to last grade (G^1 to G^n), as essential defining characteristics of age grades.

These two models are quite different in nature and aim from the ethnographic models that I am proposing. What I intend to do is identify the way in which age classes are interconnected, both structurally and functionally, in particular systems. Thus, I am trying to evaluate the principles by which the structural forms of age class systems are set in motion (initiation and generational models), and the main activities that characterize the functioning of the systems (residential, regimental, and choreographic models). In this way, I hope to be able to recognize the similarities and differences of the systems as found in the ethnographic reality and provide a key for decoding the disparate descriptions of that reality by various ethnographers.

5

The initiation model

The distinctive characteristic of the initiation model is the principle of recruitment into the class system, a principle based on postpubertal initiation. Where postpubertal initiation is practiced, children and adolescents have no social autonomy before initiation; after initiation, they are recognized as adults and thus autonomous, in a position to assume socially responsible activities. This social effect of initiation is common to all postpubertal types of initiations. What is characteristic and distinctive of the initiation model is that the undergoing of initiation places the individual in the age class system. Attainment of social autonomy occurs not simply as a result of the initiation, but through the individual's insertion into the aggregation process (the age class) and the promotion process (the age grades), processes unique to age class systems.

In joining a class, individuals acquire a social identification that, in the initiation model, is connected with the idea of age, or the time factor, defined by the time at which they undergo initiation. Therefore, although initiation provides the basis for recruitment into a class, it is the time factor that serves to group the initiates: They will be considered coevals because they have passed through initiation during the same time and are therefore ascribed a common social age. It is this characteristic that defines age classes and distinguishes them from any other type of social class.

Before I proceed in the analysis of the model, it is useful to clarify the relationship between the concept of *age class* and that of *generation*. The two terms, as I have already hinted, are sometimes used as synonyms, although generation qualifies one of the main models of age class systems. Now what is the relationship between age class and generation with regard to the initiation model? Generation is a polysemic word, and indeed I am using it in different ways even when I refer to the generation model and compare a generation to an age class. In the former sense, I imply the idea of begetting by which a son is always related to his father; in the second sense, I take it to mean all persons born about the same time and bound to replace parents. In the latter sense, generation implies the idea of equal time among its members and the idea of succession to their predecessors or parents; both ideas are also implicit in age

44

class. It is the terms of reference that make the two concepts different. An age class is a discrete group of initiates, structurally defined by its ritual beginning and closure; a generation is never a discrete unit, but rather a vague category referring to all the fathers or to all the sons at a loosely defined period, to be specified according to each context.

The Masai provide the best example of the initiation model. In describing their age class system, I will mainly refer to my previous studies on the Masai (Bernardi 1955), whereas I make use of the ethnographic literature (Gulliver 1963, Spencer 1976) in examining the Arusha and Samburu systems, which offer two variants of the same model.

The ethnic sections of the Masai

Before the colonial period, when the lands that are now Kenya and Tanzania were crossed by Arab merchants and European explorers, the Masai* were the terror of the caravans. Indeed, Thomson (1885: 134) reports that his "men had heard so many dreadful stories about the murderous propensities of the Masai that they were electrically charged with fear." However, Jacobs (1979) has recently cast doubt on the bellicosity of the "true Masai as distinct from other ethnic groups speaking the same language, referred to by the former as *iloikop*, the violent ones."

Jacobs distinguishes among various forms of Masai fighting: "war, small scale armed fights, and cattle raids," a distinction he thinks "relevant to an evaluation on the actual extent of any animosity or conflict by Pastoral Masai with their neighbours" (1979: 37). As I am not here interested in pursuing the question of the extent of Masai bellicosity, I simply note that military activity, whatever its extent, has been confirmed as an aspect of Masai social organization. Indeed, the following analysis will show that a military action is just one of the many activities that a Masai is expected to perform as he is promoted, together with his class, through the series of age grades.

The precolonial Masai territory extended from Lake Turkana in the north to Lake Tanganyika in the south. The Masai were not a politically unified group; they were divided into numerous territorial divisions corresponding to ethnic or tribal groupings. Jacobs refers to them as a "cultural confederation" of politically autonomous tribes (1979: 35).

Today, however, the situation has changed. The Masai are divided by the national border between Kenya and Tanzania, even though their cultural unity persists. The colonial governments of Kenya entered into special agreements

---

* I employ the spelling Masai instead of the alternative form Maasai for the same reasons that Somali has come to be standard spelling rather than Soomaali. Likewise, *moran* and *laibon* have come to be the standard spelling employed in the East African literature for *ol-murrani* (singular), *il-murrani* (plural), *ol-oiboni* (singular) and *il-oibonok* (plural).

with the Masai in defining their territorial reserve. There were first two reserves – a northern and a southern reserve – and then a united one in the south, which made it possible to free the lands west of Mount Kenya for the white settlers. It was during these negotiations that the government, needing a mediator, named one of the *laibon* as paramount chief and had him and his assistant elders sign the official documents with their thumbs on behalf of all the Masai. The office of paramount chief was soon thereafter allowed to lapse, as the acephalous nature of Masai traditional society became increasingly evident, though its real structure remained an enigma for the administrators.

The Masai kinship system is patrilineal, with virilocal marriage and polygyny. The normal settlement of the Masai is formed by a circular enclosure bordered by a thorny fence. The houses are regularly spaced along the border, with the cattle byre in the center. Every enclosure is inhabited by two, and sometimes up to four, families located on the sides of the entrances. Each family is at an entrance, with the first wife on the right hand of the entrance, the second wife on the left hand, and so on. The typical Masai hut is a low structure of oblong shape. The enclosures, though apparently isolated and scattered, form part of a neighborhood. Cattle transhumance takes place within the boundaries of territorial sections. There are two main sections of the Masai: the Kisongo (Kisonko) of Tanzania (with 58,000 members) and the Purko of Kenya (44,000) (see Jacobs 1979: 35). Minor sections or subsections, such as the Kapiti, the Kakonyuke, and the Dalalakotok (Dalalekutuk), do not exceed a few thousand members.

The structural formation of an age class

In the Masai age class system, ritualization is more relevant for its structural effects than for its ceremonial richness. The rituals involved may be classified as rites of passage, but we should distinguish between rites that ratify a structural form (structural rituals) and rites effecting the actual initiation of candidates (initiation rituals).

The main structural rituals are the *embolosat*, opening the general period for the recruitment of an age class, and the *ngeherr*, closing the recruitment after the completion of a fifteen-year period. This is the normal period for the formation of a Masai age class. The *embolosat* must be first celebrated by the Kakonyuke and only afterward by the other sections. The *ngeherr* is first celebrated by the Kisongo and then by the others.

Between the two main rituals, the *endungore-engibata* and the *eunoto* are held, defining respectively the opening and closing of shorter periods, normally of three years, when the initiation rites may be performed. The length of such periods depends to a considerable extent on seasonal circumstances and pastoral needs. The *endungore-engibata* and *eunoto* are celebrated by all neighborhoods having an adequate number of candidates for initiation. The most recent and detailed description of the *eunoto* ritual has been provided by Galaty (1983: 368–78). He writes that "the explicit objective of the Eunoto ceremony is to transform the state of the age-set, and its members, by bringing into being a corporate entity and promoting them to the senior warrior grade." (See also Hurskainen 1984: 3–4, 135.)

The structural value of rituals is recognized and accepted by all the Masai. When they state the right of certain sections to be the first to celebrate the two main structural rituals, they emphasize the cultural interconnection of the sections while recognizing their autonomy.

Once the general and minor periods have been opened, the initiation rituals are lawfully performed. Under the tutorship of a sponsor, candidates are ritually prepared for the great step of circumcision, which comes as a culmination of a long initiation process. During the operation, the godfather protects his candidate at the crucial moment by concealing from the onlookers any sign of weakness or suffering that the youth may show. To get through the operation showing resistance to pain is a sign of great power and maturity and confirms that the candidate truly deserves to be considered an adult. The period of convalescence is a time when the mother still provides special assistance to her son with abundant food.

Being recognized as an adult implies the acquisition of the potential capacity to take part in social activities, a capacity that will be effectively realized by progressing with the entire class through the scale of grades.

The minor structural rituals lead to the formation of at least two initiation units. The first includes the initiates of the earlier period. They will be recognized as seniors, and their units will be described as the "right-side unit" – *emurata etatene*; the second includes the initiates of the later period, who will be the juniors forming the "left-side unit" – *emurata ekedyenye*. The division into two initiation units is structurally important and effective; it creates a relationship between the unit serving its apprenticeship and the one involved in military activity as warriors. The senior and junior units exert a mutual pressure, with the seniors being made responsible for the behavior of their juniors, who do not willingly accept such supervision while claiming their right to be promoted to seniorhood. In fact, the two units are destined to merge into a single class; but there is always some overlapping between the formation of two successive classes and their units, so that the junior members of a class serve as the seniors of the first unit of the succeeding class.

At the celebration of the *ngeherr*, the closing ritual, the two initiation units cease to be distinguished in terms of seniority. They are fused into a single class with its own proper name, and its members are considered coevals and peers. At this stage, the age class is considered fully fledged, and its members, sharing the same status and power, form a single body that is promoted through the upper grades as a unit.

Age grades and their functional aspects

A characteristic of the initiation model is the structural distinction made between the initiates and noninitiates. The Masai system provides a wealth of evidence of this. Children and adolescents have no status in Masai society. For this reason, the initiation of the youths truly represents the most important moment for both the individual and the community. Indeed, it brings about the passage from a negative to a positive position and potentially allows the individual full social standing. What is important to note is that the initiation rituals simultaneously produce both the acquisition of a new status for the individual and his recruitment into a class. These two aspects are not separable. The Masai exalt circumcision as the climax of their aspirations; whether or not an individual is circumcised represents a crucial social distinction. Clearly, however, it is a kind of metonymy referring to the social changes implied by the actual operation that is important.

Circumcision, performed on each individual, implies that these social changes affect primarily each candidate as an individual; the candidate thereby joins those who have already been circumcised. The distinction among those who have already been circumcised is based on the time of their operation. Thus a class, being formed by all those who have gone through circumcision during the same period, is distinguished from other classes in terms of time, and the gradations of status for each class are similarly based on time; in other words, the classes are age classes and the grades are age grades. What matters is to be initiated. It is initiation as such that is of value, not circumcision, which is just one of the many initiation rites.

The age grades may be described, and their functions analyzed, in two perspectives. One is iterative or diachronic (see Figure 5.1), in which we consider the grades a series of stages through which all classes are destined to pass; the other is fixed or synchronic (see Table 5.1), in which the grades, in their totality, form the framework in which the classes are distributed in a stratigraphic position.

There are four grades in the Masai system. Each covers fifteen years, corresponding to the recruitment period of a class, so that the total extent of the whole series of classes covers the optimal course of human life. If a candidate who is initiated when he is somewhere between fifteen and twenty years old traverses

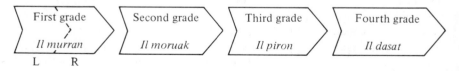

First grade · *Il murran* · L R

Second grade · *Il moruak*

Third grade · *Il piron*

Fourth grade · *Il dasat*

Figure 5.1. The iterative perspective on age grades. *First grade:* The left (L) and right (R) initiation units are formed, and the age class is formed. *Second grade:* Class members form their own families and establish their own herds. *Third grade:* The class is in full maturity. *Fourth grade:* The class is in a liminal state.

48

Table 5.1. *The fixed perspective on age grades*

Grade	Name	Activity or power
Fourth	*Il dasat*	Ritual and symbolic power
Third	*Il piron*	Decision-making power
Second	*Il moruak*	Family activity
First	*Il murran*	Military activity

the entire series of grades, he will be between seventy-five and eighty years old at the time of his death.

The scheme of grades and the functions corresponding to each can be summarized as follows:

1. Young initiates (*il murran*): military activity
2. Elders: married adult (il moruak): family and economic activity
3. Elders (*il piron*): political decision-making power
4. Senior elders (*il dasat*): religious ritual power

Let us examine the meaning and the content of each of these grades in turn.

The first grade: military activity

Completion of initiation gives the candidate fundamental adult status; in juridical terms, this corresponds to the potential capacity to claim full participation in social activities and to take autonomous individual initiatives. At the same time, by joining his initiation unit and ultimately his age class, he climbs the first step of the age grades and obtains a specific status expressed in his right to bear arms; the young initiate becomes a warrior. But, corresponding to this right, he is subject to two specific obligations, one of segregation and the other of celibacy. Although the right to bear arms represents an executive attainment, the two obligations constitute a restriction. This restriction makes it evident that, although a new class member has been recognized as an adult, with the potential rights of all other initiates, his effective capacity is limited by the scale of grades through which his class has yet to pass.

With the end of the convalescence period following circumcision, the new warriors went to live in a segregated settlement called *singira*, which was secluded yet not very distant from the family settlements. The placement of the warrior settlements was determined by strategic criteria depending on the movements of the herds and population and according to the number of warriors themselves. It is not improper, though it may be an overstatement, to call these warrior settlements barracks; it is certainly accurate to call them bachelor houses. In fact, during this period of residential segregation and military activity the warriors were not allowed to get married. The mothers and initiated girls of the same age as the warriors were allowed to enter the *singira*, both to bring certain foods and to participate in dances (Merker 1904: 89–90). Sexual relations with the girls were not prohibited, but it was absolutely forbidden to impregnate a girl. Maintenance of discipline was the responsibility of the senior members; the tension between senior and junior initiation units well served this purpose. Seniors were very exacting tutors of their juniors. Toward the end of the fifteen-year period, when class recruitment was about to close, there were increasingly numerous instances of more senior warriors who, anticipating this time, abandon military activity to settle down as married men. In fact, at the time of the closing ritual, each unit elected a ritual precursor, called *ol aunoni*, whose duty it was to speed the transition crisis. He was expected to "lead the way" into elderhood by getting married soon after his election. By that it was hoped that any blow to bad fortune would fall on him alone, assuring a safe future to all other members of his age class. His was a marginal status made evident by his attire as an elder and his feminine adornments. (See the following section titled "The leaders and individual affirmation.")

Efficiency in the use of arms in self-defense is a necessity for all the Masai and was especially in the past. After circumcision, each youth received a spear and a shield from his father that consecrated him as a warrior. Protection of the herds was the warriors' principal duty, but they occasionally took pride in planning their own cattle raids. Territorial sections were in fact ethnic sections and were the theater of military activities. In his ethnographic report, Merker (1904) shows a detailed interest in the Masai's military organization. He refers to small territorial nuclei that were able to unite into larger formations, which he calls *Korporalschaft*. Each nucleus and each larger formation chose its own leader, *ol aigwenani*. He was a guide, a strategist and, on occasion, a spokesman. His social status was not changed by the role, and he remained a peer of his age mates, who were prepared to follow him so long as he showed his capability and efficiency.

Even today, the young initiates are still called warriors (indeed, the term *moran* has entered into use in Kenyan and East African writings). But military life has changed; it is limited almost exclusively to defense of the herds. The ordinary arms of the warriors are now the spear and the club, and they are never without them (the shields have disappeared since being requisitioned by the colonial authorities). Indeed, the *moran* have become one of the most popular tourist attractions in East Africa, with their striking attire, body decoration, and hair style.

The second grade: family and economic activity

Promotion to the second grade comes as an implicit consequence of the celebration of the closing ritual; the class is thereby fully formed. This passage does not require conspicuous displays, taking place in a capillary manner with the marital arrangements made by each individual class member. Thus, being married constitutes the distinctive element of the grade. The newlyweds automatically become elders, *il moruak*. The absence of ritual display in connection with this transition has often led to this being seen as a grade of little consequence. But this is merely a misconception. In fact, it is a period of consolidation that involves individuals, as individuals, in activities common to all class members. These include the construction of one's own family and the expansion of one's own herd, perhaps on one's own settlement.

Externally, the life changes are striking. With marriage, the obligation of residential segregation ceases. Thus men settle down on their own homesteads, where they keep their livestock; or they and some other elder share a common residential enclosure. They no longer bear arms, instead carrying a stick and a stool, both symbols of elderhood. They stop doing up their hair, which they shave, and they use the *surutya* (pendular brass earrings) as a special ornament for their earlobes, another symbol reserved for the elders.

But the real, significant change is that involving status and executive rights. The elder is not only married, but he will soon become a father of a family; his social autonomy is further consolidated, as is his economic autonomy. These two activities are intimately linked and condition each other. Whereas the young initiate had to count on his father's and kinsmen's aid in raising the bridewealth for his first marriage, for his second, third, and successive marriages he must rely on his own resources. His fortune in raising livestock is what permits him to expand his family by taking more than one wife. His success in each of these spheres assures him of prestige.

The consolidation of the individual's position in this social setting is largely accomplished through these two activities that occupy the time he spends in the second grade. Through marital alliances, the elder extends his social relations; with the addition of his own livestock to the herds in pasture, he strengthens his relations with kinsmen and fellow class members.

The third grade: decision-making power

Passage to the third grade is also effected through the propelling force of the main opening and closing rituals. At least thirty years have passed from the time of the initiation of the first members of the class. In fact, all are now fathers, and some of their sons are already initiated or about to be initiated. This relationship between fathers and initiated sons is structurally significant and affects the status of the class. Those who pass to the third grade are accorded full social standing as leaders. They are between the junior elders of the second grade and the so-called retired elders of the fourth grade. Being elders at this stage assumes particular significance for them because of the special relationship that ties the class of the fathers to the class of their initiated sons. This relationship is implied by the term *il piron*, the firesticks, by which the grade is called. The little sticks are seen as symbols of the elders' authority and the consequent role of taking

51

the final decision in matters of common concern. This normally takes place in communal assemblies or in council meetings at various local levels.

The makeup of the councils is always a function of the nature and importance of the issues discussed. It is rare, however, for the members of a council to encompass those living outside the borders of their territorial section. Whoever participates in the council, from whichever part of the Masai territory he comes, sits in a position determined by the grade occupied by his class. The councils are open to all initiates, and the positioning of the participants faithfully reflects the hierarchy of grades. Along a line in the first circle sit the elders (including, if they are present, the members of the fourth grade); behind them, in the second line, are the married men of the second grade; in the third line are the warriors; in a side area are the women, who join the circle only if they have something to say.

In short, the power of the firestick elders can be effectively considered political, because they have·the last word in executive matters, because their decision is universally respected, and because they are able, in extreme cases, to command the young warriors, with the force and threat of a curse backing up their orders. Every firestick elder enjoys the same authority, though its exercise may reflect the personal character of each individual. Thus, authority and power are distributive, diffuse, and temporary. I should note that the tenure of the class in the grade is but temporary and, at the end of the period, passes to the next class in the grade.

The passage of a class from the second to the third grade seems to be celebrated throughout the country by a special ritual that involves all local neighborhoods and sections. The ritual is thus performed separately in each locality. We are not well informed on this ceremony, but Fosbrooke, in recalling it, states that "the matter is by no means clear, but there exist vestiges of a ceremony now practiced in conjunction with fertility rites . . . etc., whereby the senior elders retire and hand over the government to the junior elders" (1948: 32).

The fourth grade: religious and ritual power

Passage to the fourth grade, which is practically the last, has often been referred to by ethnographers as retirement. But the giving up of many of the most obvious kinds of daily activity, whether involving physical activity or the assemblies of the local councils, is more a consequence of the weakened physical condition of the elders who reach this grade than a negative attribute of the grade itself.

The class that reaches this level is composed of elders who are already quite old at the time of the transition and who obviously each day increasingly feel the weight of the infirmities that come with old age. Their number constantly diminishes, and for this reason the possibility of having senior elders in the community becomes rarer and more precious. Even when, as sometimes happens, isolated cases are found where there are still some survivors from the previous

The initiation model

class of senior elders, their status is no different from that of the members of the class occupying the fourth grade.

In any case, the elders of this fourth grade, whatever their class, are living on the threshold of death. In this sense, they are liminal, and liminality is a distinctive mark of the grade. For this reason, they are highly respected for their link with the afterworld, where so many of their age mates have already gone. More specifically, therefore, they represent the continuity of tradition and the sacrality of communal values. For all these reasons, their status endows them with a kind of supernatural or liminal capacity that gives them the prerogative and power to conduct sacrificial rites of value to the entire community.

Equality and inequality

The analysis of the Masai age class system indicates the differences of status and functions obtained by the age classes as they are promoted through the age grades. This poses the problem of equality within the system. How right am I in stating that the age class system, as exemplified by the pastoral Masai, assures the social equality of class members?

To avoid any misconception, let us first recognize that the problem refers only to the male sector of society. Women are kept aside and, whatever the extent of their participation, they follow their men in more limited forms, which at best could be described as parallel or complementary to men's age classes. We shall discuss the problem of women's position in age class systems in Chapter 11. At this point, I limit the question of equality to the position of men in the Masai age class system.

Our perspective on this issue is affected by whether we adopt a diachronic or synchronic view. Seeing the age class system as a series of classes promoted through a ladder of age grades leads to stress the differences that mark the classes occupying different grades; indeed, I have just described how different are the social status and functions of each grade. But there are two aspects that we should not miss in discussing this problem. One is the fact that promotion is not personal but concerns whole classes as units; as a consequence, each and every member obtains the same status and capacity to perform the same function as any other member of his own class. Class members are indeed peers, and any difference derived from personal talents will be realized in harmony with the status and functions of a member's class. The other aspect is connected to the succession of classes in the grades and hence to the temporary nature of their tenure of grades. Social mobility, in this sense of the succession of classes through the grades, is not a restricted phenomenon but involves all the classes, who in turn must always give way to their successors. Thus the diachronic perspective shows the dynamics of the Masai age system as a synthesis of the social contrast between equality and inequality. All class members share the same potential capacity, as individuals and as a group. But, again as individuals and as a group, they are only able to exercise their capacity in turn; the age class system assures that they get their turn.

When we look at the same problem in synchronic perspective, we are faced by a form of social stratification made up of a series of superimposed age grades. Grades represent the layers of that stratification, and as such they stress the inequality between the layers. Only when we consider that each layer is occupied by a single class and that the members of each class enjoy the same status and capacity – only when we combine the synchronic with the diachronic perspective – do we realize that each class will pass through the entire series of layers and see that the stratification of the age grades does not aim at crystallizing, so to speak, the social differences of class members, but rather is the result of the mechanism by which the age class system ensures the distribution and diffusion of status and power to all male members of society. It is in this dynamic sense that the age class system may be said to respond to the scope of guaranteeing the social equality of the members of society.

However, we can only speak of the equality of all class members once the class has been fully formed, and not in its period of formation and recruitment when it occupies the first grade. During this period, the initiates are distinguished into at least two initiation units, the right and the left, in terms of seniority and function. The right unit, because it is the first to be formed, is senior and has the duty of overseeing – under the supervision of the elders – the discipline of the juniors and of contributing to their training as warriors.

But the right initiation unit, even before being senior in relation to the left initiation unit, is itself junior in relation to the left unit of the class that has just concluded its period of recruitment. Indeed it is necessary to recognize that the formal promotion, even though it is ritually celebrated, is not complete, so long as it takes the warriors time to make the full transition to their new status as married adults. In this way, especially in the past when military training was of much more importance, military efficiency was assured. The consequence of this fact, from a strictly structural viewpoint, was the overlapping of the initiation units. Yet there is no contradiction between this phenomenon of overlapping and the temporal distinction between classes, as long as it is recognized that the periods of formation of the individual initiation units and the general period of recruitment into the class have only a rough calendric term, tied more closely to seasonal circumstances than to the terms provided by particular dates.

I have tried to clarify the structure of the Masai age classes and the phenomenon of overlapping that distinguishes it in Figures 5.2 and 5.3.

The succession of grades binds the classes in reciprocal positions of contiguity and alternation. The relations between adjacent classes are normally marked by tension and rivalry; the relations between alternate classes, on the other hand, are characterized by alliance and familiarity.

The tensions and rivalry between adjacent classes arise due to the tendency for the senior class to retain as long as possible the status and functions of its

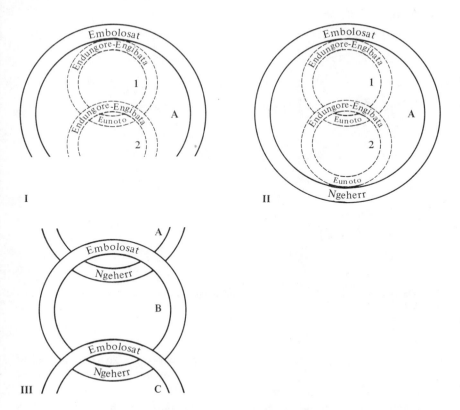

Figure 5.2. The formation of Masai age classes. *I:* An age class in its process of formation. A, the age class; 1, right-hand initiation unit; 2, left-hand initiation unit. *II:* A single age class. See I for key. *III:* The overlapping of the age classes. A, the preceding class; B, a full single class; C, the succeeding class.

grade that, by dint of the formal rite, have already been passed on to the following class. The senior class may thus be accused of prevarication, a charge that generally involves just some of its members, those who were initiated at the end of the recruitment period of their class and want to still enjoy the prerogatives and power that they should cede. The succeeding class resists this tendency, claiming more and more forcefully the rights that formally belong to it.

The leaders and individual affirmation

In describing the characteristics and functions of the first grade, we have seen two types of leaders, one military, *ol aigwenani*, the other ritual, *ol aunoni. Ol aigwenani* is an unspecified term that may be applied to any occasional head who takes the lead of a group. His basic status is not altered by being the leader of the group. There are many heads in this sense; for instance, every group of

55

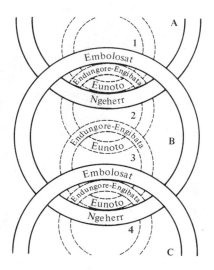

Figure 5.3. The overlapping rhythm in its entire complexity. A, the preceding class; 1, left-hand unit of class A; B, a full single class; 2, right-hand unit of class B; 3, left-hand unit of class B; C, the succeeding class; 4, right-hand unit of class C. (Adapted from Bernardi 1955: 309-11.)

warriors, whatever its composition, chooses its own head. There is also an *ol aigwenani* at the level of the entire class. He is normally selected at the time of the celebration of the *endungore-engibata* ritual.

Attainment of the office of *ol aunoni* is not the result of the individual's ambition; on the contrary, its assignment has to be imposed on the person who is chosen. Apparently, being considered "a sort of scapegoat" for the entire age class (as Fosbrooke 1948: 39 defined the *aunoni*) does not appeal to any of the class members as a rewarding position. Therefore, the elders discuss the matter secretly with the representative of the age class. The personal qualities of the nominees are discussed, as well as the "purity" of their clans and families of origin. Only when the decision has been made is the chosen one informed, and he is then expected to accept the nomination. He is henceforth obliged to settle down as an elder in fulfillment of his duties as *ol aunoni*. Yet, in spite of his initial reluctance, he reaches the highest status in the eyes of the Masai. Fosbrooke states:

But the *launon* is held in great respect by his age mates, and any demands that he makes must be fulfilled. It is stated that he is the only official whose order must be obeyed. In discussing this with an elder, I pointed out that this should give the office great political importance, in reply to which the elder indicated that such did not necessarily follow as "we can always tell the *launon* what order to give." (1948: 39)

56

The initiation model

(Among the Parakuyo, the *aunoni* is addressed as *papa lainei* – "our father" – by his age mates. It is also said that "he is supposed to live only 17–18 years after having been elected" [Hurskainen 1984: 189].)

The roles of *ol aigwenani* and *ol aunoni* afford individuals a position of distinction within their age class, though their status remains equal to that of their age mates. The idea of status equality should not be misunderstood to connote an impediment to personal self-expression. On the contrary, it is an incentive to action, for each class member is expected to give his best. Great respect is accorded to any warrior who distinguishes himself by his courageous and victorious deed, as to any of the elders who are successful in building a large family and a substantial herd of cattle. Successes of this type are certainly a cause of personal prestige. They can be further augmented by oratorial ability and debating skill, by which an elder can dominate the assemblies and councils, effectively enabling him to dictate the final decisions.

The position of the *laibon* is very different. The *laibon* are of various levels, as we know, and their realm is entirely ritual and magical. In the past, their fame was merely professional, tied up to their efficiency as medicine men. Their power, even when any of them reached the highest level of fame, was essentially equal to the power of any other successful elder. It was only because of the colonial government that the highest of the *laibon* was exalted to the political position of paramount chief of all the Masai. But as Lord Hailey has remarked (1950: 171), the paramount chief was an office that the Masai barely recognized, just as they preferred to rely on their elders for discussing cases and disputes rather than use governmental courts.

In the end, it is crucial to note that the Masai officers and individuals, however high their station and successful their lives, were not allowed to use their prestige to establish themselves in permanent position of power. Theirs was always a temporary position, as grades were successively opened to all classes and to each and every class member. Thus, prestige and authority were personal assets and could not be inherited. The promotion of classes through the grades is one of the characteristics of the initiation model, and the Masai age class system shows how the distributive nature of the system is assured against possible individual attempts at personal power.

The Arusha system

We find another variant of the initiation model in the age class system of the Arusha. Its similarity to the system of the pastoral Masai is striking; indeed it is just one of the many elements by which the Arusha are culturally equated to the Masai, especially in the Kisongo section of Tanzania. They speak the same Maa language, and except for the agricultural mode of production, their social organization is basically the same. Whereas the Masai are pure pastoralists, demographically scattered over a vast territory where they move periodically with their cattle, the Arusha are sedentary cultivators, often referred to as the agricultural Masai. They live in the relatively limited area around the city of Arusha in northern Tanzania and have a high population density. Their ethnic origin seems certain to date back to the beginning of the nineteenth century, when a number of emarginated pastoral Masai fused with some Bantu agriculturalists who settled in Arusha territory.

As for the age class system, though important differences may be found between the Masai and the Arusha systems, "the general principles of the social processes are clearly similar" (Gulliver 1963: 25). In Gulliver's opinion, the Arusha's "general dependence on and admiration for the Kisongo, and their acceptance of Kisongo leadership in the major rituals, must have been responsible for the close conformity between the two systems during the last few generations" (1963: 25). One of the significant differences is the absence of the warriors' settlements that mark the residential segregation of the *murran* (warriors; *moran* in current literature).

The entire Arusha system, like the Masai, revolves around the structural rituals, the celebration of the initiation of the youths, especially circumcision. In providing an overview of the system, Gulliver distinguishes five "formal periods" that together comprise a minimum of forty-nine years, according to a rough estimate: "These are indicators only, for in practice there is much variation" (Gulliver 1963: 27–8).

After the closing of recruitment to the last class, marked by the celebration of the *endungore ol piron* ritual, the recruits and their sponsors undertake a series of preliminary acts to obtain the "permission" of the *laibon* to start the new celebration and to get the permission of the "chief" of the Arusha. The opening of the period is marked by the celebration of the *engibata* ritual, during which the reopening of circumcisions is announced and recruitment to the new class is authorized.

The five "formal periods" described by Gulliver basically correspond to the four grades of the Masai system. In fact, the first two Arusha "formal periods" involve the junior *murran* (the first formal period) and the senior *murran* (the second formal period) and thus correspond in the Masai system to the two initiation units: the left (junior) and right (senior). At the end of the two formal periods, at the same time as the celebration of the *ngesher (ngeherr* of the other Masai) ritual by the Kisongo Masai, "the *maturation cycle*" – as Gulliver calls it – is concluded; that is, the formation of a new class is completed and the class receives its permanent name.

The celebration of these rites of class formation also determines the passage of the classes from grade to grade, or from formal period to formal period. After having been *murran* for the first two formal periods, promotion means that the initiates become junior elders for a period of about twelve years. This is followed by promotion to the grade of senior elders for a further period of twelve years. Finally, with their last passage, forty-nine years from the beginning of the pre-

The initiation model

liminary activities connected with the formation of their class, the initiates reach retirement, after which "the total cycle ends with the extinction of a group in retired elderhood by the deaths of its members" (Gulliver 1963: 28).

Initiation, as a form of recruitment to the age class system, and the passage of all class members from grade to grade, as a means of defining their social status and for the distribution of power among them to perform certain functions, represents the basic characteristics of the Arusha system and marks it as a typical form of the initiation model.

The Samburu system

The Samburu age class system offers a further variant of the initiation model. It presents, however, some peculiarities that differentiate it from the Masai and Arusha systems and that need to be analyzed. According to Spencer's (1965) ethnographic description, rather than being a means for the distribution of power, the Samburu system serves to concentrate it in the hands of the "elders." For this reason, Spencer defines it as a *gerontocracy*.

The Samburu are pastoralists who speak the Maa language and inhabit the area northwest of Mount Kenya. They remained separate from the other Masai after the Masai's forced migration to the south in their present territory.

Spencer (1976: 155) illustrates the Samburu system in Figure 5.4. The letters in the diagram indicate the total gradation process. The letter O stands for the initial recruitment into the system through initiation (circumcision), the ritual propellent of the system typical of the initiation model. The other letters – A, B, C, D – show the successive age grades. They are four in number, as in the Masai and Arusha systems. However, we find some discrepancies in their functions and mutual relationships. Let us consider the system analytically.

The first two age grades require no special comment. The division of the Samburu *moran* into junior and senior, made explicit in the diagram, corresponds to the Masai division of the two initiation units, the right (senior) and the left (junior). The second grade, defined by Spencer as "probationary elders," co-

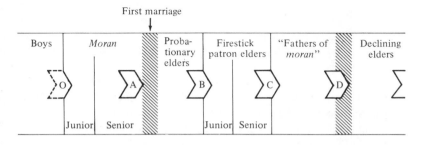

Figure 5.4. The Samburu age class system. (Adapted from Spencer 1976: 155.)

59

incides with the character of the same grade in the Masai system that I have described in terms of consolidation, with the junior elders dedicating their activity to the consolidation of their family and livestock.

It is in the third and fourth grades that discrepancies emerge. The word *il piron*, "firesticks," is also applied by the Samburu to the third grade, just as among the Masai and Arusha. Among the Samburu, however, the function of the firestick elders as commanding authorities is highly stressed, and Spencer emphasizes that the firestick elders are "godfathers," or patrons, to the warriors (*moran*), not "fathers." This peculiarity does not tally with the situation found among the Masai and Arusha, where the class occupying the third grade is regarded as the class of the fathers and their relationship with the warriors of the first grade is normally that of trust and confidence. Among the Samburu, the firestick elders – the class in the third grade – are charged with enforcing their authority over the warriors by employing the threat of a curse to bend the warriors to their will. Yet the Samburu say that no father would ever be disposed to curse a son. In fact, Spencer remarked, the percentage of godfathers who are also fathers is very low among the Samburu, just 10 percent (1976: 157), whereas among the Masai, according to statistics published by Fosbrooke (1956: 196–8), it is relatively high, about 30 percent.

The consequence of this situation is not only, according to Spencer, the concentration of power in the hands of the firestick elders, but also the deterioration of relations between the young initiates – the *moran* – and the firestick elders. From Spencer's analysis, this deterioration would seem to be due to an abuse of power by the firestick elders, not to the normal behavior of the warriors. The warriors are generally described as boastful, exhibitionistic, intolerant, and drawn to the use of physical force, whereas the behavior of the elders is fundamentally peaceful, open to dialogue, modest, and attentive to ritual duties.

The warriors' intolerance, in contrast to the elders' sedate attitude, is not surprising, for it represents the general attitude of warrior classes. Young warriors are always vying with each other to be acclaimed the best, whereas their initiation units compete in duels and violent confrontations. Indeed, they are expected to behave that way. Such encounters were typical, especially at the time when the passage from one grade to the next was about to take place. C. Dundas, with reference to the Kikuyu, reported on one of these clashes between "the young generation" and "the senior generation": "A general fight ensues which may become so severe that strangers will *mistake* it for a faction fight in earnest" (1915: 246; emphasis added).

The attitude of the Samburu firestick elders is understandable, because by withholding the right of warriors to promotion and marriage they control the availability of surplus marriageable women (Spencer 1976: 156). According to Spencer, it is the high level of polygyny to which the Samburu elders aspire and the resulting scarcity of women that lead the youths to seduce the elders' young wives, women who are their own age or even younger. Accusations of adultery are continually heard and move the elders to threaten to place a curse on the youths. Attempts at adulterous seduction have increased and been made easier by the lack of residential segregation, which in the past kept the warriors at a respectful distance from the elders' settlements. If there were such segregation, Spencer argues, sexual contact with the young wives would be avoided. He maintains that this explains what he calls the "Masai enigma," that is, the otherwise unexplainable fact that the Masai do not have such conflictual relations between the youths and firestick elders.

This reference to the situation of the past may help us understand the recent Samburu situation by leading us to suspect some development in their age class system that led the firestick elders to reinforce their authority to the disadvantage of the warriors. This development is not simply the end of the warriors' residential segregation, but also the disruption of some essential functions of the age class system, such as the activity of the warriors, brought about by the Pax Britannica. In other words, the "ethnographic present" in which Spencer observed the Samburu is quite different from the ethnographic present in which the Masai are described in the available ethnography or that in which the Arusha have been described by Gulliver. Hence, the tension that strains the relationship between the Samburu warriors and their firestick elders may not be interpreted as the result of an idiosyncracy of the ethnographer; rather, it should be recognized as a significant social characteristic.

It seems evident that the attempts to seduce the elders' young wives are conceived by the *moran* as retaliation against what they consider an abuse of power by the elders. They respond to abuse with abuse; a breach of a norm is met with a breach of another norm. Although one norm requires that the *moran* show respect for the elders' wives, the other requires the elders to facilitate the timely and smooth passage of their grade to the succeeding class.

The prevailing authority of the firestick elders has caused the Samburu system to be termed a gerontocracy (Spencer 1965, 1976). The term is properly applied to the situation of "abuse" perpetrated by the elders; if it refers to the "normative situation," then it needs to be qualified. Though the normative situation may sound ideal and hypothetical, in this perspective the Samburu system still appears as the kind of mechanism for the distribution and diffusion of power typically set up by the initiation model, that is, by the promotion of age classes through age grades.

When the abusive or gerontocratic situation of the Samburu is compared with the normative situation, the Samburu age class system raises the question of how the ethnographic present described by Spencer was the result of the peculiar historical contingency of which the strained relationship between the *moran* and the firestick elders was just one of many aspects.

61

6

The initiation-transition model

Analysis of the initiation-transition model takes us from Africa to South America and, more precisely, to Brazil. The simple initiation model is characterized first by the value given to the initiation of youths and then by the permanence of class membership for all the members throughout the entire course of their successive promotions in the grade ladder. By contrast, in the initiation-transition model the permanence of the class is more nominal than actual, for once members have reached a certain grade they pursue other channels in seeking to augment their social standing. This is not, then, merely, a variant of the initiation model, but rather a different kind of primary polity, one that merits separate consideration.

In Brazil, the only part of South America where age class systems have been documented, the situation is now becoming, and in some cases has already become, so acculturated that it is no longer possible to directly observe the functioning of the local systems. What remain are vestiges that may be more or less striking. This is the case among the Sherente, whereas the Akwē-Shavante, related to them, still had a functioning system in the second half of this century. For this reason, in analyzing this model we focus on the Shavante system, making use of the most recent ethnographic sources (Giaccaria and Heide 1971; Maybury-Lewis 1974). Maybury-Lewis devotes the fourth chapter of his monograph to a description of the age set system. He observes that, when he was in the field in 1962, there was a certain amount of resignation on the part of the Shavante to the fact that the initiation rites in which they were participating might be the last time an age class was formed.

The social organization of the Shavante

The Shavante belong to the *ge* linguistic group and currently live to the west of Rio das Mortes in the Mato Grosso. They used to live on the Serra do Roncador, but they moved away to elude contact with whites. From the end of the eighteenth century, in fact, theirs is the story of a people made distrustful and violent, almost cruel, by the treachery that greeted the friendly faith that they had given to the new immigrants. For almost two centuries, attempts at contact always failed, producing only deaths and massacres. It was only in 1953 that we find "the first continuous and amicable contact with the Shavante since the late eighteenth century" (Maybury-Lewis 1974: 5).

The first basic category necessary to understand Shavante organization is the dual division of the society in *wasi' re' wa* and *waniwiha*. Every person belongs to one of the two moieties and must marry someone from the other half. This dual division also constitutes a point of mental reference for Shavante thought and is reflected in a unique way, beyond the choice of spouse, in the constitution of political factions.

Kinship is based on patrilineal descent and on unilinear clans and lineages, on the basis of which the factions are formed. It is these factional groupings, as we shall see, that prove to be more influential than age class membership.

Residence is uxorilocal, organized in villages built in the open spaces between the forest and the shores of the waterways. The houses of the village are normally placed in a semicircular pattern facing away from the water. In the center is the communal plaza, in which social activities take place that are reserved for men; the women's world is centered inside the houses. The division of labor assigns hunting to men and cultivation to the women, whereas fishing is practiced, according to the circumstances, by both men and women.

Informal age grades and institutionalized age grades

In reading through the ethnographic sources on the Shavante, one immediately encounters a somewhat problematic presentation of the age grades, for which clarification is needed to establish the exact relationship of the grades to the age classes. First of all, the accounts suffer from an absence of univocal terminology. For example, as will be apparent from the comparison of lists provided in Table 6.1, Giaccaria and Heide call "age classes" (*classi d'età*) what Maybury-Lewis defines as "age grades". In addition, Giaccaria and Heide call "age groups" what they define as "a grouping of individuals who were born in the same period of approximately five years" (1971: 107). It can be seen that five years is the formal period of recruitment of members to a class. But, turning to the age grades, Giaccaria and Heide first list two for children and then eight for males and six for females; Maybury-Lewis lists two for children and then four for males and five for females.

A simple comparison of the lists in Table 6.1 shows that we are dealing with informal classifications, in which the division and the usage of terms are not fixed. Maybury-Lewis (1974: 143) provides confirmation for this fairly obvious interpretation of the age grades as informal rather than institutionalized, in writing that "Shavante males are divided between the uninitiates and the initiated." Along the same line, he distinguishes between "the young men's age grade" and "the mature men's age grade," observing that an age class (or age set) passes from one grade to the other. Thus it is not in the classification schemes

Table 6.1. Shavante age grades, according to the ethnographic sources

Males[a]

0. *Ayutepre:* newly born boys and girls
0. *Avute:* infant boys and girls when they begin to sit up
1. *Watebremire:* boy when he begins to walk
2. *Watebremi:* boy from roughly 2 to 7 years
3. *Ay'repudu:* boy from roughly 8 to 12 years
4. *Wapte:* boy from about 13 to 17 years
5. *'Ritey'wa:* youths from about 18 to 22–3 years
6. *Danohuy'wa:* man from about 22–3 to 26 years
7. *Ipredu:* man who has reached maturity (about 26 years)
8. *Ihire:* an elder, i.e., a person who knows all tribal secrets

Females[a]

0. *Ayutepre:* newly born boys and girls
0. *Avute:* infant boys and girls when they begin to sit up
1. *Baono:* girl from roughly 4 to about 10 years
2. *Adzarudu:* girl from about 11 years until time of her official engagement
3. *Adaba:* woman from time of her official engagement until her first child is born
4. *Pio:* married woman with children
5. *Pio ipredu:* woman whose children reached adulthood
6. *Pio ihire:* elder woman

Males[b]

0. (Not babies) (*ai repudu*)
1. Children (boys) *watebremi*
2. Bachelors *wapte*
3. Young men *ritai'wa*
4. Mature men *predu*

Females[b]

0. (Not babies) (*adzerudu*)
1. Children (girls) *baono*
2. Girls whose husband brought meat *soimba*
3. Women with children *arate*
4. Named women *adaba*
5. Mature women *pi'o*

[a] According to Giaccaria and Heide (1971: 107). Division of grades into males and females is my own.
[b] According to Maybury-Lewis 1974: 339.

64

The initiation-transition model

Table 6.2. *The Shavante naming cycle*

Shavante[a]	Western Shavante[b, c]		Eastern shavante[c]	
	0. Anorowa		0. Abariu	
1. Etepa	1. Nodzeu	initiand	1. Nodzeu	initiand
2. Abareu	2. Abariu	initiate	2. Tirowa	initiate
3. Nodzou	3. Atepa		3. Atepa	
4. Anarowa	4. Tirowa		4. Airiri	
5. Tsadaro	5. Tera		5. Tera	
6. Ay'rere	6. Airiri	elders	6. Anorowa	elders
7. Hotora	7. Sidaro		7. Sidaro	
8. Tirowa	0. Anorowa		0. Abariu	
	1. Nodzeu		1. Nodzeu	
	2. Abariu			

[a] According to Giaccaria and Heide 1971: 106.
[b] The naming cycle of the western Shavante consists of eight names: (0) Anorowa refers to infants; (1) Nodzeu refers to candidates for initiation; (2) Abariu refers to young initiates; and the other five names (3 to 7) refer to elders. The cycle is then resumed so that, at any one time, as demonstrated by the case shown in the table, there may be a situation in which the first three names refer concurrently to elders as well as to infants, adolescents, and young initiates. The same phenomenon is observed in the list of eastern Shavante, though it was not noted by Giaccaria and Heide.
[c] According to Maybury-Lewis 1974: 338.

listed in Table 6.1 that we should recognize the institutionalized age grades, but in the classifications connected with the social status of the initiates.

The Shavante grade cycle

The relevant features of the Shavante age class system are:
1. The initiation of youths as an instrument for class recruitment
2. Formal designation of the class with a cyclically recurring name
3. A strong corporate sense of the class in its first stages
4. Movement away from these corporate ties after reaching elderhood with entry into the mature men's age grade

Before analyzing the means and the forms of initiation, I believe it helpful to examine the meaning of the cyclical system used in naming the classes. Table 6.2 lists the systems described in the ethnographic literature.

It is worth noting that the discrepancies among the three lists are minimal. What is important to observe is how the nominal cycle has its own automatic progression. Indeed, when it is completed, the class of elders that leaves the cycle reacquires the first name and is thereby nominally made equal to the noninitiates. Thus, in the lists taken from Maybury-Lewis, the Anorowa (western Shavante) and Abariu (eastern Shavante) represent the zero level and find themselves in both the section of the elders and the section of the noninitiates. The name they are given certainly has an impact on the class's status, which we will examine when we consider the elders' grade.

65

Age class systems

Considering that the recruitment of a class takes place over a period of five years, after which the class proceeds as a complete unit, the nominal cycle runs its course every forty years. The recruiting process begins with the entrance of candidates into the bachelors' house between seven and twelve years of age; only afterward is their initiation ritually performed. Thus, at the conclusion of the cycle the age of the initiate will be between thirty-seven and forty-two years. There is no doubt that this is a rather brief cycle, and thus it is not surprising that at the end of the cycle there are always elders who are "survivors." If anything, it is surprising that there are so few of them. Maybury-Lewis maintains that, at the time of his research, the last four classes of the eastern Shavante (numbers 6, 7, 0, 1) encompassed just seven members, whereas in class 5 alone there were seven, in class 4 there were sixteen, in class 3 there were twenty, and the initiated youths numbered twelve. But Maybury-Lewis noted that the average life span of the Shavante is very short, and a person over fifty years of age was uncommon.

In a simple initiation system, naming cycles normally imply a distinction of institutionalized grades with specification of a particular status along with a corresponding definition of executive rights that go along with it. In the initiation-transition model, this is not the case; the acquisition of executive rights after entry into the grade of mature men does not follow from the structure of the age grades and age classes but is linked to social relations of another kind, such as among the Shavante are provided by relations of patrilineage and faction.

I would argue that it is for this reason that the institutional age grades of the initiation-transition model have little relevance and come to be reduced to the simple distinction between initiates and noninitiates. Aside from this distinction, the naming and the existing classifications can only have nominal value.

The initiation process and class recruitment

Shavante initiation rituals are extremely rich and elaborate. However, we shall not pause here to describe them in full detail, but limit ourselves to what is essential to establish the structural meaning of the age class system. Those interested in learning more about Shavante rituals should consult the original ethnographic sources (Giaccaria and Heide 1971: 118–57; Maybury-Lewis 1974: 79–83, 114–37).

Shavante initiation involves youths who have reached puberty and have entered the bachelors' house. However, more than a simple chronological calculation or physiological development of the individual is involved here. The selection of the candidates is the prerogative of the elders.

Initiation takes place in three stages, each distinct in time and meaning. The first is the residential segregation of the candidates; the second is the accomplishment of the initiation trial; and the third is the celebration of collective marriage.

The initiation-transition model

On the day set by the elders, the candidates are taken from their homes and brought to the village square. From there, proceeding solemnly, they are guided by one of the elders to the "bachelors' hut," called the *ho*, built in a secluded location but not separate from the village.

Each candidate places himself in order along the back wall of the hut and receives a penis sheath from this godfather, which he puts on immediately and ties with a cord around his belly. This is the sign that the candidate is no longer to be considered a boy. He should wear the sheath for the rest of his life; it is the only bit of Shavante clothing and is considered an indication of modesty and decency.

Segregation is obligatory but not rigid. The youths can freely visit their own families and even remain there overnight, though this is frowned upon. They are exhorted to observe chastity but "their seclusion is conceptual rather than physical and neither can nor does have the purpose of preventing their having pre-marital sexual relations" (Maybury-Lewis 1974: 109). We can see an obvious similarity to the case of the Masai *moran* behavior during their period of segregation.

In this period, the candidates are instructed by their own sponsors more by example than verbal lessons. They learn to do men's work, to make arrows and string and to do other tasks of this kind. They receive training in hunting skills, and they take part in wrestling contests, while they also learn traditional songs and dances. The ideal that the candidates are inculcated with during their period in the bachelors' hut is equality and mutual respect, but there is, above all, an insistence on a sense of solidarity. No one should gain at another's expense, but rather all should cooperate for the success of the class. It is in this perspective that friendship between age mates during the time they spend in the bachelors' hut is encouraged, transforming it into an institutionalized pact that will be honored by the two friends for their entire life.

The initiation trial represents the second act of initiation and is concluded at the third stage with the celebration of collective marriage. The first phase of the initiation test lasts three weeks. The candidates participate in daily gymnastic exercises with ritual immersion in the waters of the river. At the end of the three weeks, there is the celebration of the ear-piercing rite, a rite that entails promotion. There may be cases where such perforation is anticipated by certain individuals, but this premature performance is seen as punitive rather than promotional.

After a few months of rest, the candidates once again take part in the performance of a series of collective activities and competitions, in which the entire community participates. There are dances, foot races, and hunts. Musical instruments are made, as are the masks necessary for conducting the final phase of the initiation test. For the same reason, in this period food is gathered and stored for the solemn event to follow.

The third and final phase lasts three days, each of which is devoted to formal activities. The first two days are devoted to the ceremonies for the recognition of the officials of the new class, called *tebe* and *pahiri'wa*. These processions are richly decorated and have numerous masks. During them, the class and community make note of the ceremonial investiture of those chosen. The ceremonies last long into the night, and the newly elected officials must give evidence of their physical ability and stamina. Official recognition of these newly elected class members also implies official recognition of the new class. The class also sees itself represented by these two leaders, who will act on their behalf in carrying out the functions of disciplinary control that all members of that class are supposed to exert in the recruitment and initiation of their successors.

The third day is reserved for singing and dancing, in which women also take part, divided according to their own age classes. The solemn sound of flutes closes the day. The sound of flutes is called *teibi*, literally "it is finished," a term that makes the meaning of the performance evident.

The fourth day is the most important of all and is rich with events. It is opened with a ritual race involving the candidates, with their leaders at the head. At the conclusion, the bachelors' hut is dismantled. Then the elders give each candidate a burning ember so that he can light his own fire. There is another ritual race, and then the elders remove the decorations from the bodies of the initiates and give them authorization for the class to form its own council and to assemble in a space reserved for them in the village square. At this point, a shelter is constructed out of branches; the new class will spend the night in it.

It is there that the collective marriage rite is celebrated (Giaccaria and Heide 1971: 156 refer to this as "betrothal"). The betrothed brides then arrive, accompanied by their mothers, and obtain permission to enter from the elders. Having ascertained the groom's identity, the mother makes the bride lie down at his side, "his head turned away from her and covering his face with his hands" (Maybury-Lewis 1974: 79–80). This constitutes the official rite. The bride immediately gets up, and all girls, accompanied again by their mothers, return to their own dwellings. The ceremony concludes with the distribution of a small maize cake prepared through the contributions of the youths' families and distributed to the elders.

The brides can be very young and physiologically immature. In any case, consummation of the marriage will take place only at a later date, when the brides have reached sexual maturity.

The fifth day can be said to be ritually complementary. In fact, it is devoted to building the new bachelors' hut. The construction, however, does not always take place immediately, and its delay may slow down all the promotional passages, from the initiation of the new candidates to the transitions of the classes that have already been formed. In any case, this confirms the value of initiation as a general catalyst.

The initiation-transition model

The "young married" grade: *ritai'wa*

During the initiation celebrations, the active classes appear as the protagonists of social activity: the initiands on the one hand and the elders – or sponsors – on the other. Before examining the meaning of disengagement from the class, I believe it is important to analyze the corporate sense of the class to understand the contrast found in the initiation-transition model between the corporate class phase and individualistic phase.

Let us look, first of all, at the position of the young men. It should be evident that the terminological label "initiated youths" has symbolic value as a status marker, just as the collective marriage ceremony has a symbolic nature. In fact, with completion of the initiation process the candidates obtain recognition as adults, the right to be *ritai'wa*, "young men," to marry, and to be declared members of a class.

Being recognized as adults means being recognized as mature enough to take autonomous and responsible social action. Recognition constitutes the basis, or juridical title, for the potential capacity class members enjoy to obtain the powers and take the actions appropriate to the grade attained by their class.

The first of these effective powers is marriage. The fact that the marriage rite is celebrated collectively at the moment in which the class is formed not only reveals its symbolic value, but also means that it is not possible to separate membership in a class from the attainment of such executive power. Thus the class is the mechanism for social promotion. "The members of the young men's age grade," writes Maybury-Lewis, "are, of course, also married. They have not, however, for the most part taken up residence with their wife and begun to lead the lives of married men" (1974: 141 n.).

In addition to marriage, the young men also attain the executive right to hunt and participate in councils. Hunting implies some kind of military organization and requires training beyond that required of a sport. Thus the Shavante young men are also called warriors. As soon as they have completed initiation, the youths make their own personal clubs. Though the comparison may seem obvious, it does not appear that Shavante military organization is comparable to that of the Masai. More revealing is their relationship with the elders. Although they have no authority, they have little responsibility. As Maybury-Lewis (1974: 141) observes, "they are sometimes directed to go out hunting by the mature men's council, but they consider this excellent sport, and anyway may disregard this injunction if they feel like it" without suffering any sanction or negative consequences of any kind. This provides further confirmation of their autonomy.

The executive right of participation in the councils involves both the class council and the village council. The difference between the norms that regulate participation in these two bodies is an indication of the progressive nature of the acquisition of effective power on the part of the young men. In the class council,

69

the leader demands rigorous respect for the norms; indeed, these follow such formal rules that Maybury-Lewis was led to compare them with the debating societies found in British universities. But in the village councils, participation takes place more freely, though it must pertain directly to the matters being discussed; only someone with something important to say gets up and speaks.

Any delay in the celebration of the rites, as I have noted, brings about a delay in the promotional passages. As a result, it can happen that, at least for a certain period of time, two classes of young men exist at the same time. Relations between them are not easy, and each of the two classes tends to close ranks, further developing the esprit de corps that they acquired during initiation. The distinction between the two classes naturally is maintained in terms of seniority, on the basis of precedence in initiation, but this does not prevent tensions and conflicts from arising. These tensions are never totally overcome until the senior class is promoted to the elder grade.

The elders' grade and disengagement from class

In the context of the nominal cycle reported in Table 6.2 we find eight classes of mature men or elders among the western Shavante and seven among the eastern Shavante. In both cases, five are included within the cycle, with the rest remaining out of the cycle. The nominal identification between the senior elders who are at the end of the cycle and the infants who are at the beginning of the cycle is not a unique phenomenon. It is found, for example, in the generational model of the *gada* system of the Oromo (see Chapter 7). Although when elders and children are assigned a common liminal status they generally exercise a joint ritual function, this is not the case among the Shavante. Two reasons for this can be advanced: One is the purely nominal value of the grade cycle; the other is the phenomenon of disengagement of the elders from the classes as a means of social promotion.

For whatever reason, the only elders who emerge from the initiation celebrations as a corporate group are the sponsors. Thus, from the structural point of view, there are just two effective promotional grades in the system: the grade of young men and the grade of the mature men. The passage from one grade to the next takes place after five years. Once having completed their period in the grade of sponsors, the category of elders is not further distinguished from the point of view of the grades: The classes remain, but no importance is given to any further grades and, as a result, the classes lose their corporate link and their characteristic as a means of promotion. It is this phenomenon of loss affecting the classes that must be examined in considering the position of the elders in the Shavante system.

The Shavante elders' grade appears as a long and apparently undifferentiated status. Classes are not dissolved, but they persist only in name, as terms in the nominal cycle. Class members continue to socialize and come together as age-mates and friends, but the class itself no longer represents a corporate bond. All the elders' attention and ambition is turned to the attainment of power. To reach any form of higher power, the individual must be successful, and this is possible through demonstration of oratorical ability within the councils and the ability to win over the other council participants to one's own opinion. But in addition to this mechanism, itself normal in every initiation model, the Shavante also make use of, and give priority to, ties of kinship. They rely on their own lineage and the factions with which they are associated.

In this way the factionalism is released that, in the words of Maybury-Lewis (1974: 190), constitutes "a basic fact of Shavante life. It is part of the scheme of things, in terms of which people regulate their behavior and order their conceptual categories. The factions are in perpetual competition for power and prestige and the ultimate prize of chieftaincy." The dialectic of the factions entails the continual struggle for the individual to reach a position of prestige and power. The position of the Shavante "chief" emerges in this way, the fruit of factionalism and even more the product of individualism. The difficulty of defining "what the powers of a chief are or even to determine who is a chief" (Maybury-Lewis 1974: 190) derives precisely, in my opinion, from the implicit contradiction in abandoning an initiation-type system that necessarily entails the fundamental equality of all the class members and, in successive order, of all the classes.

It is nevertheless the case that the so-called chiefs of the Shavante are not formally installed, for they are neither elected nor appointed: "They are in effect men who exercise leadership and thus lay claim to the status of chiefs" (Maybury-Lewis 1974: 190). They do so because they are the expression of the factions and sometimes of a faction within a faction. The "chiefs" are almost always – though not necessarily – the same leaders who were elected during the celebrations surrounding initiation.

The contradictions of the Shavante system

The political struggle appears to be the true cause of the disengagement of the members from their own class. In this struggle, the relevant structural elements are the clan, the lineage, and the faction, and it is in relation to these elements that individualism is unleashed, undermining the corporate sense of the class. The class, in the culminating phase of elderhood, recedes in the face of the prevalence of the kinship system and the factions. In other words, the age class remains a simple category of social reference and the age class system becomes, as such, a secondary – nominative – model of the primary polity.

At this point, reference to and comparison with the Nuer system becomes inevitable. Among the Nuer, as is noted, the age class system is secondary, an alternative point of reference of the primary polity. But it is just this comparison with the Nuer system that casts light on the unique nature of the Shavante system and the initiation-transition model. Whereas among the Nuer the secondary significance of the age class system is a permanent and constant feature in comparison with the kinship system, among the Shavante it becomes secondary only in a particular phase, as a consequence of disengagement. In the phase in which the classes are active, the Shavante age class system prevails over the kinship system. It constitutes "a model of a certain kind" of which the Shavante are explicitly conscious (Maybury-Lewis 1974: 156).

In this perspective, the age class system is seen as a vehicle for harmony. It overcomes the dual divisions, even if these are employed in the organization of sport and ritual activities. In the same way, the divisions based on kinship are overcome, and the young initiates are inspired by a sense of solidarity.

Yet, as Maybury-Lewis (1974: 307–8) observes, although maintaining that it is a "vehicle of harmony" for the Shavante, the system "nevertheless appears to be the very institution that inculcates the values of aggression, which lead to disharmony in their society."

The contradictions in the system are undoubtedly considerable. There is the contradiction between the equality established by common initiation and the inequality that follows once the organization of the class has reached its pinnacle. There is a contradiction between the continuity in the formation of classes and the discontinuity that leads to disengagement and, ultimately, the ascendance of individualism. Hence, the initiation-transition model, exemplified by the Shavante system, involves a life-course transition from corporate participation to individual competition.

7

The generational model

The distinctive characteristic of the generational model is its recruitment principle, defined by the structural distance between father and son fixed in terms of age grades. Thus, for example, among the Oromo the rule dictates that the individual be placed in the age class of the *gada* system at a distance of five grades or forty years, from the grade occupied, at the moment, by the father.

The generational principle is fundamental and underlies the structural order of this model. As a result, postpubertal initiation, which in the initiation model is the determining factor in marking individual autonomy as well as in establishing the structure of the model, is not central. In the societies that reflect this model, a boy can enter the system in infancy, provided the rule of the structural distance from his father is respected. Moreover, certain rites, normally tied to postpubertal initiation, as, for example, circumcision, are not rendered essential; if they are carried out, they are performed at times and in ways that seem incongruous because they appear to be removed from the normal concept of postpubertal initiation.

It is worth stressing, also, that the term *generation,* with reference to the generational model, does not necessarily mean that the class is the aggregation of fathers or of sons; rather, it emphasizes the structural distance by which the position of a son within the age class system is defined by the position of his father in the same system.

What draws most of our attention is the fact that, despite the complexity and negative consequences that the rigidity of the structural principle produces, the generational model represents one of the most efficient primary polities. Confirmation of this fact may be found in the Oromo age class systems, which, as I have noted, provide the most significant example of this model.

The Oromo Boran

In the literature on Ethopia, the Oromo are usually referred to as Galla. Only recently have scholars shown a preference for the name used by the people themselves, discarding the term Galla, a name spread by the Amhara conquerors.

73

Age class systems

The Oromo, residing in the southern regions of Ethiopia, have long been moving toward the northern region, and fighting the Amhara, who finally made them subjects of their Ethiopian empire. However, the Amhara were never successful in assimilating the Oromo. The Oromo's resistance and pride were motivated, it seems, by the structure of their age class system. About the end of the sixteenth century, in his history of the Galla (see Guidi 1907, Beckingham and Huntingford 1954), Bahrey describes the periodic military attempts of the Oromo to expand toward the northern regions and explains this expansionist thrust of their warriors as an exigency dictated by their membership in the *gada* classes. Bahrey's explanation has been recently confirmed by Legesse (1973: 74 n.) on the basis of his own research on the Boran.

It is estimated that the Oromo today number between 8 and 10 million and thus represent one of the largest and most important ethnic groups in Ethiopia. They are divided into numerous groups, many of which are quite acculturated as a result of the prolonged domination of the Amhara and the penetration of both Islam and Ethiopian Christianity. Though traditionally pastoral nomads, many of them have become sedentary agriculturalists. The only ones who retain their ancient way of life and traditional institutions in nearly intact form are the Oromo Boran.

Part of the Boran live in Ethiopia and part in Kenya, whereas a few, known locally by the name of Qotu, are found in Somalia. Liban in Ethiopia, in the area of Negeli, and Isiolo in Kenya are the two extremities of the ethnic diffusion of the Boran. Among the Boran, too, some people have taken up cultivation using oxen-pulled plows, though this remains rare.

Their kinship system rigorously emphasizes patrilineal descent. The father's position, as has already been mentioned, is preeminent, even in the structure of the age class system. The descent groups, clans, and lineages are divided into two distinct moieties, Sabo and Gona, which also have ritual significance.

The analysis that follows is based on Pecci (1941), Legesse (1973), and Baxter (1978), whose works should be consulted for further details.

The complexity of the generational model cautions us to follow an analytical path, distinguishing between essential structural elements and purely functional aspects. The complexity of the generational model is further complicated in the Boran system by the overlapping of the two recruiting principles: initiation and generation. The result makes the Boran system a combination of two systems, one generational and known as the *gada* system, the other based on initiation and known as the *harriya* system. We begin with an examination of the *gada* system.

The *gada* system

Formally speaking, the *gada* system consists of a cycle of ten grades through which the classes move. Each normally lasts eight years. There are two grades

Table 7.1. *Listing of gada grades*

Ordinal number	Name	Length in years	Ordinal number	Name	Length in years
1	*Daballe*	8	1	*Daballe*	8
2	*Gamme,* junior	8	2	*Gamme*	16
3	*Gamme,* senior	8			
4	*Cusa*	8	3	*Cusa*	8
5	*Raba*	13	4	*Raba didica*	8
			5	*Raba dori*	5
6	*Gada*	8	6	*Gada*	8
7	*Yuba*	3	7	*Iuba*	27
8	*Yuba*	8			
9	*Yuba*	8			
10	*Yuba*	8			
			8	*Gada mogi*	8
Total		80	Total		88

Source: Based on Legesse (1973) and Baxter (1978).

Source: Based on Pecci (1941: 308–9).

of different duration, but these compensate for each other, so that altogether the length of the cycle is eighty years. (Pecci [1941:308–9] includes a grade outside the cycle in the series, the grade referred to as *gada moji*, and thus he describes the total length of the cycle as eighty-eight years.) Besides the variation in years, repetition of grade names should also be noted: *Gamme* and *raba* are repeated twice, *yuba* four times. This is the reason why the cycle has not been recorded in a consistent way in the various ethnographic sources. Sometimes grades that share the same name are assigned the same total duration as if they were all part of a single grade, whereas other times repetitions of the same name are distinguished, with each assigned a duration of a full grade. Comparison of the sources provides ample demonstration of this. Legesse and Baxter, for example, maintain that *raba* is a single grade lasting thirteen years, and they distinguish *gamme* into both junior and senior grades, just as they insist that *yuba* is repeated four times. By contrast, Pecci considers *gamme* and *yuba* single grades with durations of sixteen and twenty-seven years, respectively, whereas he distinguishes *raba* into *didica* and *dori*. It appears, then, that the phenomenon of repetition is not a simple matter of naming, but relates to the status of the grade, as can be seen from an analysis of the individual grades. In Table 7.1, the list of *gada* grades collected by Legesse and Baxter is compared to that collected by Pecci.

The arithmetic precision of this description is the feature that strikes us immediately. The compensation in duration among the grades having repeated names makes this even more evident. Here we have an observation that attributes an automatistic effect to the cycle. And it seems that it is just this aspect of automatism of the cycle, implicit in the rule of the structural distance between father or son, that is the cause of the generational model's rigidity. Legesse

(1973:136) attributes this phenomenon to "the fact that the Cushites have fairly precise calendar systems. Gada System developed out of a common eastern African institution on which the Cushites imposed rigid generational rules." It is difficult to prove this assertion, but it is possible to recognize the mentality it reflects. The cycle moves and ticks like a ritual and social clock; the rites follow the time, and the ticks of time determine the succession of the grades and influence the social condition of the individuals involved. Unfortunately, however, the automatism of the cycle does not always fit the variety and unpredictability of the human situations, and its observance generates intrinsic contradictions in the social system with negative consequences that require remedies and corrective measures. These, in turn, add further complexity to an already complicated situation.

The grades of the *gada* system

The description that follows is limited to the essential characteristics of the individual grades.

First grade: *daballe*. This grade is entered at birth and occupied for the following eight years. Whoever at birth is found to be forty years distance from his father is considered *daballe* and will pass through the entire series of grades. The members of the grade automatically form a class, in the sense that all are considered to have the same status and function. Their status is sacred, and their function is ritual. The *daballe* are children, morally pure and holy, and for this reason they are held to be "the principal mediators between man and God" (Legesse 1973: 53). For the same reason they participate in rites; their status as liminal, rather than sacred, is emphasized by their feminine clothing. People call them *intal*, that is, girls. As a consequence of such characteristics, the *daballe* are thought to be similar to the elders (*jarsa*), whose social status is equally liminal.

Second grade: junior *gamme*. This grade extends from eight to sixteen years of age. The *gamme* abandon feminine style clothing and hair. Promotion to this grade represents, in fact, as the Boran say, the true "birth of the sons," because only from now on are the sons considered truly male. The transition in social status that thus takes place is the only function of the grade.

Third grade: senior *gamme*. One belongs to this grade from age sixteen to twenty-four. Passage from junior to senior is automatic, determined by the diversity of activity. Pecci does not distinguish between junior and senior and lists it as a single grade. In any case, the seniors are considered apprentices because they are admitted to take part in both military action and pastoral life, activities that are, strictly speaking, the exclusive property of the later grades. In the *gamme* period of apprenticeship, the youths are able to learn and demonstrate their own abilities.

Fourth grade: *cusa*. This grade extends from twenty-four to thirty-two years.

The generational model

It signals the end of all apprenticeship terms: Individuals are now adults. Solemn rites are celebrated during this period. Some involve the initiation of individuals as members of groups within the *harriya* system. However, the principal rituals involve the formal institution of the class within the *gada* system and the election of its ritual leaders. These are the six councillors, elected according to criteria that take into account both their personal qualities and the position of their kinship groups, including their patriclass (see section on the patriclass later in this chapter). Those elected have a common title, *Abba Gada*, but normally, when used without further specification, the term refers to the first of the elected, who is considered to be the Father of the *Gada*. Within the council, a hierarchy is established, with the first councillor recognized as the leader of the class and called *Abba Gada Arbore*; the next two are called *Abba Gada Kontoma*, and the other two are simply *Abba Gada*. Nothwithstanding these distinctions, the status of the councillors is that of equals, and moreover is not distinguished – except ritually – from the status of the other members of the grade. According to Legesse (1973: 63), the class council constituted in this way represents "the Boran version of 'government by committee'."

Fifth grade: *raba*. One remains in this grade from thirty-two to forty-five years of age, according to Legesse and Baxter. According to Pecci, two *raba* grades are to be distinguished: *raba didica*, from thirty-two to forty years, and *raba dori*, from forty to forty-five years. This is no idle distinction, for it is of considerable aid in helping us understand the way the system works.

The *raba* grade is connected with the achievement of two kinds of effective powers: contracting marriage and begetting sons. These powers are differently conditioned by the generational rule specifying the structural distance between father and sons in the grade cycle. The effective power to marry is obtained on becoming *raba didica*. A marriage during this phase of the grade is a privileged marriage, in the sense that it bears all the characteristics of a socially recognized union and entails the right to a virgin bride. Whoever, by consequence of the generational rule, is excluded from entering the *raba* grade or enters it in early childhood, and is thus incapable of sexual union, will have to be satisfied later with occasional unions, which are tolerated but never recognized as true marriages.

The person who enters the cycle at birth and marries as *raba didica* has not yet completed forty years in the cycle, and therefore, though he achieves the right to marry, he has not yet covered the distance that would allow his sons to enter the cycle of grades. As a consequence, he is not permitted to bear children; if he does so, they will have to be given up.

In the second phase of the grade, on becoming *raba dori*, and hence having completed the required forty years in the cycle, the man will be in a position to bear and keep children who can enter the cycle at birth, but only if they are male. His female children, at this stage, may not be kept.

This feature of infanticide is perhaps the most negative aspect of the *gada* system. But the structural exclusion of some people from the form of privileged

77

marriage also has negative effects. To cope with these negative consequences, the Boran have developed certain corrective measures, which we will analyze in the section titled "The negative consequences of the *gada* system."

Military activity is another of the effective powers connected with the *raba* grade. If the *cusa* are apprentices, the *raba* are the expert warriors. It is they who bear the weight and glory of all bellicose acts during their period in the grade. Without doubt, the rules regarding timing of marriage and siring of children are related to the military function of the *raba*, which is the members' primary duty.

Sixth grade: *gada*. This grade is occupied by men from forty-five to fifty-three years old. The passage to this grade signifies attainment of elderhood. Military duty is no longer preeminent, and the *gada* members are able to devote their time entirely to family and community activities. The rites of promotion to the grade are led by the *Abba Gada* of the class being promoted and the *Abba Gada* of the class supposed to leave the grade. This is the moment when a class achieves the apex of the social hierarchy because the *gada* grade entails the decision-making power. The significance of the passage is well symbolized by the name of the rite, called "exchange of the sceptres" (*balli walirrafudu*). The sceptres, *balli*, are the insignias of the *Abba Gada*.

Another rite of great importance celebrated during the *gada* grade is circumcision. It takes place in the third year of the grade and, according to Pecci, signifies the time at which the *gada* cease being contemporaneously *raba dori* and *gada* (the first three years of the *gada* grade are considered a continuation of the *raba dori* grade while belonging also to the *gada* grade).

As we thus see, circumcision does not have the character of a postpubertal initiation; rather, it marks the passage from adulthood to elderhood. Ethnographically, this is certainly unusual. Indeed, a century ago Cecchi (1886: 529) expressed his surprise at the extraordinary timing of the circumcision ceremony. Having undergone circumcision, the man acquires the right to sire female children.

Seventh, eighth, ninth, and tenth grades: *yuba*. A man is in the seventh grade from fifty-three to fifty-six years, in the eighth from fifty-six to sixty-four, in the ninth from sixty-four to seventy-two, and in the tenth from seventy-two to eighty. *Yuba* is thus the grade in which men truly become elders, *jarsa*. During this period, increasing physical disability leads the elders to a progressive and constant disengagement from public life. However, their participation, especially but not exclusively in the ritual realm, is always sought after and considered valuable. All *yuba*, without distinction, are regarded as having prestige and wisdom. They are consulted in both the local councils and the pan-Boran assemblies, *gumi gayo*, where representatives of all the Boran convene to discuss important issues.

Eleventh grade: *gada moji*. Only Pecci lists this as a grade. The other sources indicate it as a position outside the cycle. In any case, it is reached through celebration of a "consecration" (Legesse 1973: 131) or "culmination" (Baxter

1978: 160, 175) rite. The *gada moji* are people who have completed the cycle and are outside it. They occupy a marginal position with a liminal status. In fact, they are equated with the *daballe* children and, like these, are considered pure and holy, effective mediators between man and God. For this reason, people ask them for their blessing.

This portrait of the totality of the *gada* grades reveals a well-defined structure that is clearly organized for the distribution of the effective powers between the classes and their members and shows the serious contradictions that result from the rigidity of the generational rule. It remains to note the corrective devices that have been developed to counteract those negative consequences. One minor device that may be pointed out here is the possibility for an individual to perform privately any of the rites that his class has performed before he came of age, or that took place before his birth. (See Legesse 1973: 105–7.)

The generational rule

From an examination of the *gada* grades, it is clear that the eighty years of the cycle not only cover the whole life course of a normal person, but may exceed it by a considerable amount. We might also ask what value the so-called grades outside the cycle have, namely, the *gada moji* and *jarsa*. How is it possible that some people may be excluded from participation in the *gada* system? The only possible answer consists in recognizing these situations as a result of the rigidity of the generational norm.

According to this norm, there should be a structural distance of five grades or forty years between a father and his sons within the *gada* system. In a polygynous system such as that of the Oromo, the same man can become a father at twenty years of age and can continue to produce children from young wives until an advanced age. As a result, the physiological ages of his sons may be far apart, yet there are no grounds, given that they are sons of the same father, for them not to meet the obligation to be at the same structural distance from him. Thus, youngsters and their old brothers, being sons of the same man, belong to the same grade. For this reason, *jarsa* "sons of the old men" do not even gain the right to enter the *gada* system.

The following list gives the ideal generational–age correspondence:

Daballe (0–8 years of age)	Sons of *raba dori* (40–5 years) and *gada* (45–8)
Junior *gamme* (8–16)	Sons of *gada* (48–53) and seventh-grade *yuba* (53–6)
Senior *gamme* (16–24)	Sons of eighth-grade *yuba* (56–64)
Cusa (24–32)	Sons of ninth-grade *yuba* (64–72)
Raba didica (32–40)	Sons of tenth-grade *yuba* (72–80)
Raba dori (40–5)	Sons of *gada moji* (outside the cycle)

This list reflects a social order that has been reported, time and again, by various ethnographic witnesses. The exactness of the generational rule has demographic consequences, and the generational norm works as a latent and indirect

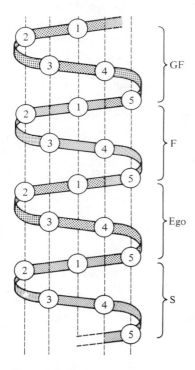

Figure 7.1. Boran age sets and generation sets. (Adapted from Baxter 1978: 157.)

method of birth control by precisely fixing the time at which men are able to bear and breed children. All methods of birth control imply some negative and even disconcerting aspects, but they bring about some sort of demographic and social equilibrium.

The patriclass – *gogessa*

Among the positive effects of the generational norm is the formation of a corporate sense among the members of the so-called *patriclass*. Baxter (1978: 157) provides a description of this in illustrating the workings of the generational norm. The five grades that, according to the norm, should separate a father from his sons are arranged in five lines. The spaces that separate the individual grades on the same line are eight years each. As a result of the helicoidal movement that represents the succession of grades, the same figure is always found along the same line and at the same distance of five grades, equal to the forty years of a generation. Each line, then, represents a generational line.

The generational model

This phenomenon could be considered the workings of an ingenious helicoidal system. However, the Oromo give it a cultural value and conceptual meaning in terms of their social and ritual structure that they express with the term *gogessa* (or in Pecci's spelling *goghessa*). According to Baxter, this word refers literally to "the dry foreskin of circumcision." Conceptually, it designates the totality of the generations that reappear, from fathers to sons, along the same line with the same grade. Therefore, he translates it with the term "set-line," whereas Legesse coins the expression "patriclass" (Baxter 1978: 158; Legesse 1973: 189).

The similarity of the patriclass to the patrilineage may seem clear, but the similarity is only apparent. In reality, it is neither descent nor the attempt to concentrate wealth in the paternal line that brings about the formation of a patriclass, as happens in the case of the patrilineage. There are no problems of production or reproduction in the patriclass, but rather of allocation of roles in the social and ritual spheres. The ritual aspect is the part that Pecci (1941: 309) most emphasizes when he defines the patriclass – *goghessa* – as "a group of people who conduct particular ceremonies at the time of the passage of the successive age classes until they complete a gada cycle." In other words, the relationshp based on a patriclass concerns the ritual activity connected with the structure of the age class system and, more precisely, with the rites of passage of the classes from grade to grade.

The generational norm is categorical: Sons must always be recruited into the *gada* system respecting the structural distance of five grades from their father. The initial point from which this distance is measured is, obviously, the time of birth of the sons. But because a man can become a father at different ages, it is clear that a person can become a father at times in which he occupies different positions in the *gada* cycle. These possibilities do not change the nature of the patriclass, because the sons, whatever the moment in which they enter the *gada* system, are always found at the same distance from their father and along the same generational line.

The patriclass concept thus seems to have a special importance in Oromo thought. Baxter (1978: 158) refers to the fact that "Boran said that they have five *gogesa* as given property of their culture." The importance that the Boran give to the patriclass leads us to understand more precisely the importance that the age class system has assumed in Oromo social organization and to understand the difference between this system and the kinship system. It is the underlying principles that distinguish the two systems: descent in the kinship system, joint participation in the structural rites in the *gada* system.

The negative consequences of the *gada* system

Let us now examine more closely the negative consequences of the *gada* system that have already been pointed out. There are at least three structural norms whose effects seem to contradict the distributive and egalitarian aspects of the system: the privileged marriage, the norms of childbearing, and military organization.

I have already noted that a marriage performed in the *raba* grade is a privilege both because it is the only type of approved marriage and because those who are not *raba* at a physiologically correct age for marriage are excluded from it. The unions permitted to them are not true marriages.

Legesse has justly observed that a norm of this kind "appears quite unrealistic, if not unworkable" (1973: 67). Too many people are excluded. The most common remedy is tolerance for sexual unions that Legesse, with some descriptive liberty, calls "cicisbean unions." This is a compromise solution, a kind of imperfect marriage. The cicisbean Oromo is not simply, like his seventeenth-century prototype, a gallant and well-mannered companion, but a man who enjoys full sexual rights with respect to the woman. The women who enter into such an arrangement are already married, and their relationship with the cicisbean takes place with the tacit, and sometimes expressed, consent of their husbands. In fact, remarks Legesse (1973: 68), "cicisbean has much wider significance" but serves as a corrective to the evident insufficiency of marriage regulations.

Infanticide is the pernicious consequence of the norms on childbearing. As we have noted, the right to marry does not entail the right to have children. This right is consigned at two times. The right to bear sons is obtained at the time of promotion to *raba dori*; for this reason, the rite of passage to the *raba dori* grade is called a rite of paternity, *dannisa*. The right to bear daughters is not reached until a man has achieved the *raba* grade. Children who are born before and outside the allowable period must be abandoned. Legesse has attempted an explanation by supposing in the structure of the *gada* system a lateral aim toward birth control. He argues by a simulation operation on the computer, based on modern census data (1973: 155). But although it can be admitted that population control might be an indirect effect of the system, this explanation does not seem to be sufficient as it does not take into full account the actual context of the *gada* system. Of particular relevance here is the system's military function, for it is military service that is the primary activity of the *raba* grade.

The *raba* are the expert warriors, just as the *cusa* are the apprentices. The passage from *raba didica* to *raba dori* was signaled, especially in the past, by the war ceremonial called *butta*. Only after the *butta* war had been waged could the fatherhood rite – *dannisa* – be performed. Legesse (1973: 74, 76) has gathered recent accounts of the *butta* wars. It is this kind of war that Bahrey refers to in describing the expansionary tendency of the "Galla" toward the northern regions of Ethiopia and that he attributes to the impulse of the warriors of the *gada* classes, driven by the ritual requirements of the system. The *butta* war was fought to vindicate the raids suffered by their warriors' fathers. It was a war of conquest, but with a ritual and structural motivation.

Legesse distinguishes between a ritual, "traditional" war and a "contemporary'' war. Traditional warfare was preceded and accompanied by special rites, including the election of the leader called *Abba Korma*, Father of the Bull. He took care of a sacred bull (*korma*). Upon his arrival in enemy territory, leading the warriors, the Abba Korma "stealthily approached one of the enemy's kraals and released the sacred bull among the cattle. A territorial fight broke out between the dominant bull of the kraal and the sacred bull. If the Borana bull won, the warriors proceeded with the campaign . . . '' (1973: 75).

Contemporary war is not of this ritual type but is rather the result of tensions existing in the relationship between the populations bordering the Boran, arising from disputes over rights of pastorage and water, and over livestock raids. Now, in a pastoral society such as the Oromo, military efficiency must always have been an imperative for the protection of cattle, though it had always to be combined with the structural rigidity of the generational rule. As a consequence, whereas on one side the regulations on marriage and childbearing assured the continued provision of warriors, on the other side the rigidity of structural norms caused a series of negative consequences that imperiled the required military efficiency. In fact, not only was privileged marriage precluded to many, and not only was infanticide a cruel imposition, but a number of able-bodied youngsters were forced to remain outside the *gada* system and were thus precluded from the use of arms. To cope with such negative consequences, the *harriya* system developed. This system is not opposed to the *gada* system; rather, at the moment when the class is promoted to the *raba* grade, the *harriya* system is activated to recruit those youngsters who would otherwise remain outside the military formation.

The *harriya* system

Physiological maturation, which makes the youths physically able to bear arms, is the principle of *harriya* recruitment. Recruitment takes place following the structural rites of the *gada* grades. It is opened with the promotion of the *gamme* to seniors, in the third grade (about sixteen years), and closes with the passage to the *cusa* grade (about twenty-four years). During these eight years, each year in the summer, when food supplies are abundant, the *cuc* (*harriya cuch*) rite is celebrated, marking the formalization of membership in the *harriya* class. A *harriya* class is a culmination of an aggregation process, which is begun by age mates in their childhood through their informal association in games and the petty activities of pastoral life. The celebration of the structural rites of the *gada* system affords the occasion for the *harriya* class to be formalized. Such a class includes all age mates without any reference to their fathers' and their own position within the *gada* system. Formalization takes place by public acknowledgment of the existence of the class, an acknowledgment obtained by class members traveling from place to place, where they are received festively and generously by the local people. In this way, the *harriya* class makes known its name and the election of its own leader.

The *harriya* naming system is linear: Class names are not cyclical, and their names are connected, as in all linear systems, with historical events related to them. I report the list recorded in 1963 by Legesse (1973: 60); note that *wakor, darara,* and similar terms are not class names, but rather generic designations.

Name	Ages
1. *Wakor Duba*	12–19
2. *Darar Godana*	20–7
3. *Dambal Bule*	28–35
4. *Wakor Liban*	36–43
5. *Dambal Arero*	44–51
6. *Wakor Sora*	52–9
7. *Dambal Taddacha*	60–7
8. *Wakor Dida*	68–75
9. *Udan Bukko*	76–83
10. *Wakor Mallu*	84–91

The characteristic feature of the *harriya* class is that of encompassing all youths of the same age without any discrimination. As such, it helps redress the restrictive consequences of the *gada* system.

As a result of military needs, the *gada* and *harriya* systems are interwoven: The *raba* classes and *harriya* classes unite and constitute unitary regiments, called *cibra*, each with its own leader, called *Abba Cibra*, Father of the Regiment. Each regiment can initiate its own bellicose activities autonomously, but when the situation requires a strategic plan, general control of military actions is given to a Father of Warfare, *Abba Dula*. The unitary formations of *gada* and *harriya* warriors acknowledge and respect the authority of the *Abba Gada*. In this way, the double affiliation of the warriors allows the *Abba Gada* to extend his power to cover the *harriya* classes and thus to encompass those excluded from the *gada* cycle.

Assembling together as age mates, forming united regiments, and sharing military experiences and the triumphs and defeats of war – all give the *harriya* and *gada* class members a sense of identity and brotherhood, made explicit and memorable by the names of their classes. As a result, the distinctions created by the *gada* system are mitigated and the voids are filled in.

The *gada* system as primary polity

In describing the position of the *Abba Gada*, Pecci states: "The *Abba Gada* is the effective head of all Boran and he has the greatest civil, political, juridical and religious powers; a sentence pronounced by the *Abba Gada* cannot be appealed" (1941: 315). The literal meaning of these words might induce one to think of the Boran organization as a monarchic system. But, though we respect

The generational model

Pecci's trustworthiness, for he was an informed and sober ethnographer, his words must be taken in their proper context. To do this, we must understand the nature of the *Abba Gada's* power and the duration of his tenure.

Supporting the breadth of powers attributed by Pecci to the *Abba Gada* is the symbol of the scepter, *balli*, which is used to indicate the whole batch of powers that the outgoing *Abba Gada* hands over to his successor. In fact, the *Abba Gada* himself embodies all the rights – and therefore the power – acquired by the class, of which he is a member, during its tenure of different grades in the *gada* cycle. Since the time of his election, all the ideals of the class are reflected on his person: He performs a privileged kind of marriage; he celebrates the fatherhood rite (*dannisa*); and, finally, he is expected to hand over the scepter to the next *Abba Gada*. Yet, though his position is one of preeminence, he is considered an equal – *primus inter pares* – not only with regard to other councillors who were elected with him to form the executive council of the class, but also with regard to the rest of the class members. Within the council, the authority of the *Abba Gada* is decisive; his final words in resolving a dispute or deciding any political affairs are listened to with high respect and bind the entire population.

The *Abba Gada's* power may be, as Pecci says, "maximal," but in a moderate and not an absolute sense, because it is effectively tempered by both the participation of his councillors and the limited duration of his term. "The exchange of sceptres – *balli walirrafudu*" signals the term of office of both the *Abba Gada* and his council. In the choice of *Abba Gada* and his councillors at the time of their election, we find evidence of corrective elements designed to prevent the excessive accumulation of power. It has, thus, been remarked that councillors are selected alternately between the two moieties, *Sabbu* and *Gona*. So that the accumulation of power might not become the prerogative of the same kinship groups, the new *Abba Gada Arbore*, the first of all the councillors, must be from the opposite moiety from that of the current *Abba Gada;* the second and third councillors are selected from within the *Gona* moiety, which is recognized as having greater ritual significance; the other three councillors must be chosen from the two moieties "however, observing an alternation" (Pecci 1941: 14). As Legesse (1973: 86) observes, "In peacetime the *Abba Gada* is a common herdsman who makes every effort not to stand out from the crowd. In time of crisis, however, his role is defined in a language so extreme that it does not seem to be part of the normal language of the Borana." He is, in fact, equated with God. The symbolic and ritual aspects of the *Abba Gada* might be likened to the nature of the *Kallu*, yet the two must be sharply distinguished. "The Callu," writes Pecci, "is a great Saint or Sorceror, thought to be of supernatural origin, who has great influence over the Boran populations. His dwelling is believed to be sacred and enjoys protection as a place of refuge. In it, magical rites are performed, and it is the pilgrimage destination for all Boran, including those of Kenya."

Traditionally, there were six *Kallu*, four from the *Sabbu* moiety and two from

85

the *Gona* moiety. Legesse (1973: 44) describes the *Kallu* as "ritual leaders of the moieties," emphasizing their political power: "Their villages are the spiritual centers around which political debate is organized." He adds that "Borana say that the *Kallu* are kings (*moti*)."

From this viewpoint, it is particularly interesting that the *Kallu*'s authority, undoubtedly ritual, was used by the Ethiopians for their political goals. Pecci (1941: 317) tells us how "the Abyssinians invested the highest civil and political authority in the two most important Callu of each moiety (*gossa*)," giving them "titles and privileges" such that "they did not hesitate to impose themselves on the *Abba Gada* themselves, resulting in considerable loss of the *Abba Gada*'s importance."

Pecci's information not only explains the different emphasis given to the authority of the *Kallu* by Pecci in comparison with Legesse, but also shows the colonial action of the central Ethiopian government. This episode brings to mind the colonial intervention of the British in Kenya, when during the first phase of colonial occupation they declared the *laibon* to be "paramount chief" of the Masai. Besides, the analogy between the figures of the *Kallu* and the *Mugwe* of the Meru, Kenya, both described as "king" (for the *Mugwe*, see Bernardi 1959: vii–viii passim) should be taken as a warning against attributing to the term *king* a literal value (cf. also Legesse 1973: 4).

In conclusion, the *gada* system, in many respects, shows itself to be very complex. The fact that it has gone through many important alterations in the course of its long history has been emphasized by all scholars. According to Bahrey's account, it seems certain that at the end of the sixteenth century there was a closer relationship between the circumcision rite and recruitment into an age class and its entering the *gada* cycle. Age classes were, and sometimes still are, referred to as *luba*, from the verb *lubomu*, to circumcise. In any case, the generational rules now represent the distinctive characteristic of the *gada* system, and circumcision has lost its structural significance. Indeed, circumcision is now just one aspect of the ritualization found in the *gada* system.

The *gada* system certainly cannot be considered the only basic component of Boran social organization; kinship is important, as are numerous ritual beliefs and the territorial system. But more than these other systems, the *gada* system affects and characterizes the entire Boran social organization. The continued repetition of its structural rites bolsters its prominent place and makes its significance felt more strongly by the people. But its most profound effect, that which makes of it a primary polity, is the distribution of potential and effective powers among class members that it accomplishes, assuring the passing of decision making, or political, power through the succession of the classes and their leaders along the ladder of grades.

Tradition and change among the Guji

Comparison of the Boran system with the *gada* system of the Guji is both inevitable and also stimulating, for the latter has been cited as evidence of the cognitive and ritual functions that for some are the only real significance of age class systems.

The Guji (Guggi) live to the north of the Boran, between Lake Abaya (Margherita) on the west and the Galana River on the east. The Guji have suffered much more than the Boran from the consequences of long-time Amhara domination. Near the end of the past century, Menelik's government established some military garrisons among the Guji; deprived the *Abba Gada* of all decision-making power; imposed chiefs named by imperial authority; and among these chiefs, included the *Kallu*, who took on a politically preeminent position.

The transformation of the *Kallu* from a characteristically ritual position into a political one merits further analysis. We have here a phenomenon that is the opposite of that which occurred not only to the *Abba Gada* but also to the entire *gada* system of the Guji, depriving them of their main political significance and limiting them to ritual significance. "Today, three quarters of a century after the conquest of the Guji: it is only the powers associated with the *gada* ritual which remain," states Hinnant (1978: 231). As a consequence, in his field research Hinnant focused on the ideological conceptions that underlie the entire *gada* complex, leading him to define it as a "religious system" (Hinnant 1978: 231).

This is certainly an interesting perspective. It emphasizes an aspect that other ethnographers have considered implicit in the system and described in passing. But we should never lose sight of the fact that the ritual and religious characteristics that today seem so apparent among the Guji are the result of changes brought about by acculturative contact with the Amhara rulers. It is worth noting, in fact, that the emphasis on traditional religious values, rather than on other values, is a typical consequence that subject peoples suffer when living in a colonial situation. Their political power has been totally alienated and their economic power also greatly reduced. In colonial situations, the religious sphere is the last to be affected; but there comes a time when this too collapses, and the ancient religious values are abandoned to embrace the values of the rulers. It is the time of religious conversions and other revivalistic and syncretistic movements. Among the Oromo, for instance, the situation reflects the pressures of the colonial situation. The Boran, who have been the most marginal to the center of Ethiopian feudal power, have remained the most attached to the old ways; the Guji, having lost their political traits, have maintained and emphasized their religious values; the Shoa have long been converted to the Ethiopian church.

There are two basic concepts of Guji ideology: destiny (*kayyo*) and virility (*kallacha* or *kallacia*). According to the Guji, destiny and virility, as well as the entire *gada* system, were created by God (*Waka*: literally, sky).

The concept of *kayyo* "subsumes the entire philosophy of interaction between man and God" (Hinnant 1978: 210). Ideally, it assures order and well-being and, because it is jeopardized by life's evils and dangers, these are combated through divination and ritual observances. Each individual has his or her own destiny, as does each age class. When the class takes over the stewardship of the country, its destiny reflects on the entire population. Accordingly, in taking possession of his duties, the *Abba Gada* spends a year passing from place to place transmitting the beneficial energy of his own destiny and the destiny of his class. When he later gives up his power, he tells the members of his class to stop contracting new marriages and cease procreating because the destiny of the class has diminished.

Hinnant writes that "*kallacha*, or virility, is the key symbol of the *gada* system and its leadership" (1978: 212). Virility is the male fertility force, comparable to that of God, whereas women's force is similar to that of the earth. Promotions through the *gada* system represent the continual acquisition of virility. It is possessed by *Abba Gada* to its maximum extent; his kinsmen are called "the men of virility." Virility is symbolized by a metallic phallus that the *Abba Gada* wears on his forehead every time he undertakes one of his duties.

The *Abba Gada*'s authority is the expression of the class that elects him and thus differs from the *Kallu*'s authority, which emanates directly from God. The first *Kallu* is believed to have descended from the sky. In olden times, the *Kallu*'s power was the power of sanction, expressed both through benediction and curse. What the Guji feared most was the *Kallu*'s curse, which they compared to a snake's bite, and the snake was therefore the symbol of the *Kallu*'s power.

The two powers – the *Abba Gada*'s and the *Kallu*'s – were supposed to be distinct. It was thought also that any confrontation of the two would cause danger. Therefore, to avoid conflicts and maintain peace, the symbols of the two powers were exchanged: The *Kallu* was, thus, given the right to bear a metallic phallus on his forehead, just as the *Abba Gada* did, whereas the latter, at the moment of his assumption of power, was given the right to kill a snake and burn its ashes on his metallic phallus in order to acquire the power to curse, just as the *Kallu* did (cf. Hinnant 1978: 212–23).

The Guji variant of the *gada* system

Knowledge of the Guji's present conceptions is useful in placing the religious meaning of the *gada* system in the proper light. However, it would be inappropriate to take this as sufficient evidence for concluding that the cognitive and ritual functions of the *gada* system are the only true functions of the age class system. In any case, the acculturated nature of the present Guji system undermines any such sweeping conclusion. For these reasons, it is pertinent for us to consider Hinnant's (1974, 1978) reconstruction of the pre-Amhara *gada* system of the Guji, based on information he collected from elderly informants in the field. In fact, Hinnant (1978: 230) reports, on the basis of such information, that "one of the vital roles of the system in the past was to provide and legitimise political, legal, and religious leadership." In other words, the Guji *gada* system constituted a primary polity.

Hinnant (1978: 227) offers us a "prototypical" chart of the Guji *gada* system.

Table 7.2. *A prototypical gada system*

Ego's rank	Ego's age when he changes rank	Father's rank
		Raba mido
		Marries; children abandoned
Born – *daballe*[a]		*Dori*
		Children legitimate
Makabasa ceremony	8	
		Gada
Karra		
		Batu
		Yuba
		Gives up wealth;
	28	*New children unwanted*
Kussa	32	
Raba mido		*Yuba guda*
Marries; children	40	
Dori		*Jarsa gudurru*
Children legitimate	44	
Gada	52	*Jarsa kolulu*
Batu	60	*Jarsa raka*
Yuba		
Gives up wealth;	68	
New children unwanted		
Yuba guda	76	
Jarsa gudurru	84	
Jarsa kolulu	92	
Jarsa raka	Until death	

[a] The name *daballe* has been added.
Source: Hinnant (1978: 227).

(See Table 7.2) From it, we can clearly see its similarity to the Boran system. The placement of the grades in the chart gives evidence of the forty-year structural distance separating father and sons, following the generational rule.

Some of the effects of the generational rule may be noted here. The first effect is the social autonomy of the two adjacent generations of the father and his sons (Ego). One succeeds the other, so that both reach the same social status, but at different times, avoiding any competition for the same status and effective powers. The Guji are conscious of this effect, and they maintain that the separation of adjacent generations is "necessary." They argue that adjacent generations are "antagonistic and dangerous, " whereas alternate generations are "equivalent and harmonious" (cf. Hinnant 1978: 214). All this makes it clear that the age class system has a structural effect; that is, it creates a social order that distributes roles and statuses. Accession of the age classes to the various grades and with it the acquisition and exercise of effective powers is regulated according to a system of careful timing.

Let us examine the character of each of the grades. There is a clear corre-spondence between the father's acquisition of the right to bear legitimate children, upon his completion of forty years in the cycle, and the entrance of his son (Ego) into the cycle at birth. These children are *daballe*; their position is liminal, and they are described in feminine terms until the *makabasa* rite, the naming rite, is performed.

Karra consists of a number of grades, in spite of its single name. Three *karra* periods are distinguished, two of eight years each and one of four, for a total of twenty years. The first phase covers the time of adolescence, leading to the passage to adulthood. *Karra* members are apprentices; they learn how to be good shepherds, how to use arms to defend the cattle. Indeed, they are junior warriors, whereas those of the *kussa* grade are senior warriors. Neither the *karra* nor the *kussa* is allowed to marry. The right to marry is only achieved at the next grade, *raba mido*, and it is only in the following grade, *dori*, that the right to bear children is obtained. Following this is the *gada* grade, which is the most pres-tigious of them all, for it entails decision-making power. This is the moment when power is handed to the *Abba Gada* of the class and the class takes on the responsibility for leadership of the people.

The *yuba* and *jarsa* also each consists of a number of grades, with their members gradually retiring from public life. The *yuba batu* stop taking more wives and having more children; the *yuba* hand their herds over to their sons, keeping just a few animals for themselves. The role of the *yuba guda* is exclu-sively ritual.

The *jarsa's* position is liminal: "The first *jarsa gudurru* wears the same braided hair style as children of *daballe* rank. Members of both are referred to in the fem-inine gender, have no daily responsibilities and are cared for by kinsfolk" (Hin-nant 1978: 219). The parallel between the similar position of the children and the retired elders in the *gada* systems of both the Guji and the Boran is striking.

It has been a long time since the Guji practiced infanticide. In those situations where, in the past, infanticide was compulsory, they now practice adoption by persons who are in the correct grade for having children. Adoption thus serves as a corrective for the negative consequences of the generational rule, but at the same time it confirms the rigidity of the rule.

The similarity of the Guji system and the Boran system also extends to the concept of patriclass. What the Guji call *missensa* presents the same character-istics as the Boran patriclass, *gogessa*. Both consist of five groupings, with one formed every eight years. The formation of such groups respects the generational rule, and therefore a son is always found in the same group as his father and forefathers. Hinnant states that the basis of the *missensa* among the Guji is the patrilineage. But because we are dealing with the same phenomenon in the two *gada* systems, and because the idea of patrilineage does not fully coincide with the phenomenon, it is advisable to use the term patriclass for both the *gogessa* and the *missensa*.

The significance of the Oromo variants in comparative perspective

One of the reasons for the great interest in examining the variants of the *gada* system is the substantial similarity found among the different ethnic groups. In its essential traits, the system can be seen to be an effective primary polity and, as such, it offers an illuminating example of the generational model. Other peoples in southern Ethiopia have today or had in the past some form of age class system. Among these are the Konso, a sedentary agricultural mountain people who are distinguished by a robust age class system in which both a *gada* system and a *harriya* system are intertwined in much the same way as the Boran system (cf. Hallpike 1972).

The Konso, too, had been long in contact with the Amhara, who subjected them to their rule. The Amhara feudal system was imposed on all these groups as political domination, as well as a religious advance marked by the traditional antagonism between the Ethiopian church and Islam. The stage of transformation of the ethnic characteristics of the *gada* system may be measured by the degree of penetration of Amhara influence. Indeed, it is due to such Amhara domination that the *gada* system has lost much of its political significance. This is true of the Boran, as it is true of the Guji. Among the latter, Amhara penetration has been more lasting and more effective, so that their *gada* system is today most notable for its ideological and ritual aspects. However, it would be unwarranted to emphasize these aspects without considering the acculturated situation in which they exist. Through the interrelation of classes and grades, the structure of the Guji system served to introduce and prepare children and adolescents for community life. It also served to regulate the structural time for marriage, childbearing, and more recently for adoption.

Among the Oromo, Amhara domination has led to a colonial situation and, as in all situations of this kind, the subject people have lost political power, leaving room only for those aspects of their traditional social organizations that did not contrast with the power of the rulers.

This conclusion finds further confirmation in the *gada* system of the Shoa Oromo. The Shoa are the most northerly of the Oromo, and they have been in contact with the Amhara longer than all others. They are today a sedentary people dedicated to a type of mixed agriculture. They cultivate cereals and keep goats, sheep, horses, and cattle, as well as chickens.

The loss of previous characteristics of the *gada* system is much further advanced among the Shoa than among the Guji. Even during the past century, ethnographic reports revealed the presence of foreign principles within the structure of the *gada* system among the Shoa. Thus, for example, wealth had become a major source of political power, so much so that the rich landowners tended to take on the role of "landed nobility." This process was fully encouraged and accelerated by the Amhara, who themselves had a stratified monarchic society with social classes of aristocrats and plebes.

Age class systems

Blackhurst (1978: 258) observes that "the Amhara did not simply abolish *gada* officials and the *gada* system and replace them with their own political and administrative officers. There was rather an element of indirect rule in the administration of the incorporated areas." It was this impact, that only euphemistically can be described as "indirect," following the established jargon, that affected the *gada* system. As Blackhurst remarks: "First, it exaggerated tendencies already within the system towards a further weakening of its political functions, and second, it created a situation where two political systems were in competition with each other for the allegiance of the people."

Currently, the Shoa *gada* system has just five grades, each covering a period of eight years. Recruitment follows the generational rule, and hence sons are always found at five grades, or forty years, distance from their father. The five grades are:

1. *Itimako*, 0–8 years
2. *Daballe*, 8–16 years
3. *Folle*, 16–24 years
4. *Doroma*, 24–32 years
5. *Luba*, 32–40 years

There are two promotional transitions that maintain the system intact: promotion to the third grade, *folle*, and promotion to the fifth grade, *luba*. Though the behavior of the members of the two grades seems antithetical, together they encompass the current significance of the entire Shoa system.

Whereas the first two grades, *itimako* and *daballe*, represent a common period of apprenticeship, the third grade, *folle*, involves the attainment of autonomy for the individual and the class. The young *folle* are at the height of their physical powers and show off in exhibitions of arrogance, through both their language – libertine or obscene – and their actions. However, they perform certain functions in maintaining order; for example, it is up to them to punish an adulterous man who is caught red-handed by subjecting him to public pillory. It is very important to emphasize this fact. Even though it is of limited significance, it reveals a function that goes well beyond the simply ritual or symbolic.

Promotion to the fifth grade, *luba*, signals the attainment of full elderhood. In entering this grade, the class acquires a status of great respect. Its members must always maintain a dignified bearing, the opposite of that of the *folle*, because they are responsible for the political guidance of the people.

Once the five-grade cycle is completed, the man becomes *yuba*. However, this is not considered to be a promotion of grade; that is, *yuba* does not constitute a grade, as it does among the Boran and the Guji, but simply an undifferential category of people.

As can be seen, the current significance and functioning of the Shoa *gada* system represents barely the shadow of the complex working of the Boran and the Guji *gada* systems. However, nothwithstanding this fact, the Shoa system is of great comparative interest. At present, *gada* celebrations are aimed at

92

protecting the health and fertility of both people and animals, and the system has been reduced "to a series of almost wholly domestic ritual" (Blackhurst 1978: 245). Following this perspective, Blackhurst attributes importance to the *gada* system as a model of the structure of Shoa family, household, and village. At the same time, he does not neglect the broader and more involved meaning of the system. After what we have seen of both the Boran and Guji systems, we can recognize the validity of Blackhurst's (1978: 266) conclusion:

The past involvement of *gada* in a tribal political system gave it a specific form and significance. The disappearance of this political system has directly affected *gada* firstly by narrowing the ceremonial arena of *gada* celebrations and secondly by highlighting the religious, as distinct from the political, features of the system.

8

The residential model

Among the various ways in which structural age is used as a principle of social organization, a unique place is held by those societies that employ age in the organization of residential settlements. Reference here is not to the temporary residential segregation that is often part of initiation rites and that, for example, characterizes the young warriors grade in the initiation model, but to settlements such as villages.

The Nyakyusa of Tanzania, studied by Wilson (1951), have become renowned in the anthropological literature for their so-called age villages. Wilson's interpretation has substantially withstood the heavy criticism directed at it, criticism that we will take into account in our analysis. But the Nyakyusa age villages are only one of the forms, and perhaps the least significant, of the use of structural age for residential organization.

Other forms specifically directed to residential organization and the maintenance of order of communal life display more complex structural and functional characteristics. The best-known cases, at least with respect to the available ethnographic information, are the Afikpo villages of Nigeria and the ethnic groups of the Lagoon Peoples of the Ivory Coast.

The existence of residential systems that make use of structural age as an organizing principle is documented among a number of other populations as well, such as the Yakö of Nigeria (Forde 1950: 267–89), the Ndembu of Zambia (Turner 1955: 121–37), and the Lele of the Kasai in Zaire (Douglas 1963: 68–84). In such cases, however, we are provided only with sketchy information that does not allow satisfactory comparative analysis. It is only because structural age is the principle underlying the peculiar forms of residential organization that we are justified in defining such social organization in terms of age class systems. Although the nature of class recruitment and the distribution of effective powers differ from system to system, it is the effect of the class system on residential organization that is the primary characteristic of these systems. It follows that the functional model that emerges in this context can be appropriately termed residential.

The residential model

We start by examining the Afikpo system, turning then to the system of the Lagoon Peoples of the Ivory Coast and finally to the Nyakyusa age villages.

The Afikpo village group

The Afikpo belong to the ethnic and linguistic group of the Igbo of southern Nigeria. They live on the west bank of the Cross River in villages whose compactness distinguishes them from other Igbo villages characterized by more spread-out settlements. In the current Nigerian administration, the Afikpo are in a territorial division that is named after them but includes an area greater than that occupied by the *Afikpo clan*, the term used in the colonial period to refer to the Afikpo village group, with a total population of 35,000 and an average village population of 1,500.

One of the Afikpo's distinctive characteristics is their dual system of kinship. This is almost certainly the result of the cultural mixture brought about by the fusion of the Igbo immigrants with a preexisting local population. However this may be, the Afikpo currently rely on their paternal line to organize their residence in the village and follow their maternal line in defining their property and inheritance.

Each village is divided into compounds and wards. The compounds are enclosed clusters of private dwellings, whose inhabitants are members of the same patrilineage. Entrance into the compound is provided by a single gate. The ward is composed of the aggregation of a number of compounds, and the complex of quarters constitutes the village.

Each compound has its own separate spaces and services, just as it has its own shrines or altars, around which communal ritual activities take place. In the same way, each village also has its own communal spaces and places: The shrines are widely scattered throughout the village and are dedicated to a large number of gods and ancestral spirits.

The Afikpo village group is sometimes referred to as a town, but perhaps it is better described as a district. Uchendu (1965: 44) notes that the village group is neither "a federation nor a confederation." In fact, each village retains its autonomy and names its own elders to the district council.

Within the intervillage markets, the centers of commercial exchange on the district level are communal houses reserved for the elders of the district council. Cultivated fields surround each village. The Afikpo are primarily agriculturalists, though they also, albeit to a lesser extent, engage in riverine fishing. Yams, taro, and manioc are their principal crops. Cultivation of yams is considered prestigious and is reserved for men; cassava and manioc are cultivated by women.

Politically, we are told, "There are no village chiefs in Afikpo: rule is by the elders as a group. In this sense it is a genuine gerontocracy" (Ottenberg 1971:

95

91). Just what is meant by this last term must be inferred from a careful reading of the ethnography.

The Afikpo age classes at the village level

Descent and age are the two principles on which village structure is based and which, according to Ottenberg (1971: 52), "create the groundwork of village life." As has already been noted, descent is patrilineal, and consequently the social configuration of the village is also patrilineal. Age mates are grouped together on the basis of their common age without regard to kinship, and in this way age classes are formed. It is through age classes that the social status of village members comes to be defined and with it the distribution of responsibilities in communal life. According to Ottenberg (1971: 52), "There are usually between fifteen and twenty age-sets in the community, each one covering a span of approximately three years." Such a large number of classes indicates that the Afikpo system needs to be placed in its own perspective. First of all, class recruitment is not directly connected with initiation, and thus the system does not conform to the initiation model. In general, initiation is not practiced in a formal manner among the Igbo, and its performance differs from village to village (cf. Jones 1962: 205). The Afikpo, too, hold to their own tradition. They perform both circumcision and clitoridectomy at a quite young age, but these operations do not entail any structural effect.

Age mates start grouping together in adolescence, but this occurs as the result of spontaneous attractions: The boys of the same age tend to spend time together, work together in the communal labor assigned to them, and participate together in competitive sports, especially wrestling, the most popular sport among the Afikpo.

It is in connection with wrestling that a first informal promotion takes place along a series of grades. These are purely sports-related grades, but they are considered preliminary to the institutional formation of age classes. The number and series of sports grades varies from village to village. However, commonly there are three: an initial grade – *mkpufu mgba*; a middle grade – *isogu*; and an upper grade – *ikpo*. Youths are admitted to the first grade at roughly fifteen years of age, to the second between eighteen and twenty years, and to the third between twenty-eight and thirty years.

As is evident, the members of the third grade are already mature men. In fact, they have already gotten married, for the right to marriage is not a function of membership in any particular class. Those promoted to the third grade are admitted to one of the various secret societies connected with the cult of some divinity. All these promotions afford a peculiar type of initiation process. In any case, on reaching the third sports grade one is considered adult and comes to be part of the category of elders, becoming at the same time members of an age class.

96

The residential model

Formation of a class involves a number of formalities, which may vary from village to village but which may only be held with the consent and control of the senior elders. Admission into a class does not take place by group, but rather by individual; each person must pay a fee to cover the expenses of the communal celebrations and pay a tax to the senior elders. During the communal celebrations, the new class is host to its senior classes. Whoever is absent during these celebrations will be accepted as a member of the class only after he has paid his fee. When these communal celebrations have been completed, the new class receives its institutional name.

There are villages in which no formalities are involved, and a new class is considered to exist with the promotion of the candidates to the third sports grade. The normal frequency of the formation of a new class is one every three years. Members of the institutionalized classes are no longer expected to engage in manual labor nor to take part in sports competition except as advisors and instructors, and this also on an individual basis.

Each class is free to decide on its own internal organization, specifying its own rules and the activities of its members. However, members are always considered equals.

On the basis of this internal equality, each class plans its activities in response to external events. Only rarely has military activity been one of the activities of the Afikpo age classes.

Although the sets would appear to be well organized for warfare, and have names associated with strength and bravery, they have rarely been the basis of warrior groupings. Fighting groups in Afikpo seem to have been organized on the basis of village, ward, and major patrilineage, with all the able-bodied men of the group concerned taking part without a great deal of formal organization or leadership, or to have been a matter of small parties of men of different ages going out to take heads for ceremonial purposes. (Ottenberg 1971: 64)

Each class is divided into segments corresponding to the internal divisions of the village, ward, and compound. As a result, just as the residential structure is patrilineal, so the age class comes to be patrilineal in the arrangement of its segments. Each of these segments enjoys full autonomy in its initiatives, because it must respond to the local exigencies of the moment. Thus, as Ottenberg (1971: 67) observes, "From the point of view of the individual, membership in a set fixes a person's authority role not only in the village, but in the ward and the compound as well as in his matrilineal groupings and in Afikpo as a whole."

The triennial rhythm of class formation necessarily leads to the multiplication of sets or classes, and as a result, to a finely graded stratification and an elaborate division of functions and responsibilities. As has already been noted, the number of sets or classes varies from village to village. But whatever the number, there always exists a gradation in their status and the status of their members. The Afikpo speak of this in rather broad terms, distinguishing a series of grades in terms of juniors, young elders, and elders, but considering them all as one against the youths who are still involved in sports contests. Ottenberg clarifies this arrangement. Within a village, when sets or classes are formed on completion of all wrestling grades, they can be distinguished as "junior sets" (the first three sets), then as "executive sets" (two or three sets), then as "young elders" (two or five sets), and finally as "elders" (normally nine sets, rarely more). Though each village may keep its own tradition, the passage from one grade to another is always solemnized with rites, feasts, and the payment of fees to the elders to secure their consent for the promotion of the sets from grade to grade.

The set or class of the so-called executive grade is responsible for the organization and oversight of public works in the village, such as the clearing of roads, the construction of bridges, and the preparation of communal celebrations, including the gathering of the necessary foods, the inspection of the public works carried out by the youths, the youths' conduct in sports competitions, and, finally, the prevention of any outbursts of violence.

The elders are responsible for the general oversight of everything that takes place in the village, dictating, if necessary, new norms and issuing decisions of a judicial nature. However, these rights are not exercised in an authoritarian fashion but rather in the framework of the councils, where the various questions are freely discussed. Whoever is interested in the matter can speak up and express his own opinion. Only at the conclusion of such a discussion do the elders issue their decision or decide on a sentence, and these are considered binding.

The Afikpo age classes at the district level

Beyond the village, at the district level, the elders enjoy an eminent position and theoretically are all equal. In practice, however, there are at least two elements that introduce distinctions among them.

The first of these arises from differences in individual oratorical capabilities, especially as these have an influence on council debates. The second derives from the position of the elders and of their classes in the stratigraphic gradation of classes at the district level. Three grades or subgrades, as Ottenberg calls them, (1971: 224–5) are recognized here: junior, middle, and senior.

The junior elders belong to the most recently formed classes of the villages, and they range in age from roughly fifty to sixty years old. Their position is subordinate to that of the middle elders, whose orders they carry out. In fact, the junior elders, at the district level, constitute a police force for the maintenance of social order, and it is up to them to collect fines, arrest criminals, and repress any abusive behavior.

The middle elders, ranging from sixty to seventy years old, have both legislative and judicial decision-making power affecting the economic functioning of the markets and the amount of bridewealth, as well as the promotion of the junior classes to the senior grades.

The senior elders are all of advanced age, roughly seventy to eighty years

Table 8.1. *Afikpo age class system*

Village	District
Wrestling grades (informal class groupings): 1. *Mkpufu mgba* 2. *Isogu* 3. *Ikpo*	District elders, *nde icie ehugo* Junior elders: 3 village classes, executive function (50–60 years old), *ekpe uke ato*
Formal institutionalization of the set or class, with or without initiation	Middle elders: 6 village classes, judicial and legislative functions, (60–70 years old), *ekpe uke esa*
Junior sets: from 1 to 3 classes, *nsu ekpe* Senior sets: from 2 to 3 classes with executive functions, *uke ekpe* Young elders: from 2 to 5 classes, *ohale nde icie*	Senior elders: 3 village classes, (70–80 years old), few survive, *oni ekara* Residual category: over 80 years old, *ho ri*
Elders: from 9 to 12 classes, *nde icie*	

Source: Ottenberg (1971: 170).

old. They retain the prestige that comes with old age, but their active participation in community life recedes with the fading of their own physical strength.

Clearly, the hierarchy of Afikpo age classes is rather complex. The elders belong at the same time to the class structure of the villages and to the class structure of the district, which operates autonomously. To describe such a system as a "genuine gerontocracy" is certainly simplistic and deceptive.

Because in the Afikpo language the categories of youths and elders, of juniors and seniors, are characteristically broadly defined, it is necessary to take a closer look at the actual structural organization of the system and the resulting differentiation of functions it provides. In fact, it must be observed that the two levels of village and district not only supply a difference in structure and functions but also a difference in attitudes. At the village level, cohesiveness and unity of action prevails, whereas at the district level the elders are inclined to follow their own individual interests, as happened in the past in response to the central colonial governments and as even now happens in the face of the national federal government.

To synthesize the characteristics of the residential model that can be garnered from the Afikpo system:

1. At the *village level*, the grouping of age mates originally takes place spontaneously, influenced by the grades that are distinguished within the context of sports competitions.
2. The institutional formalization of age classes is bound to the advancement to the third sports grade or takes place as a result of it. Distinctions among classes facilitate the distribution of responsibilities for the internal administration of each village.
3. Although locally reflecting kin-group membership, age classes constitute the only comprehensive criterion for uniting people at the village level.

99

4. At the *district level*, the elders represent a broad category effectively divided along a stratigraphy of grades, within which the various classes progressively move.
5. Differentiation of the grades occupied by the classes serves to define and allocate the administrative responsibilities for governing the entire district.

A graphic illustration of the system is given in Table 8.1, which adapts the scheme originally formulated by Ottenberg.

The Lagoon Peoples of the Ivory Coast

The *Lagoon Peoples* is a term of convenience used to denote the peoples who live along the low-lying portions of the rivers and lakes that surround the region of Abidjan. The principal groups are the Ebrie, the Aboure, the Mbato, the Atie (considered part of the Lagoon Peoples more for their cultural characteristics than their ecological situation), the Adjoukrou, the Alladian, and the Avikam. All show obvious cultural similarities, yet there are also notable differences among them and indeed even within each of them.

The age class system of these peoples has been most specifically studied both in monographic and comparative form by Paulme (1971 a, b, c), but references to it are found in all the published studies of the Lagoon Peoples, particularly in the works of Niangoran Bouah (1964, 1966) and Augé (1975).

The Lagoon Peoples are currently engaged in cultivation and river fishing, but at one time they were known for their aggressiveness. They used to return from their war ventures carrying triumphantly the heads of their enemies, so that they were also renowned as headhunters.

A characteristic that the Lagoon Peoples shared with many other West African populations was their village organization. Each village was normally planned perpendicularly to the flow of the water, on the sides of a single central street. In recent times, with increased population size, two or three streets parallel to the main street have been added. The village was normally divided into three sections: high, medium, and low. Each section included a number of compounds, or courts, each formed by one or more homesteads and an internal courtyard. The closed side of the homesteads bordered the street, whereas the entrance opened on the side of the space between one compound and the next. Communal gatherings and village-council assemblies took place in the central street.

In many respects, the village of the Lagoon Peoples was structured by matrilineal kinship organization, and its historical foundation was always traced back to the ancestor of the dominant matriclan. As regards marriage rules, the village constituted an endogamous unit, with exogamy practiced among the clans and matrilineages of the village. There was a preference for patrilateral cross-cousin marriage, with virilocal residence. In fact, the articulation of the matrilineal and patrilineal elements was an important characteristic of the social organization of all the Lagoon Peoples.

Table 8.2. *The age class systems of the Lagoon Peoples*

	Society			
	Ebrie	Aboure	Mbato	Atie
Class	Blessue	Bruswe	Bresue	Bresue
	Niando	Nowe	Niando	Niando
	Dougbo	Bele	Dugbo	Dyigbo
	Tiagba	Taba	Monakua	—
Initiation unit or	Diehou	Atible	Dyewo	Gyewo
subclass	Dougba	Bawule	Tyagba	Tsogba
	Agban	Jamia-Malimbe	Mundone	Bunto
	Assoukrou	Jamia	Adeyehera	Asungba
	—	—	Ataba	Agbri

Politically, the village enjoyed full autonomy and represented the basic unit of the system. Within each village, social relations could vary to a greater or lesser extent. For example, the village organization of the Alladian exhibited, in the words of Augé (1975: 28–9), an "emphasis on the village," whereas the organization of the Avikam showed a "clan emphasis." This dual distinction emphasizes, on the one hand, the importance of the kinship system – involving both clan and lineage – which, in relation to the village structure, is always of great importance and sometimes even predominant. On the other hand, it points out the prevalence, or at least the significance, of certain institutions more directly connected with the village organization, such as the division into village sections, the physical distribution of the dwellings, the role of the village leader, and the age class system.

The importance of the age class system in relation to the village was greatest among the Atie and the Ebrie. Among these people, the residential distribution of the inhabitants into village sections was governed by class membership, to the extent that there was a certain coincidence between village section and age class. Of all the Lagoon Peoples, the Atie and the Ebrie provide the most typical and significant example of the residential model of age classes.

The formation of age classes among the Lagoon Peoples

As with the other social institutions of the Lagoon Peoples, the form of the age class system generally differs from one people to the next, though with obvious similarities. The system is normally organized into four classes (the Atie have three, the Adjoukrou seven) and each class is subdivided into four or five initiation units or subclasses. Table 8.2 gives a comparative outline.

Recruitment was governed by two principles: postpubertal initiation for the initiation unit, and generational relationship for class membership. Initiation was normally celebrated every four years, and the age admission was around sixteen

years. Within a family, the firstborn preceded his younger brothers and consequently always belonged to a senior unit. All the sons of the same father were,
however, supposed to be admitted to the alternate class to that of the father.
Although this represents a generational norm, it cannot be equated with the basic
rule of the generational model. In this model, it is the structural distance between
the father and son that determines the admission of the son into the class system,
whereas in the case of the Lagoon Peoples admission into the system first comes
through initiation. Moreover, among the Lagoon Peoples the relationship between
father and sons not only determines class membership but also determines their
residential distribution in the village sections. However, the generational distinction of the classes among the Lagoon Peoples is rigid. Sons of the same
father, though they may find themselves in different initiation units as a result
of the difference in the timing of their respective initiations, are always assigned
to the same class on the basis of their common paternity. In contrast, among
the Adjoukrou recruitment was based only on the initiation age of the candidate
and not on his generational relationship to his father.

The cyclical repetition of class names created a constant relationship between
the classes: the senior alternate classes were always the "fathers," the junior
alternate classes the "sons." Among several of these societies, such as, for
example, the Ebrie, the constancy of this placement of the classes gave rise to
two moieties, each of which was formed by the classes of "fathers" and "sons,"
in patrilineal relationship. Paulme (1971c: 208) discerns structural value in these
moieties, especially emphasizing their patrilineal character:

	First moiety	Second moiety
"Fathers"	Dugbo (1)	Tsagba (2)
"Sons"	Blesue (3)	Niando (4)

The structure has only been uncovered through anthropological analysis and, as
Paulme (1971c: 208) remarks, "this dual division is not explicitly recognized:
Although there is a term used to designate the classes, there is no such term for
indicating the 'moieties'." Therefore, if any value is to be attributed to this
phenomenon, it must be that of latent structure, though it is significant that this
should be patrilineal.

The latent structure is in fact apparent in the relations between the classes.
These relations tend to create tension between adjacent classes, whereas between
alternate classes the elder class always displays some solidarity toward and
support of the junior class. According to Paulme (1971c: 208 n.7), this phenomenon brings to mind similar relationships found among the classes in East
African systems. From this perspective, it is logical to recognize the cause of
such tensions between adjacent classes as arising from confrontations produced
by class succession. There is resistance on the part of those who must leave the
grade and pressure on the part of those who aspire to the grade. In practice, the

confrontation is manifested in almost banal, yet impressionable ways: in the disciplinary control that the class exercises over the class junior to it. This junior class, for its part, will act in the same way with respect to the class that follows it, so that the members of the junior class are always the scapegoat for the oppression suffered from the class senior to it. However, the "fathers," of the senior alternate class, protect their "sons," in the junior class.

Another observation should be made with respect to the patrilineal nature of the "moieties." The terms "fathers" and "sons" with which the alternate classes are called are a typical feature of age class systems; they are not at all unique to the Lagoon Peoples. Indeed, the language in which relations between members of the various classes are expressed is normally taken from kinship terminology. In the case of the Lagoon Peoples, this terminological borrowing assumes special significance, however, not only because it highlights the latent structure described by Paulme, but particularly because it emphasizes the patrilineal aspect of the age class system in contrast to the predominantly matrilineal character of the Lagoon Peoples' social organization.

Solidarity and equality characterize the relations among age mates within each initiation unit and also within each class. Yet as a result of the lineage principle, there is considerable room for individuals to assert themselves and thus for the development of different positions within the groups. In brief, it can be said that the ideal of solidarity and equality embodied in class membership is deeply felt and, in the past, was especially binding when members were involved as warriors in military actions. This contrasts with the ideal embodied in lineage membership, where solidarity pertained only to the members of one's own lineage and, in the past, emphasis was on the acquisition of wealth and gold to enrich one's own lineage (see Niangoran Bouah 1964 and Augé 1975). Lineage membership was also a means for the allocation of offices within the village and, to a certain extent, within the class. Among the Atie, for example, offices were passed from uncle to nephew along the matrilineal line. This represents yet another point of articulation between the lineage principle, which was matrilineal, and the class principle, which was patrilineal.

The succession of classes in time and status necessarily implies a series of grades. This matter has not been entirely clarified in the literature on the Lagoon Peoples. Paulme provides an outline of the grades found among the Ebrie, which can be taken as typical of the Lagoon Peoples; see Table 8.3.

From the genealogical perspective, the series of grades covers the entire normal life span. The designations of the grades provided by Paulme in her French terminology are not comparable: Aspects of physical maturation are referred to in three of the grades, whereas for the second grade the military function is emphasized. Clearly the matter is more complex; we need further clarification of the relationships existing between the age class system, the residential settlement pattern in the village sections, and the political system. It is worth repeating here, too, that the meaning of the expression "holding power" with reference

Table 8.3. *Grades among the Ebrie*

Grades	Ideal age	Actual age
Youths (*enfants*)	16	8–24
Adults (*guerriers*)	32	24–40
Mature men (*hommes mûrs*)	48	40–56
Elders (*viellards*)	64	56–death

Source: Paulme (1971^c: 260–1).

to the class of ''mature men'' is rather imprecise and ambiguous, even though this phrase is very common in anthropological writings on age class systems.

Lagoon Peoples' village polities

In every model and in every system, membership in a class involves the allocation of a status, which changes with the movement of the class along the line of grades. Along with this, membership involves the exercise of the effective powers inherent in each status. ''Among the Lagoon Peoples,'' writes Augé (1975: 131), ''this attainment basically corresponds to the entry into a political relationship which goes beyond the simple lineage relationship.''

Political relations among the Lagoon Peoples are rooted in village organization. In fact, whoever belongs to a class acquires: (1) the right to live in a particular section of his village of origin, though one's right of residence is based on one's lineage membership; (2) the right to undertake certain activities based on the grade occupied by his class; and (3) the right to compete for village offices.

Attainment of the right to live in a village section should be interpreted, first of all, as an expression of the individual's autonomy with respect to his family of origin. Individual autonomy is one of the most important effects of all forms of postpubertal initiation. Once they had successfully passed through the great trial, the members of a new class demolished the dwellings currently standing in the section of the village that had been assigned to them and, in the same place, constructed their own new dwellings. ''Without breaking their kinship ties, by having an independent residence, beside neighbors who had the same family problems, the youth were able to escape strict oversight and class solidarity was strengthened'' (Paulme 1971c: 211).

The residential mobility associated with the succession of classes is perhaps the most characteristic feature of the Lagoon Peoples' age class system in the context of the residential model. At a distance of a generation, the members of a new class followed the same movement of the classes that preceded them.

Among the Atie, the high village section was reserved for the ''warriors,'' the low section for the ''sons,'' and the middle section for the ''fathers.'' The

104

spatial division reflected simultaneously a distinction in structural age and a distinction in status and function.

Among the Mbato and the Aboure, movement took place only at initiation, when the new class took possession of its own village section, where it remained permanently (Paulme 1966: 108). It is understandable that, in this way, there came to be a kind of identification between village sections and class; "a Mbato man lived all his life in the village section where he went to live upon the formation of his class, so that the same term was used to refer, according to the context, to both the class and section. *Giefio* not only indicates the village section where one lives, but also indicates age class" (Paulme 1971c: 250).

The bilineal principle emerges continuously in the Lagoon Peoples' village organization: The principle of matriclan and matrilineage provides the basis for the right of residence and the principle of age class membership is the basis for the distribution and succession of inhabitants in the sections of the village. The two principles are also expressed in relation to the internal functions and offices of the village, but with different effect. Augé (1975: 37) observes that among the Ebrie, for example, "residence prevails over descent"; in other words, the age class principle, connected with residence, is for the Ebrie more influential than the lineage principle.

Among the powers deriving from class membership, aside from that of residential autonomy, which has already been discussed, the right to marriage must be mentioned. Though the choice of spouse among the Lagoon Peoples was governed by lineage membership, the timing of marriage was determined by class membership. Paulme (1966: 111) justly observed, in noting the late age of initiation, that "the functioning of a system of this kind cannot be understood apart from its role in population control."

To these powers must be added the right to provide instructional assistance on the part of the "sponsor" or "tutor" who was responsible for the formation of the youths into a new class. Each of the sponsor's children was required to give him a "gift," and all of them were required to do whatever work he requested of them in his compound or his fields.

The instruction covered knowledge of traditions and behavioral and military training. The youths' military activity was so absorbing that, in people's minds, it assumed an exclusive importance. There is no doubt that this was emphatically thought to be the case by the people, yet putting the military aspect in proper perspective does not necessarily mean belittling the importance of this element. Today, the "warriors" of one time are, as Paulme states, "unemployed." This is one reason, though certainly not the only one, for the transformations that have taken place in the age class system and in the entire social organization of the Lagoon Peoples.

Participation in political life reached its zenith when, having become "mature men," the class obtained "the power." Though this grade can be considered to hold the maximum prestige and decision-making power, participation in political life came first through exercising the right to police the village. This was a real form of power, though tempered by the fact that the last word on all village matters was entrusted to the class of the "power-holding elders."

Paulme considers the right to hold the office of headman in the village as a typical manifestation of the power of the "mature men." In contrast to this view, Augé (1975: 51) cites the opinion of Niangoran Bouah, who maintains that the office of headman was a colonial creation and had no traditional tie to the age class system. Augé holds that "at the most, the age class system served as a basis for chronological reference." In any case, headmanship involved the clear articulation of the lineage system with the age class system. The choice of the head was determined not only on the basis of his membership in the proper class, but also by the quality of the man's lineage of origin. The headman, rather than being a kind of king or political chief, was more in the nature of a dean or senior elder. Paulme (1971c: 210–11) describes the office in terms of its "priestly nature," for the man's initiatives as headman – *akube nana* – were especially sought after in disputes regarding land, where it was necessary "not to upset the hidden masters of the soil," that is, the ancestors. Tenure in office ended with the promotion of the following class to the grade of "mature men."

The choice of headman took place within a small council elected by the class, taking into account the lineage of origin of the members. Among the Atie, two of the counselors belonged to the senior initiation unit, and the first one named had precedence over the others and was considered in public opinion destined to become the new village headman. The third counselor belonged to the second initiation unit, and the fourth belonged to the third unit.

Other offices were assigned within each class, such as, for example, the positions of judge, assistant judge, town crier, musicians, etc. A special place was reserved, among the Ebrie, for the *taprognan (tapronya)*, chosen for his excellent physical appearance and moral qualities. He was the hero in times of war and the best dancer in times of peace. He had to be capable of making noble gestures, because he personified the ideal of class perfection and symbolized the class itself. Contrasted with him and with the *duassanowo (dwasama)*, the select group of warriors, was the coward and idler, *kwitawo*.

Paulme (1971c: 212) summarized the general characteristics of the Lagoon Peoples' age class system with the following points: (1) solidarity among class members; (2) the organization and execution of public works; (3) the exercise of political power; and (4) organization, in the past, of military activity. To these, we would add a fifth characteristic, the residential distribution of classes in the village sections.

All things considered, the residential model expressed by the age class system of the Lagoon Peoples appears to be a global institution. From the political viewpoint, Paulme compares it to the "diffuse government" described by Mair. In this sense, we can understand Paulme's (1966: 117) hypothesis, offered in relation to the Atie, that it is likely that the succession of classes to power served as a check impeding the formation of a centralized state.

Paulme's (1971c: 212) summarizing description of the Ebrie system reiterates the significance and the value of the age class systems among the Lagoon Peoples as a primary political organization based on age. She writes of: "matrilineal clans but virilocal residence and patrilineal age classes; the village as a political unit, self-sufficient and whose daughters marry locally; the class of 'mature men' in power, who must take into account the councils of the elders and at the same time restrain the enthusiasm of the 'warriors,' who themselves are under pressure from the youths (*enfants*) jealous of their successes; a fragile structure in which we can discern the concern that no clan and no class, or no party, stay in the limelight too long.''

The age villages of the Nyakyusa

In the age villages of the Nyakyusa, we face a unique institution. First of all, in contrast to what happens among all neighboring peoples, the Nyakyusa are not organized on the basis of kinship but rather on the principle of age. We must ask, consequently, to what extent we are justified in seeing this system in terms of age classes.

The Nyakyusa are a Bantu population numbering about 50,000. They live in southern Tanzania on the Livingstone Mountains, which rise from the northern point of the Lake Malawi. In precolonial days, the territory was divided into a hundred chiefdoms, each composed of a cluster of villages. The chief belonged to an "aristocratic" clan, for he was a descendant of one of the first Nyakyusa to come to the lake: His office was hereditary. Presiding over each village was a headman selected by popular election.

The kinship system is essentially patrilineal, but great emphasis is also given to cognatic and bilateral ties in enlisting people's cooperation and aid. The Nyakyusa practice mixed agriculture, currently supplemented by cash crops such as coffee and rice. Their cult of ancestors, a characteristic of all the Bantu, is mixed with a strong belief in witchcraft, "the breath of men.''

Since the 1930s, the Nyakyusa have been the object of study of Godfrey and Monica Wilson. To the latter, in particular, we owe a series of monographs on Nyakyusa social organization and their villages. Although the analysis and description of these villages have raised considerable hermeneutic problems, their importance for comparative study is unquestionable.

A new village begins to take shape before its first residents reach puberty. Normally, a youth is separated from his parents' home when he is about ten or eleven; he is then sent to a secluded residence, where he may find other boys like himself already present. One hut is built after another so that all the youths are housed, and the result is a satellite village on the margin of the parental village.

107

Age class systems

The segregation of boys is a widespread practice, commonly connected with the initiation process. It is not in this feature that the uniqueness of the Nyakyusa villages is found. Rather, as Wilson (1951: 159) observes, it "consists in the fact that contemporaries live together permanently through life, not merely as bachelors." Sharing the same residential location thus acts as a means of social aggregation. Living together in the same village, the age mates form a distinct residential group, which is made homogeneous by their commonality of age. It is in this sense that the inhabitants of a Nyakyusa village may be compared to an age class. But it is clear that the similarity is based on a rather broad analogy. An age class recruits its members without regard to residential or kinship ties; the Nyakyusa village, on the contrary, is not only by definition a residential institution, but is seems to be conditioned, at least to a certain extent, by kinship. This is the case because the boys who are originally segregated belong to kin-related families, and in their relations with each other they express the values and solidarity of their kin group (cf. McKenny 1973: 94).

Although the young residents of a village tend to develop common social interests, not all their social life is conditioned by their village membership. For example, marriage, celebrated normally between twenty and thirty years of age, is attained according to norms strictly governed by the kinship system and are not regulated, nor were they even in the past, by membership in an "age village."

The establishment of new villages brought about a special relationship among existing villages in terms of age and social stratification. In fact, a chiefdom was normally divided into two sides, each comprising: (1) "two or more villages of old men, contemporaries of the chief's father" with ritual functions; (2) "two or more age-villages of contemporaries of the chiefmen of the ruling generation" with administrative and military functions; (3) a number of new "boys' villages made up of young brothers and sons of contemporaries of the chief." The latter were entirely dependent on the chief and his contemporaries and fought under their leadership (Wilson 1951: 31).

This structure was modified and renewed by the celebration of a solemn promotion ritual when the two sides of the old chiefdom became chiefdoms on their own. The old chiefdom disintegrated, with the old chief adhering to one of the new chiefs, a person who normally belonged to his own lineage if not in fact one of his own sons.

The promotion ritual (which was described by Wilson as a "coming out" ceremony) was celebrated "eight or ten years after the young men of the senior boys' village had begun to marry" (1951: 22). By that celebration, all the boys' villages were publicly recognized as full-fledged villages, and therefore for each of them a headman was elected and a territory for cultivation was set aside. At the same time, a chief for the new chiefdom was also elected, and the headmen were expected to declare their allegiance to him in the same way that all village inhabitants were expected to state their allegiance to their own headman. Loyalty to a chief entailed the right to a chiefdom's membership, whereas loyalty to a

108

headman entailed the right to reside in his village. Adhering thus to a chief and a headman meant recognizing their capacities as ritual mediators in the maintanence of harmony and order in the chiefdom and the village.

The continuous formation and fissioning of new chiefdoms was brought to a halt in the colonial period. Among the purposes of the Nyakyusa promotional or "coming out" rite was the attempt to guarantee the fertility of the families and of the fields and herds. As is apparent, such a rite was not a normal initiation rite; it did not involve single individuals as such, but rather the entire village as a community. It served to clarify and ratify the whole panoply of relations – territorial, residential, and political – brought about by the formation of new villages.

Behind the motives that move the Nyakyusa to segregate their youths in secluded villages, beyond physiological age and development, there is also their concern to maintain certain cultural values. Wilson synthesizes these values in the concept of "good company," expressed by the Nyakyusa term *ukwangala*. Good company consists of friendship and understanding, which bind together the age mates: "A main end of age-villages, in the Nyakyusa view, is to allow men the enjoyment of congenial company of friends and equals" (Wilson 1951: 162).

It is friendship more than equality that is emphasized. And this involves people who, according to Wilson, are bound together by ties of kinship and affinity. It is a matter of keeping peace among kinsmen, who feel constantly threatened, especially by the fear of witchcraft, to such an extent that they may abandon the company of their own kinsmen. As the Nyakyusa say, " 'It is not good for a son to live close to his father, they will quarrel.' 'When we move to another village we consider friendship not kinship is selecting it' " (Wilson 1959: 93).

Segregation may, in fact, be seen as avoidance. The attempt is made to stifle any sexual competition between father and son and also to ensure that there is no opportunity for the son to observe, much less spy on, the parents' sexual relations. Moreover, residential segregation is a means of preventing the sons from having incestuous relations with the young wives of their polygynous fathers, just as it prevents the fathers from having such relations with their daughters-in-law (Wilson 1951: 159–62).

Kinship and witchcraft

Wilson is adamant in maintaining the contrast between kinship ties and residential relations:

> Kinsmen are bound together by their common interest in the inherited stock of the lineage and in the cattle coming in for its daughters; by co-operation in cultivation and building; and by the belief that they are mystically interdependent – the contagion of defilement and of certain diseases caused by sorcery travelling along the roads of kinship. Village neighbours are bound together by occupation and ownership of common land;

by cooperation in herding and cultivation; and by common defence against enemies "by day and by night." (Wilson 1951: 170)

McKenny (1973: 96) offers a more flexible interpretation. He claims that the absence of kinsmen from the age villages is not a rigid norm but rather "ties of kinship and age were utilized by persons to accomplish certain things in a large arena – the economic and ritual system of the chiefdom."

In any case, even if it is true that witchcraft – which the Nyakyusa define as "the breath of men" – works among kinsmen, it also threatens the good company of the village. Indeed, Wilson (1951: 165) argues, the village residents are more exposed to the jealousy that inspires witchcraft than are kinsmen. In seeing the wealth in cattle of one's relatives and affines, kinsmen do not become jealous because they know that they will one day take part in it through inheritance. But neighbors who are not kinsmen and see such bounty without having any claim on it feel jealous and their "breath" becomes malevolent. For this reason, reciprocal accusations of witchcraft are frequent in the village and recourse is continually being made to the headman's mediation.

The only effective remedy for witchcraft is keeping good company and observing the rules of social exchange, ever ready to share one's milk, meat, and other foods with one's neighbors and to cooperate in the communal tasks of the village. From this perspective, not only are fellow village residents no longer feared, they also come to be seen as one's defenders against the danger posed by witchcraft.

McKenny's criticism of Wilson's interpretation of the concept of authority is quite cogent. He notes that "authority was an attribute of certain categories of individuals regardless of the relative standing of their age-villages within a generation or between generations. In a small-scale society age itself counts for something, but most particularly through the things that go with it – wives, children, affinal alliances, control of cattle, the allegiance of dependents, things which accrue to age with or without the age-village system." Village structure, according to McKenny, has no relation to power. The promotional "coming out" ritual "was crucial in defining relations between chiefs and commoners." Renewal (Wilson cites the phrase from the Apocalypse, "I will make everything new"; Ap. 21: 5) produced by the promotional rite is only symbolic, according to McKenny: "But the ceremony itself does not reveal any clear-cut transition in the relations of authority within the chiefdom." McKenny argues that village structure was fluid: With time, immigrants entered who had nothing to do with the age of the original inhabitants; "what gave the age-village its continuity was not so much its personnel as its headman, the focus of the village, who in his turn was identified with the chief by virtue of having gone through the 'coming out' with him." (1973: 100–1).

According to McKenny, the true source of the solidarity of age mates, inspired by their common residence, was the difficulties and limitations that the youths confronted in their kinship sphere in attaining autonomy with respect to land control, women, and livestock. In such a situation, "an ideology of age-mate association could have been important in forming a natural alliance group" (1973: 103).

Thus, in this view, it is not just age that stands at the origin of the Nyakyusa villages, but a complex of different reasons and social interests. McKenny raises similar arguments with respect to the chiefdom. In his view, there are three sorts of social relations in a chiefdom: (1) relations of kinship, (2) age mate relations, and (3) relations of chief and headmen and their consciousness. He contends that "a man without kin, age-mates, or a chief was scarcely a social personality: but it seems that, though they were of importance, age-mate relations were the most easily dispensed with" (1973: 101).

In conclusion, it seems beyond doubt that the age principles had a structural and determining, though not exclusive, weight in formation of new villages. However, this is not tantamount to saying that residential segregation as practiced by the Nyakyusa was transformed into a corporate grouping of the village inhabitants matched by a gradation of status and, consequently, of power, such as to mark it as an age class. Aside from the villages, the Nyakyusa give age a certain value as a principle of differentiation and participation, but only in an informal, not institutionalized, way.

9

The regimental model

In the next two chapters, we will examine some systems that, though no longer in existence, have a unique historical value. This value stems from both the fact that they have lain behind the social structure of important societies, and because they present unusual models for the use of the age principle.

The two models to be considered are called, respectively, the regimental and the choreographic, because in the first military organization is the predominant characteristic, whereas in the second the *principal* aim is the organization of traditional songs and dances. The regimental model is represented by the ancient *Nguni* population of southern Africa. The choreographic model is found among some of the ancient Indian groups of the North American prairies.

The ancient Nguni

In the history of southern Africa, from the eighteenth through the entire nineteenth century, the Nguni were famous for the long chain of wars and continuous resistance that was their response to the territorial expansion of the colonial powers, whether Boer or English. In the course of these hostilities, internal rivalries among clans led to the splitting off of the Nguni peoples, giving rise to the formation of autonomous ethnic groups that have by today been displaced into different states of southern Africa.

The Zulu are now found in the Republic of South Africa, where they were once part of the province of Natal, but are now considered to constitute an "independent" state, an autonomous "Bantu territory" called Kwazulu, with Ulundi as its capital.

A second ethnic group is the Swazi. They live in the little independent state that has been named after them: Swaziland. Formerly a British protectorate, it lies to the north of Natal along the Mozambique border.

A third ethnic group is formed by the Ndebele in what is now Zimbabwe. They live in the southern regions of the new state and cluster around the city of Bulawayo.

112

The regimental model

A fourth ethnic group is the Ngoni, the only one that still bears the ancient ethnic name. After legendary raids that brought them from South Africa to the shore of Lake Tanganyika, they ended up establishing their residence in Malawi, where they still live.

Another group of the same ethnic stock is the Xhosa-speaking peoples of southern Africa. Both the internal migrations of the Nguni and the intercontinental migrations of the Europeans were movements of expansion and conquest. The Nguni were driven by the necessity of finding new lands for their herds and crops and moved along the southern highlands that face the Indian Ocean toward the northeast regions of Africa. Along their journey and in their new settlements, they were frequently confronted by the white colonists. In rapid succession, they met first the English, who had landed in Natal; then, coming in from the Cape, the Dutch-Boer *vortrekkers*; and finally the column of English pioneers financed by Cecil Rhodes who were to settle the land that was named after him, Rhodesia. The method followed by all the Europeans was substantially the same: First, with various enticements and gifts, they requested hospitality from dominant African leaders; then they defended the rights they had acquired by employing force; finally, they always proclaimed the annexation of the entire territory for their mother country or else imposed their own local European-style government.

It was in this way that the Nguni expansion was blocked, but not without a series of conflicts, misunderstandings, and suspicions that permanently poisoned the relations between Africans and whites. The Nguni, whose military pride had made them the feared, dominant power over vast territories, were defeated and humiliated. This military decline exasperated their internal divisions, leading to a process of social and political decline and profound changes, from which the present Nguni ethnic groups were born.

Two characteristics explain the ancient Nguni's military efficiency and expansive force: the emergence of able and astute military leaders and the regimental organization of the population. The Nguni's traditional social structure, typical of the Bantu peoples, was articulated around a series of patrilineal clans. But it is neither in the vitality of the clan organization nor in the emergence of outstanding individuals that the uniqueness of Nguni history is to be found. The exceptional fact that distinguishes the Nguni from the other Bantu populations is the skill with which certain clan leaders designed and implemented radical reforms in warfare tactics and military organization. Thanks to this success, certain clans assumed a position of great authority, transforming the kinship system into a monarchic system and, in this way, giving their clan the prestige and continuity of a dynasty.

Of the dominant clans at the end of the eighteenth century, the most powerful was the Mthethwa clan, headed by Dingiswayo. At that time, the Zulu clan was of little importance. It was with Dingiswayo, however, that Shaka of the Zulu clan, the man destined to become the most famous of all the Nguni leaders, found refuge and protection. Dingiswayo was responsible for the beginning of the transformation of the ancient age class system into a regimental organization. Shaka was to bring Dingiswayo's reform to completion, carrying "the evolution of military and political institutions to a new stage." He armed his regiments with short-handed stabbing spears to substitute for the long-handled javelins (*assegai*) that used to be hurled from a distance. The stabbing spear was, instead, to be retained throughout the battle. He also introduced new tactics – the so-called cow's horns – by which two regiments, one on the right and one on the left, would trap the enemy as two encircling horns. Shaka also abolished the circumcision ritual to avoid the warriors being immobilized during convalescence. Omer-Cooper (1976: 327) concludes:

The introduction of these new tactics necessitated prolonged drilling and was related to a further development, the introduction of continuous military service and the barracking of the age-regiments in special military settlements at the royal households, where they remained until formally dissolved and given permission to marry. As a result of this change the value of the age-regiment system as a method of integrating tribal aliens into the community was greatly increased. What was more, the whole balance of power within the political system was radically altered.

The Nguni reforms provide us with a case of particular interest because they reveal a plan of radical intervention both in the age class structure and in military tactics and organization. Gluckman (1940: 31n) notes that Dingiswayo's reform took place "on the basis of old age grades." The term age grades is used here by Gluckman as a synonym for age classes or age sets. The old Nguni age class system was of the initiation-model type, and initiation included circumcision. It was circumcision, not initiation, that was abolished by Shaka, though as a consequence the entire initiation process was profoundly modified, making the young initiates observe a more severe and rigorous discipline. Shaka's motivation behind the abolition of circumcision was clear. He intended to avoid altogether the period of immobilization of the circumcised youths who were obligated to await the healing of the wound left by the operation. With circumcision abandoned, the conscripts were immediately available for all the instruction and drilling that their military life required.

The segregation of the conscripts in training camps and the delay in marriage imposed on them bring to mind the initiation model exemplified by the Masai. As has been noted, during the period of recruitment of a new class, the young Masai warriors – *moran* – were required to live in the segregated dwellings that were reserved for them, and they only acquired the right to marry upon the completion of their military obligation. However, the Masai's discipline was not nearly as rigid as that found among the Nguni.

Shaka's achievements, which completed the reform begun by Dingiswayo, were not only accomplished by his genius for reform but also by his cruelty as a tyrant. Shaka died, the victim of a conspiracy, in 1828.

The regimental model

Zulu initiation and conscription

After Shaka's great reforms, the Zulu became the most powerful Nguni clan and, of all the Nguni groups, they remain the best known. In fact, their social system may be considered typical of the regimental model.

Until the last few decades, even during the colonial period, although only indirectly, Zulu society retained its politically centralized, or monarchic, organization. The king, or supreme leader, was the center of the entire society and the source of all authority and power.

Several observers have provided information on the long process involved in the traditional Zulu initiation ritual. Within this process, a series of four rites signaled social recognition of the attainment of one of the four grades into which, within this perspective, the Zulu divided the ages of a man:

1. *Qumbhusa*, the ear-piercing ceremony signaling the childhood grade
2. *Tomba*, publicly recognizing the attainment of puberty
3. *Ukubutwa*, recruitment of a candidate into a regiment and his attainment of full youth
4. *Kehla'ing*, conferring a head-ring on the candidate and thus signaling his attainment of elderhood status, implying the right to marry

Mahlobo and Krige (1934), the authors from whom our data are taken, observe that the rites of childhood and puberty could either be celebrated individually or in groups, but, in any case, did not give rise to institutionalized corporate groups.

It is interesting to examine the postpubertal *tomba* rite, both because it fully embodied the cultural conception of the Zulus concerning the vital force and because it was performed anew when a candidate joined a regiment and was promoted to full youth status. The essential meaning of the rite concerns the growth of the virile force of the candidate. In the first phase, the adolescent was expected to gather the scattered livestock and bring them into the *kraal*, in which he, too, was enclosed, to emphasize symbolically the force he had acquired with puberty. In the second phase, the candidate was treated with vegetable and animal medicines, which were used to massage him and which, in part, he had to ingest. There followed a third phase of segregation in the initiation hut, where the candidate lived for some time under the community's control and protection. During this period, he was given sexual instruction and was not permitted to leave his isolation, still less to converse with women. The fourth phase was devoted to sacrifice: Once again, the candidate was enclosed in the *kraal* together with the officiant: The invocation was directed to the ancestors, who were urged to recognize the initiand as a son. By the 1930s, the *tomba* rite had become rare, and the Christians celebrated it only in reduced form, without sacrificing animals (Mahlobe and Krige 1934: 180).

In spite of the individualistic nature of the first two rites, the age mates, following their natural tendency, spent their time together, forming spontaneous and homogeneous age units. As Mahlobo and Krige describe it, "Any group of children in a neighbourhood, differing in age by not more than three years, belong to the same *intangu* or age set and call each other *ntanga* – my equal" (Mahlobo and Krige 1934: 158). Rather than a formally institutionalized age class or age set, we find here a spontaneous and informal, though clearly indicative, anticipation of youthful aspiration. The greatest of these aspirations for Zulu adolescents was formal recruitment into a regiment. That could take place only with the celebration of the *ukubutwa* rite and the formal assignment of a name to the regiment. From that moment, the regiment was formally constituted and the period of membership recruitment was definitively closed. Again we see a similarity between this system and the formal creation of a class in the initiation model.

Admission to a regiment required frequent repetition of the *tomba* rite. Such repetitive rites were meant to strengthen and renew the physical and moral force of the recruits as warriors. The rite indeed had a practical effectiveness, as it involved physical massages, which undoubtedly served as preliminary preparation for the exertions and fatigue that came with the life of a warrior.

Recruitment into a regiment was seen as the culmination of the social promotion of an adolescent. By becoming a warrior, a young recruit was given the opportunity and power to exhibit his abilities. Moreover, the aggregation of candidates into formal regiments provided them with a position and status within an institution whose composition extended well beyond the limits of local groups and was thus universally recognized.

Formation of a new regiment depended on the king's decision alone. It was up to him to indicate the propitious time for the celebration of the *ukubutwa*. This term literally means "to make the regiment," *butwa* being the regiment. The word *ukujutshwa* has the same meaning and could be used as a synonym. The rite itself was complex and lengthy. The time chosen for the celebration was normally the dry winter season, immediately after the harvest, when there was an abundance of food.

Upon the announcement of the king's decision, the columns of participants, under the leadership of their chiefs, and with the provisions being carried by each warrior's younger brother or cousin, moved from their various territories toward the king's residence. Mahlobo and Krige (1934: 183) described the scene as follows:

> The general rule at the *Jutshwa* ceremonies in the old days used to be that all the men of the tribe were present for the first few days; the oldest regiment formed the council of the chief and in this they were aided by the other married regiments; the younger unmarried regiments looked to the order and welfare of the kraal, while the regiment that had been *jutshwa'd* last was in direct charge of the young men whose turn it was to be grouped. The life led at the *Jutshwa* is "that of soldiers."

As can be seen from this description, the Zulu polity, under the authority of the king and chiefs, reflected the military organization. Even the elders maintained intact their corporative regimental identity, although they did not perform any special political function.

The first task entrusted to the recruits was construction of the provisional huts for nighttime shelter. Their main daily activity, however, was to train in physical exercises and perform songs and dances. They were also required to do some work in service to the king. This involved cultivating the king's fields and caring for his livestock. Sports competitions and matches aroused great rivalry, not only among the recruits coming from various districts, but also among individual competitors. Considerable tension surrounded such events. The chiefs looked on with great attentiveness, for they were responsible for recognizing the champions and proclaiming their success.

During their stay at the royal residence, the recruits were absolutely forbidden to have any relationship with women. All their attention was to be devoted to absorbing technical instruction and advancing their moral education. Norms of conduct were inculcated with much severity and great attention to detail. These involved, above all, honor and respect for one's elders, one's parents, and the chiefs who represented the king. Other important norms included the premarital ban on relations with women, except with one's female age mates, whom, however, it was forbidden to impregnate; glorification of the work ethic, which makes a real man and allows him to be rich in livestock, giving him the opportunity to build a large family; and the importance of the community, whose well-being one must always have in mind. One informant commented, "There are so many 'don'ts' that I can hardly remember all of them, especially as not many of them are observed generally" (Mahlobo and Krige 1934: 185).

It was up to the king to determine both the length of time that the recruits remained at the residence and the duration of the *ukubutwa* celebration. Normally, everything was completed within six months. The celebrations were closed by the formal naming of the regiment in the presence of the king. This rite also included the formal handing over of arms – the *assegai* and shield – by each chief on behalf of the king.

From military activity to folkloric function

According to Bryant's estimate, in Shaka's time the regiments were formed by youths from all the clans and had about 1,000 men each, with the entire army numbering roughly 20,000. It should be borne in mind that in this period the splitting off of ethnic groups had not yet begun. In another estimate, regarding the years around 1870, Gluckman (1940: 36n) calculates that "the later regiments consisted of nearly 8,000 men."

On their return, the members of the regiment stopped at the residence of the chief of their district. The stop lasted at least one day and was aimed not only to pay homage to their local chief, but also to hand over their arms to him: It was up to him to keep them and to distribute them in time of need.

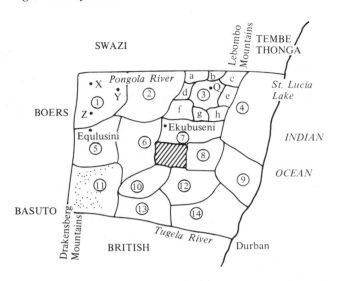

Figure 9.1. Zulu territorial organization. (Adapted from Gluckman 1940: 27.)

Although they returned to their families and fields, the men always remained attached to their regiment. In precolonial times, they were required to return each year to the barracks at the royal residence to strengthen the royal forces and renew their training. All the men, both chiefs and followers, always had to be ready for the king's orders. The king's authority was absolute. As has been noted, he alone determined the formation of the regiment and determined the time when the members of a regiment were free to get married.

The repeated stationing of the regiments with the king was a necessary means to assure their loyalty. Locally, the chiefs represented the king, to whom they owed their authority and office, but they too were required to present themselves periodically to the king. The observation of this practice forestalled possible attempts at rebellion and secession.

As can be seen, everything in the formation and organization of the regiments glorified the king's centrality. Gluckman (1940: 27), in a brief sketch shown here in Figure 9.1, gave a rough idea of the Zulu territorial organization, making clear its centralized character as it existed at the time of king Mpande, around 1870.

Gluckman comments as follows on this sketch:

This is a sketch of the territorial organization of the Zulu nation under King Mpande. It is presented only as a plan, and not as a map.

The shaded area is the King's, containing his capital, other royal homesteads, and military barracks (which are also royal homesteads). Numerals show tribal areas: there were many more then fourteen.

In tribe 3, of which Q is the capital, small letters show wards under indunas.

118

The regimental model

In tribe 1, X, Y, and Z are the homesteads of the chief and two of his important brothers: the men of the tribe are attached to these homesteads to constitute the military divisions of the tribe.

In tribe 11, the dots represent homesteads spread over the country. Equlusuni and Ekubuseni are royal homesteads which were the heads of national army divisions, though they lay outside the King's area.

During the colonial period, construction of and residence in the traditional barracks were forbidden. However, formation of the regiments continued with a certain regularity, each seven or eight years, until "military organization [had] been broken and peace established" by the British government (Gluckman 1940: 47).

The last occasion when a regiment was formed was in 1925, for the visit to South Africa of the Prince of Wales, but the event turned out to be without any true significance, simply folkloristic and decorative (cf. Mahlobo and Krige 1934: 181).

Shaka's revolution lasted just a century. It is worthwhile here to consider Gluckman's (1940: 46) observations:

The evolution of the barrack system affected Zulu social life considerably: it controlled marriages, and though the old secular labour division values remained, it was necessary for girls to assist in the world of herding and milking. The young men were not available for work at home and food had to be sent to them at the barracks. For the moment when they would be enrolled as warriors they waited eagerly, longing to join a regiment.

In conclusion, the Nguni regimental model is especially striking for the reforming initiative that generated it. Compared to the other models, it demonstrates both the importance and limits of the military function of the age class systems. The function is important, but not exclusive: It was only the historically unique reform found among the Nguni that made it so central. But such a manipulation of the military function altered the nature of the entire social organization. Shaka's reforms not only affected "the sexual labour division," but had even greater consequences for the distribution and exercise of power. Shaka's true goal, beyond his technological and organizational reforms, was that of concentrating in the supreme chief all forms of power and command. Although this concentration was the basis for extraordinary efficiency, it altered the traditional nature of military activity. From a right/duty, exercised in a polity that, if not acephalous, was certainly not highly centralized, military service became an obligation imposed from on high and entirely subordinated to the wishes of the king. The military ideal and the regimental organization of the Nguni are not to be found in any of the other models, even in the initiation model, where military activity, though admired and sought after by the young initiates, is not a permanent activity.

The regimental model is clearly unique, contrasting sharply with all the other models, including the initiation model, with which it shares certain similarities. This contrast is clearly the direct result of the reform that changed a traditional polity into an absolutist political system.

119

10

The choreographic model

In the anthropological literature, the term *age societies* has come into use to refer to a type of association found among certain peoples of the North American prairies. These associations show certain clear similarities to the age class systems found in Africa. There were basically five Indian societies involved here: the Mandan, the Hidatsa, the Arapaho, the Blackfoot, and the Gros Ventres.

The prairie Indians, just as all North American Indians, over the past two centuries have traversed an ineluctable process of cultural transformation. The changes that have occurred over this tragic period have irreversibly brought these people into the complex structure of advanced industrial society.

From the ethnographic vantage point, our only firsthand accounts of these independent societies are the descriptions provided by the first European explorers of the eighteenth century. Later research and reconstructions, even that conducted by Lowie earlier in our century and employing professional criteria, have had to be content with indirect sources of information and not participant observation. A few years ago, Stewart (1977), in the second part of his book on the fundamentals of age groups, compared the various ethnographic sources, from von Wied-Neuwied (1839, 1841), to Lowie (1913, 1916, 1919), to Bowers (1959, 1965), coming up with a well-documented and intelligible descriptive synthesis, which I will rely on in the analysis and descriptions that follow.

As has already been mentioned in Chapter 4, because it is dancing, singing, and the decorations connected with their performance that constitute the central element around which the structure and functions of the age societies develop, we refer to the model represented by these societies as choreographic.

Buffalo hunting was common to all the prairie Indians. In the past, the buffalo moved freely throughout the immense spaces of the prairies in a seemingly infinite number of groups. Hunting was not left to individual initiative, for it required a complex organization that involved the entire community. The large-scale hunt took place during the summer season and was the annual occasion on which all members of the same people united at the same camp. The grandeur of this organization was so characteristic of these people that the prairie Indians have come to be ethnologically classified as the great hunters of the prairies.

The choreographic model

Yet notwithstanding their common hunting activity, there were notable cultural and social differences among these ethnic groups. The Mandan and Hidatsa were largely, if not exclusively, sedentary. The Blackfoot and Gros Ventres were nomadic and divided into bands, who only united during the summer season to hunt together. We will not refer to the Arapaho in our analysis because unfortunately information on their age societies is too limited.

The acquisition of age societies among the Mandan and Hidatsa

At the time of their first encounter with the Europeans, at the beginning of the eighteenth century, the Mandan lived in six fortified villages along the northern portion of the Missouri River. The Hidatsa were located even further to the north along the same river as well as the Knife River. Among the main evils, and few benefits, brought by the Europeans was a series of epidemics. By the end of the eighteenth century, both the Mandan – who were more numerous – and the Hidatsa had been decimated. In 1837 a final, virulent smallpox epidemic reduced them even further, to such an extent that the Mandan were practically extinct. The survivors came together in a single village, called Like-a-Fishhook. There they tried to keep their ancestral traditions alive. Unfortunately, however, their social disintegration could not be arrested, due both to the extinction of the buffalo around 1880, destroyed by the ruthless massacres of the herds by the new European migrants, and to the federal government's repression. Their age societies had been entirely destroyed. Our description of the system, then, is based on a reconstruction focusing on the period from 1781, the year of the first epidemic, to 1837, the year of the great smallpox outbreak.

Both the Mandan and Hidatsa villages consisted of residential agglomerations surrounded by palisades. Each village was independent. General governance was exercised by the council of elders, whereas for each particular group activity there was a leader elected or chosen by appropriate means. The elders' council was not the expression of the age associations. These latter were groupings directly tied to social and recreational activities and sometimes, but almost always indirectly, involved in military, political, and ritual activities.

Ethnographic reports contain references to age groups (which Stewart compares to age classes because they were formed through the aggregation of age mates) and age societies (which Stewart equates with age grades). The age societies within each village constituted a social gradient along which the groups (or classes) succeeded one another through the rhythm of precisely timed promotion.

Membership in a society constituted the juridical title for the acquisition and exercise of specified rights and, in particular, for the prerogative of performing certain songs and dances and possessing certain decorations to the exclusion of all others.

Recruitment into a society took place with the collective purchase of the rights associated with it. The holders of the rights indicated a price, and the candidates assessed an appropriate tax among themselves, thus participating collectively in its acquisition. There was a true transaction of buying and selling, whose object was acquisition of the decorations and rights connected with membership.

In addition to its economic aspect, the transaction had a promotional value and determined the succession of one group (or class) from one society (or grade) to another. The time for this transition – that is, the time of the sale on the part of the group that owned the rights of a society and the time of purchase on the part of the aspiring group – was not fixed. Each group was free to decide and agree on its own time. However, possession of a society by a group did not normally last more than six years. The youths were the first to exert pressure for the acquisition of the rights, because to become members of a society and enjoy the rights that came with it meant attainment of the autonomy and prestige associated with adult age and elderhood.

The dances were all substantially the same in rhythm and type, but not in the content of the songs and the timing of performance. Each society had its own calendar specifying when the dances were to be performed. The themes of the songs were varied: love, war, sport. The decorations consisted of all aspects of the costume, including clothes, decorative bands, haircut, masks, and body painting. An integral part of these decorations was the musical instruments, including various kinds of flutes, bull-roarers, and drums, which were valued not only for their sound but also for their aesthetic quality.

Because the acquisition of an age society meant social promotion, it was always the occasion for a celebration. The celebrations that accompanied it lasted for days, from a minimum of six days for the lower societies to a maximum of twenty – and even forty – for the most important societies.

The series of societies varied from village to village. The diversity involved the lower societies, that is, the first in the series, which were distinguished by different names and duties in the different villages. In fact, they were the property of the youngest groups, whereas the last societies were the property of the eldest groups. The middle society was the most sought after because it had unique functions and privileges. The lack of precise definition of the timing of succession and of acquisition of the age societies was occasionally the cause of a certain overlapping, whereby the same group owned two societies while another group had none. These were possible, but temporary, situations; but they do indicate the elasticity of the system.

The series of age societies reported by Stewart (1977: 257) for a Hidatsa village is:

1. Stone Hammers
2. Little Dogs
3. Crazy Dogs
4. Crow Imitators (the reference here is to the Crow tribe)
5. Half-Shaved Heads
6. Black Mouths
7. Dogs
8. Old Dogs
9. Buffalo Bulls

The choreographic model

The middle society was the sixth, Black Mouths, whose prerogatives will be explained in the next paragraph. Here we are particularly interested in understanding the general functioning of the system in terms of the succession of groups (or classes). If, as mentioned, the rhythm of succession from society to society was on the order of every seven or eight years, a youth who entered the first society – the Stone Hammers – at age twelve and continued to pass from society to society through the entire series would arrive at the end of the series at about age eighty-four. In other words, the entire series covered a period longer than the normal life span.

Passage to the sixth society – the Black Mouths – signaled promotion to adult age, while passage from the sixth to the seventh society signaled entrance into the category of elders.

The first societies, those of the youths, had the right to perform dances and songs of love and war, whereas the last societies, those of the elders, enjoyed the right to perform all other types of dance and song. As has already been noted, the group that sold the society lost the right to perform the dances and songs associated with it. However, Lowie (1920: 327) relates that one of his informants, "a man named Poor-wolf considered himself at 90 the master of a complex bought at 7; of another obtained at 20; of a third held since he was about 27; and of a fourth purchased at about 45." If this is true, we might conclude that this situation was due to the advanced disintegration of the ancient system by this time. By the time of Lowie's research, after all, the process of acculturation was already far advanced. But one could also argue that this fact provides evidence of the normative fluidity of the age societies for which, as has been repeatedly stated, the rules of succession and ownership were neither rigid nor compulsory.

The structure and function of the Mandan and Hidatsa age societies

All activities of the age societies took place under the control and direction of a leader. The leader, a kind of choreographer who presided over the organization and performance of the dances and songs, was elected by the members of the group (or class). The choice was not only based on who was distinguished by his valor and courage, but also on who was notable for his skill in dancing and singing. These leaders had the right to own and wear special decorations.

The choral performances took place regularly inside the society's lodge, or in the open with solemn, public displays. Membership in the same society and joint performance of the same dances and songs, both in public and private, nourished and reinforced the corporative sense of the group. Its members considered themselves brothers and aided each other. For example, they made sure that a comrade did not diet excessively in his attempts to obtain supernatural

123

power; they provided consolation to those who experienced misfortune; and, in cases where a man was away, they monitored his wife's behavior.

During the transactions of buying and selling, and the consequent succession, the purchasers were considered the "sons" of the sellers. Such a relationship was not a collective one but rather involved individuals, though it could only be established at the time of negotiations between the two groups. At the time of this transaction, every member of the buying group placed himself in a relationship with one of the sellers, possibly one of his "clan fathers," that is, a person of the same kin group as the buyer's father. An exchange of gifts took place between the two men, and the "father" took it on himself to instruct the "son" in the society's songs and dances, passing on to him the relevant decorations he owned and also sometimes passing on his own supernatural powers. This took place with a simple incantation of blessing or, according to the tradition, with the "father's" sexual relations with his "son's" wife. Although this was a personal relationship, a "father" could have more than one "son," a situation necessitated by the fact that the number of elders who were available for "paternity" was always less than the number of purchaser candidates.

The specific function of the Black Mouths society could be described as that of police. Stewart (1977: 269–70) summarizes these responsibilities as follows: (1) to maintain order during communal activities and to stop or severely punish anyone who tried to hunt alone, since such activity might scare the herds; (2) to prevent conflict within the village, especially in the case of murder; (3) to ensure that the village did not drift into war, especially by maintaining peace among trading parties of different villages; (4) to defend the village according to the instructions of the council, especially at night. Stewart (1977: 268–71) emphasizes the "secular," or nonreligious, character of the Mandan and Hidatsa age societies. However, he does argue that it is necessary to take into account their basic religious conceptions to understand the meaning of the entire system. Indeed, there were some direct ties between religious activities and the age societies.

The religious conceptions of the Mandan and Hidatsa can be summarized in a few points: the supernatural character of all power; the derivation of power from supernatural beings; the possibility of obtaining power from supernatural beings through isolation, fasting, and mortification of the flesh to the point of mutilating a part of the body; and conserving the symbols of sacred things connected with this power in personal or tribal bundles or parcels. (It is clear that, in this context, the concept of power involves all individual capacities.)

Although the decorations associated with the age societies were not equated with the sacred bundles, the members of the group did make individual offerings to their society's insignias in the same way they made offerings to their own bundles. In other words, they treated the insignias of the age society to which they belonged like they treated the sacred bundles.

The choreographic model

The veneration directed toward these bundles, especially the tribal bundles, was tremendous. To be custodian for them was considered a privilege and was not only the source of prestige, but also of power. In practice, only the eldest men could hope to attain such a position and, in fact, membership in the last of the age societies, the Male Buffalo, was reserved for those people who cared for the tribal bundles. In other words, it was an age society whose members were "men with a great deal of supernatural power." With the dances that were reserved for them, the Buffalo Bulls were in a position to assure the continual presence of the buffalo and to guarantee the success of the hunt. Because custody to the tribal bundles could only be acquired at a high price, only the rich elders were able to obtain it. Thus, wealth and supernatural power converged to make the elders who belonged to the Buffalo Bulls extraordinarily successful men.

Stewart (1977: 271) maintains that the religious character of the Buffalo Bulls society constitutes an "exception." It is true that the age societies of the Mandan and Hidatsa were a unique kind of structure founded on the selling and purchase of the rights of each society, the acquisition of which automatically implied succession to the next grade of the system. But on the basis of such a structure the system incorporated multiple functions that emphasized, through dance and song, the position and power obtained in other ways. In fact, the choreographic model appears to run structurally parallel to the social models expressed by kinship and religious systems.

Stewart takes issue with Lowie's and Bower's claim that the military content of the songs is evidence for the military nature of the Mandan and Hidatsa age societies. Stewart notes that no one would claim that the same societies were of an erotic nature just because the songs of the first societies – of the "youths" – have an amorous content.

Stewart's argument seems compelling, though we must warn against seeing the age society system in terms of a single function, but rather in its entirety. The age society system is in fact an age class system, or a system of social gradation, implying the succession of the groups (or classes) who possess the "societies." The gradation and succession entail – in the same way as do the other age class systems – a differentiation of functions that, though they are expressed by the dances and songs, reflect the social position of the groups possessing the societies. Thus, the gradient of the various societies may be distinguished by the following characteristics: first, the amorous character; then the military activity; then policing (as in the Black Mouth society); then decision-making or political power (at the time when the group enters the category and councils of elders). Finally, there are the societies having prestige and religious power (like the Buffalo Bulls society). However, the common characteristic distinguishing the entire system is the purchase of the right to perform some dances and songs as their exclusive property; this is the reason why the system may be correctly referred to as choreographic.

The Blackfoot age societies

The Blackfoot lived around the border separating the United States from Canada, in northern Montana and southern Alberta. They were the most numerous and warlike of all the Prairie Indians. Essentially nomadic, they were divided into three principal groups: the Piegan, the Blood, and the Siksika (or northern Blackfoot). The three groups were subdivided into relatively small bands. Their principal activity was buffalo hunting, which was conducted on horseback.

Band membership was open, and there was great mobility in membership from band to band. The basic units within each band were teepees, with a normal band consisting of about twenty teepees, although some had as many as one hundred or even more. Each teepee contained, on the average, eight people.

In general, their entire social organization was "fluid and competitive" (Stewart 1977: 298). Equality among the members was a basic principle, but practical control was entrusted to the leaders, who were chosen for their valor and leadership capabilities.

The bands gathered together all during the summer season for the great buffalo hunt, but then they would separate again for the rest of the year. Thus there was a certain parallel between the seasonal movements of the bands and those of the buffalo. With the disappearance of the buffalo, which until 1880 had provided the principal source of food and raw materials, the entire Blackfoot economy had to change, and with it the social organization as well.

Internecine wars, a frequent cause of population decline, weighed heavily on the people, bringing about decadence and change. Their intolerant individualism made the Blackfoot prone to rebellion and the use of violence, whether the problem was an overbearing leader, a rival companion, or the necessity of punishing an adulterer. The last great fratricidal war occurred in 1870. In the following five years, from 1870 to 1874, an epidemic of alcoholism spread among the people. In 1877, the Canadian government created three Blackfoot reservations, one for each group. Yet, despite this, the social decline and cultural changes were slower among the Blackfoot than among the Mandan and Hidatsa. Among the Blackfoot, the age societies and, especially the Sun Dance, persisted for a long time.

The age societies only functioned in the summer when all the bands came together. The series encompassed nine or ten societies arranged in a gradient. In general, the system appears to be quite similar to that found among the Hidatsa.

The age of first entry into an age society is not entirely clear. Some informants maintained that by the age of between eight and ten years boys were affiliated with the first society; other informants have claimed that this first affiliation only took place when a boy was between fifteen and twenty years old.

Membership in an age society was purchased, as among the Mandan and Hidatsa. However, the Blackfoot were obliged to sell their society within four years of having acquired it. On the basis of these figures, we can calculate the time it would take to pass through the entire series of Blackfoot age societies. We find that a Blackfoot would complete the series between the age of fifty and sixty years old, marking a considerable difference from the Mandan and Hidatsa system.

Another significant difference involved the type of transaction that occurred. For the Blackfoot, the payment was not collective, nor did relations of seller as "father" and buyer as "son" need to be established at the time of the transfer. There was maximal freedom. Each seller, in fact, was free to sell to more than one individual: This meant that in exchange for payment he could distribute the decorations of his society and the supernaturally infused personal powers that he possessed.

Thus, individualism is a typical characteristic and dominant value of the Blackfoot. In this context, the unifying effect of the age societies is notable. It is true that the criterion of affiliation with a society was typically individualistic, so much so that each person was free to join a society without regard for his kinship group or the teepee to which he belonged. But once a person joined a society, he came to live with age mates who belonged to other kin groups and other teepees, and he took part in communal singing and dancing activities with them. The society's name itself came to emphasize their common affiliation, a commonality sustained by the obligation of providing aid to one another, especially during battles and in times of personal difficulty.

The bonds of solidarity among members of the society were also renewed during the annual Sun Dance celebration, the principal collective ceremony of the people, even though this ritual was not directly connected with any age society. The Indians lived in scattered small groups through much of the year, when the buffalo themselves were scattered about the plains. But in the summer, when the buffalo gathered in larger herds, the people, too, could come together in large groupings. It was during such annual gatherings of the tribe that the Sun Dance was held, encouraging the tribal members to renew their bonds and celebrate their tribal identity.

Among the Blackfoot, maintenance of public order was not the responsibility of any single society. Each year, during the summer gathering, the leaders of the individual kinship groups and the council of elders decided which society or societies were to be responsible for internal policing. Normally, three societies were chosen. The task was considerably more difficult and demanding than among the Mandan and Hidatsa, who were sedentary village dwellers. The Blackfoot circular camp, around which the tents were erected, could extend for more than a mile in diameter. The teepees were right next to each other and, when a child or a horse was lost or there was a dispute, those charged with maintaining order had to act quickly and efficiently.

In this regard, Stewart's (1977: 307) observation strikes me as quite significant: "The fact that the age societies were of much greater political significance among the Blackfoot than among the village tribes is obviously related to their sharing the police work.'' It is hardly necessary to add that this confirms, for the Blackfoot as well, the multifunctional character of the age societies.

The classes and dances of the Gros Ventres

The Gros Ventres were less numerous than the Blackfoot, but their band organization was quite similar. They lived to the east of the Blackfoot, in northern Montana and southern Saskatchewan. Although there are some excellent ethnographic studies of the Gros Ventres (Cooper 1957; Flannery 1953), they represent historical reconstructions based on material collected in a period when the organization of classes and dances had already been moribund for almost a century. Yet what little information exists, even though not always terribly precise, is of precious value to us for comparative study. (For the Arapaho, the information available is even spottier. But, from what we can tell, it indicates a system quite similar to that of the Gros Ventres.).

According to Stewart (1977: 321), the Gros Ventres had ''a true age-set system.'' In fact, it appears that they had classes in the sense of groupings of age mates who had a permanent name, formally instituted to carry out, according to a precise gradient, particular dance activities. In short, among the Gros Ventres a series of grades corresponded to the age classes, with these grades identified with varying forms of dance. The classes completed their duties when they had passed through the entire series of dances.

The timing of class formation is not well known, but it appears that it could take place every two or five years. According to others, however, the formation of a new class took place only when a class exhausted its own right to perform certain dances (or grades), and when its members, before retiring, acted as sponsors in the recruitment of young candidates.

The age at first recruitment is also uncertain, but it seems to have been at around fifteen years.

Because succession in the exercise of the rights to the dances was not marked by rigid timing, a varying number of classes could exist at any one time, from a minimum of twelve to a maximum of twenty-four. The imprecision of the data seem to mask a lack of accurate knowledge of the actual mode of operation of the system. We can, however, calculate approximately that a candidate who was recruited at age fifteen would reach the end of his dancing rights between sixty-five and seventy-five years of age.

The method of formalization of the class, as a grouping of age mates, is itself none too clear. It seems that it took place with the assigning of a collective name to the class. Membership in the class was open, in the sense that it was not determined by membership in any particular kin group, teepee, or band.

Once it had been formed, the Gros Ventres class was assigned to one of two moieties, or streams, into which the entire population was divided. These were called the Stars and the Wolf-Men. There was a dialectical relationship of competition between the two moieties, and in effect it seems that they served to order the performances of the class activities in the dancing competitions, horse races, verbal games, and other such activities.

As has already been noted, the principal function and activity of the classes was the performance of dances. The gradient was represented by a series of the six dances, and it is with reference to these dances that a gradient was established (Stewart 1977: 323):

1. Fly Dance
2. Crazy Dance
3. Kit-Fox Dance
4. Dog Dance
5. Drum Dance
6. Law-Enforcers' Dance

Two other sacred dances were comparable to these six dances: the sacrifice dance, which only marginally had a tie to the age classes, and the old women's dance, which had no tie at all.

The dance performances required buildings where the dancers could gather and be protected from inclement weather. The dances were thus performed in buildings normally referred to as sacred lodges, and, for this reason the term lodge was sometimes used as a synonym for dance.

All dance among the Gros Ventres had a sacred character. The Gros Ventres' religious concepts were not substantially different from those of other prairie Indians. It seems that they gave more emphasis to their belief in a Supreme Being and in an indefinite number of other supernatural beings, from whom the Gros Ventres hoped to derive and increase their power. The Gros Ventres also practiced solitary fasting and the mortification of the flesh to the point of mutilation as a means of obtaining a spirit vision and thus assuring themselves instruction in how to make a sacred bundle in which their personal power would be condensed. The Gros Ventres referred to their sacred bundles as *pipes*, for a pipe was the principal component. But the Gros Ventres also believed that it was dangerous to obtain supernatural power, because such power could shorten one's life. As a result, there were those who never sought it and those who, having obtained it, were glad to immediately transfer it to others.

Of these bundles, there were two tribal bundles of great importance, the Flat Pipe and the Feathers Pipe. The annual ritual cycle was oriented around these. Celebration of the festivals connected with this cycle could be requested by anyone who made a vow, and the celebration always included performance of certain dances. The performance of these dances was always an important occasion, in which virtually the entire population was involved in one way or another. Aside from the rituals connected with the pipes, which were the most solemn, the sacred dances mentioned above were the only religious solemnities connected with the bundles.

The old women's dance was the only dance that the women could vow. In contrast, the men could pledge the performance of the sacrifice dance or of any of the dances corresponding to the grade to which their age class belonged.

A dance vow was never made idly. In the case of the sacrifice dance, it could only be made once in a person's life, and thus it was pledged only in the most serious circumstances. In any other situation, if a person wanted to obtain a power or a supernatural benefit, he could vow the dance connected with his grade.

Before the pledge was made, there was presumably some kind of consultation with classmates, for the performance of the dance by the class could only be repeated one or two times, especially for those societies at the beginning of the series.

A dance performance could be extended over a number of days, according to the dance's importance. At the beginning of the series, the dance could conclude within a single day, but for the more advanced levels the performance could last four days. During the performance of the dance, the camp was guarded by an ad hoc council, formed by the pledger of the dance assisted by three or four councillors belonging to the adjacent class senior to the pledger's class, whom he referred to as "older brothers."

The council had to be very familiar with the methods and contents of the dance being performed. Such knowledge was previously obtained from instructors who were of the higher classes – those at least two grades above – and who belonged to the moiety (or stream) opposite that of the pledger. In any case, each council member had to choose a sponsor for his own personal instruction, who had to be duly compensated. The pledger's age mates did likewise, dividing themselves into little groups of no more than four to obtain the same paid instruction.

Lowie gave great weight to this payment, seeing in it an analogy to the system of age societies of the other prairie Indians, both in terms of ethnological origin and especially as an economic transaction. Stewart takes issue with this interpretation. Indeed, it seems that among the Gros Ventres we are not dealing with a buying and selling transaction of the same kind as is found among the other Indians. In any case, the buying and selling among the Gros Ventres does not involve so much the acquisition of the exclusive right to perform the dance, but rather simply the acquisition of the knowledge of how to perform it properly. In the end, the Gros Ventres system shows an interrelationship between age classes and age grades, with the latter expressed in terms of dance rights, and the gradient of dances being a means for distinguishing status and powers.

The choreographic model, as exemplified by the age societies of the old Prairie Indians, reveals itself as a peculiar kind of primary polity. However, one should not be prevented from realizing the multifunctional character of age societies by their apparently recreational nature. Through dance and songs, such societies promote an aggregating force by which members of society are classified and stratified as groups. In creating such groups, economic transactions in terms of purchase take place, a method of recruiting entirely absent in all other models. The fact that dances and songs are considered the property of age societies affords their members a corporate bond as strong as, if not stronger than, what is found among the age class members in other models. Moreover, it is noteworthy how age societies perform a definite political activity in being responsible for the organization of the social activity connected with dance performances and in keeping order during those performances. Finally, the connection of age societies with ritual activity further demonstrates their multifunctional character.

11

Women and age class systems

Up to this point, I have omitted almost entirely any reference to the position of women in age class systems because my intent has been to describe the basic features of the models of these systems. In the past, omissions of this sort have had a critical, if implicit, meaning. Age classes were thought to involve predominantly, if not exclusively, the male members of society and to be directly related to the postpubertal initiation of male youths. As a result, much attention was paid to this kind of initiation, whereas the initiation of girls and their social status were considered to be of no great interest. Kertzer and Madison (1981: 110) are correct in observing that "in many ethnographic reports, women are totally ignored, with references to 'everyone' or 'all the youths' signifying only males." In fact, the position of women in age class systems was not considered an issue of any value. Yet today no study of the problem of age classes could be considered systematic and objective without taking into account the position of women. We must clarify which forms of institutionalized age groups, if any, involve women, and we must understand why age class organization is more frequently found among males in a society, just as it has been possible to clarify the relationship between postpubertal initiation and age class systems, and between generation and the military and other functions of those systems.

The ethnographic data: the Kikuyu and Meru

There are some cases where the existence of age classes for women has been described as an established fact. Kertzer and Madison (1981) have gathered the ethnographic data regarding several East African societies, producing a comparative table that affords us with a good starting point; see Table 11.1. Of the twenty societies they review, all of which have men's age classes, three (the Kikuyu, Konso, and Latuka) are signaled for the "presence" of women's age classes, three (the Kipsigis, Meru, and Zanaki) are distinguished for the "assimilation" of women's classes into the men's. As for the remaining fourteen, women's age classes are either "not mentioned or absent."

The value of this overview in providing a general orientation is beyond doubt.

132

Women and age class systems

Table 11.1 *Women's age classes in East Africa*

Society	Present	Assimilated to men's classes	Not mentioned or absent
Arusha			X
Galla			X
Jie			X
Karimojong			X
Kikuyu	X		
Kipsigis		X	
Konso	X		
Kuria			X
Latuka	X		
Masai			X
Meru	X		
Nandi			X
Nuer			X
Nyakyusa			X
Pokot			X
Rendille			X
Samburu			X
So			X
Turkana			X
Zanaki		X	

Source: Kertzer and Madison (1981: 122).

But let us begin by examining the case of the Kikuyu. Ethnographic data seem to prove the existence of some forms of women's groupings, but it is not clear if these constitute institutionalized age classes or merely forms that are in some more general way parallel to the men's age classes.

In 1908, K. R. Dundas reported (1908:181) on a series of "age classes" among the Kikuyu women of the following kind:

Morika ya moireka: the age of uncircumcised girls
Morika ya moiretu: the age of girls eligible for marriage
Morika ya moiki: the age of married women who have not yet given birth to a child
Morika ya wabai: the age of those who are mothers
Morika ya mutu mia: the age of mothers of circumcised sons

These categories were similar to the men's and apparently served to regulate the participation of women in ritual and other ceremonies as well as in dances and songs. Thirty years later, Kenyatta, in discussing the principles of Kikuyu organization, recalled a norm by which "women should be given the same social status as their husbands" (1938: 189). Kenyatta also refers to "the same parallelism of grade privilege and knowledge" that, in Kikuyu tradition, should mold the training of both boys and girls. In addition, he describes the "council of women" (*ndundu ya atumia*), remarking that "women of this rank deal with all matters concerning circumcision of girls, births and other religious duties" (1938: 111).

133

Lambert sheds no greater light on this problem. Although he does detail a few matters in which women are involved, he does not specify the type and structure of their groupings. Thus, for example, he mentions that in every territorial section (*mwaki*) in case of rain shortage a sheep was to be slaughtered and "if it is not readily forthcoming *the older women in a body* demand it from some head of a homestead who had not yet paid. Though they do not eat meat, *it is their business* to see that the sacrifice is made. The sheep is called *mburi ya aka* (goat of the women) or *mburi ng'otho*" (1956: 95; italics added).

Whereas Kertzer and Madison distinguish the Kikuyu from the Meru in their survey, Lambert discusses them together. Indeed, he refers to the Kikuyu and Meru interchangeably, stating that "whether there are formally constituted women's lodges it is impossible at present to say with any certainty. Men sometimes talk of a *kiama kia aka* ("women's lodge'), but generally mean an *ndundu ya atumia* ('secret meeting of dames') in reference to some particular subject" (1956: 95).

The word *kiama*, which Lambert translates "lodge," is better rendered by "council," in the sense of a gathering. In any case, Lambert, with reference to both the Kikuyu and Meru, summarizes his interpretation in the following way: "Whether or not the women have lodges they certainly have the means and the will to mobilize themselves with speed over a wide area for concerted action when they feel that their rights have been disregarded or their sphere invaded" (1956: 100). To prove this, he recalls a few historical events that took place during the years immediately before the Second World War. Then he concludes:

It would seem that hitherto the women's assemblies, however constituted, have restricted their activities to matters generally regarded by the men to be within the women's sphere. These are (a) purely domestic affairs, (b) agricultural matters, such as food crops, rainfall, and the use (not the ownership) of land, and (c) the discipline, and the regulation of the social life, of girls and women. (1956: 100)

If we may make any conclusion regarding the Kikuyu and Meru, it would seem to be beyond doubt that women's corporate groupings were not autonomously institutionalized; rather, they worked parallel to men's age classes, the only ones formally constituted. Perhaps it would be appropriate to add my personal experience here. During the years I lived among the Kikuyu and Meru, I never found any specific evidence of formally constituted women's age classes, though I had always cause to argue that there was a striking correspondence between the social evaluation of age among both girls and boys with respect to initiation, and a close correspondence between the social condition of women and that of their husbands and sons. It was this correspondence that served as a basis for women's corporate initiatives of the kind indicated by Lambert.

Parallelism and subordination

The second case of the "presence" of female age classes that Kertzer and Madison present is that of the Konso. This is a population of sedentary cultivators who live in the urbanlike clusters surrounded by walls. They are known as one of the few African populations who work the soil through terracing, using animal manure for fertilizer. The Konso are culturally quite close to the Oromo and especially to the Boran, with whom they share a complex system of the generation model.

The position of women in this society is not as clear as its placement in Table 11.1 might lead one to believe. According to the information provided by Hall-pike, the condition of women varies among the three regions into which the Konso territory is divided. Normally, girls belong to the same grades as their brothers, but in contrast with their brothers they get married at an earlier age and consequently make an earlier change in social status. After marriage, the gradation in which women are involved has an entirely different significance than the men's. In particular, in the Garati region, once women have been married, "they retain the same grades as men, but only in relation to their maternal role"; in the other two regions, Takadi and Turo, "women are ex-cluded" from the system "once they have reached the grade in which marriage is allowed" (Hallpike 1972: 204).

In practice, Konso women belong to the system in the sense and with the limitation of belonging to the first grade, called *farida*, which "is essentially the grade of childhood," during which "the chief restriction on boys and girls is that they may not marry" (Hallpike 1972: 188). On reaching puberty, boys are not yet allowed to get married, whereas girls are, because, according to Hallpike (1972: 190):

Since the grades above Farida are basically concerned with the social categories of warriorhood and elderhood, from which women are excluded, it is regarded as socially beneficial not to restrict the numbers of marriageable women beyond the limit imposed by the Farida rule.

Thus, among the Konso, too, the "presence" of female age classes is limited, beyond women's maternal function, to a bland form of parallelism with men's age grades. Certainly there is no instance of female groupings that can be con-sidered formally institutionalized age classes.

The third case of the "presence" of female age classes that Kertzer and Madison identify is the Latuka. The two authors concentrated their attention on this population, first studying the male system of age classes (Kertzer and Mad-ison 1980), then the female system (Kertzer and Madison 1981).

The Latuka are sedentary agriculturalists of the southern Sudan. They speak a Nilo-Hamitic language and live in villages divided into hamlets. The male age class system has the characteristics of an initiation model, applied to the gov-ernment of the individual villages. There are four male grades: the children, *aduri*, who have no recognized social responsibility; the youths, *aduri horwong*, who are assigned communal labor tasks as a group under the direction and control of the adults; the adults, *monyemiji*, who are responsible for the leadership of the village, exercising decision-making power; and the elders, *amarwak*, who no longer have any executive activity, but who are respected for the prestige that comes with age and wisdom. The elders have the right to special treatment in the distribution of meat and are turned to when disputes must be mediated.

Latuka women are also divided into four grades: *aduri, odwo, angorowo monyemiji*, and *amarwak*.

Whereas for the males formal institutionalization of the class takes place with promotion from the second grade, *aduri horwong*, to the third, *monyemiji*, for women the passage from grade to grade is always made on an individual basis and is informal.

The *aduri* consist of small girls and, as in the case of the males, they have no social responsibility. The *odwo* are adolescents and, like the boys, they too take part in collective labor for the hamlet or the village. However, although recruitment into the male groups is left to the males themselves, the girls are individually brought together by the *monyemiji*, the "owners" of the village, who assign certain tasks to each group.

Passage to the third grade – *angorowo monyemiji* – takes place upon marriage: "Marriage is considered performed when the bride-wealth is paid and *ipso facto* the girl becomes part of *angorowo monyemiji*" (Kertzer and Madison 1981: 115). The marriage transaction is an individual process in the sense that it is not contracted in the corporative manner with a common effect on all the members of the same group. However, despite this fact, the *angorowo monyemiji* have a strong corporative sense, which is revealed especially in the autonomy of their initiatives and the coercive force that derives from these initiatives. Although the activities of the *odwo* girls are organized as a result of the initiative and under the control of the men *monyemiji*, the activities and the organizations of the married women are under their own control. There is no village space reserved for gatherings of married women, so that their activities are always catalyzed by some enterprising woman or by request of some interested person. Once a decision has been made, the women go from house to house to let the members of the grade know the time, the place, and the work that needs to be done: "Those who deliberately absent themselves from such collective labor are subject to the sequestration of their property (*abiala*)" (Kertzer and Madison 1981: 116).

Kertzer and Madison compare the men's and women's systems among the Latuka to clarify their similarities and differences. I think it useful to summarize these here for their comparative value. There are four points of similarity: (1) universality of membership, for all males and females, at a certain point, become part of a grade; (2) similarity of the male and female grades; (3) social equality among members of the same grade; and (4) utilization of the grades for organizing collective labor.

On the other hand, they note ten differences between the male and female systems: (1) There is a lack of formalization and ritualization in the female passages from grade to grade. (2) The female passages have an individualistic nature. (3) The *odwo* girls are recruited by the men. (4) Females are recruited into age groups by the time of *odwo* and thus become members at a younger age than the males, who only form age classes with their passage from the second to the third grade. (5) The names and compositions of female groups differ among themselves even within the hamlets of a single village, whereas for the males the names and the structures of the classes are similar throughout the territory. (6) Because the girls are recruited into age groups at an earlier age, there is a larger number of female than male groups. (7) There is no correspondence in age between the members of a male grade and the members of the female grade of the same level. This difference is most evident in the case of the male grade of *monyemiji* and the corresponding female grade of *angorowo monyemiji*. (8) Age class membership involves more activity and is more important for men than for women. (9) There is no comparison between the powers associated with the male and the female grades of the same level; the *monyemiji* are the "owners of the village," whereas the *angorowo monyemiji* do not even have responsibility for recruiting or commanding the girls. (10) Women have no part in the exercise of political and juridical power.

In conclusion, even in the case of the Latuka we see that the "presence" of female classes and grades is no more than a bland form of parallelism to the male system.

In fact, such parallels can also be found among a number of the peoples listed by Kertzer and Madison in the last column of their comparative outline (see Table 11.1). Among the Samburu, for example, the "circumcision" of girls who are about to marry

follows the same pattern as that of her brothers, and they should be circumcised in exact order of birth. The parallel is extended to her marriage which is sometimes compared with the boy's first *il mugit* ceremony when he becomes a *moran* . . . ; the new duties laid on her are the new prohibitions laid on the *moran*. (Spencer 1973: 106)

On the other hand, there are cases in which women's subordination is total. For example, among the Boran, if a widow lives with her sons,

she is neither the head nor the center of the family. The oldest male has jural authority even if the youthfulness of the "senior male" sometimes makes this legal fiction rather implausible. He is senior to his mother in all ceremonial and political matters. (Legesse 1973: 35–6)

A similar situation is found among the Masai and the Arusha and, in general, wherever there exists a patrilineal system in which, as Gulliver (1963: 142) writes, "women remain permanently jural minors."

Matrilineality and patrilineality

The case of the Lagoon Peoples of the Ivory Coast is especially significant for the analysis of the position of women in age class systems. There we find societies with matrilineal kinship systems that for this very reason provide a valuable comparison in the study of age class systems.

Age class systems

Among the Lagoon Peoples, each village, which forms the basic sociopolitical unit, traces its origin from the matriclan ancestor, and membership in the matrilineage establishes one's basic right to village residence. However, the internal order of residence, or the distribution of residence by hamlet, is determined by age class membership. These two principles of lineage membership and age class membership interact and, in a certain sense, conflict, for the lineage has a matrilineal character while the age class structure has a patrilineal character. This bilineal antinomy is a characteristic feature of the Lagoon Peoples' age class system. In saying, in relation to village organization, that residence prevails over descent, it is implicitly argued that the age class organization – which is of a patrilineal nature – prevails over the lineage organization.

The intersection of matrilineality and patrilineality emerges in the constant tension in the application of the norms that govern the allocation of responsibilities within the village and within the age classes. In the choice of the class councillors and the village headman, consideration is given, as we have already observed, to the lineage of origin or membership in the maternal descent group. The same criterion is essential in the selection of town crier, assistant to the headman, and official musician.

The patrilineal nature of the age classes is not substantially altered by the existence of female classes. The organization of these classes is the same as the men's. Among the Ebrie, for example, each female age class elects its own president, or *abeoma*, who "règle les palabres entre femmes à l'interieur de la classe d'âge" (chairs the discussions among women within the age class). Likewise, the women select their own *taprognambia* who, like the *taprognan* of the men's classes, personifies the idea of the female class and must know how to direct the dances performed for the feasts (Paulme 1971c: 227, 228). Among the Mbato, the women create their own class organization, which is less complex than that of the men. They have their own council, directed by a president, or *okobemo*, who is elected by the council itself from its own members.

Le conseil dirige les travaux collectifs des femmes, veille à la propriété du village, assure la réception des hôtes importants, aujourd'hui deputés et ministres.'' (The duty of the council is to organize women's collective works, to supervise the village's property, and to provide for the reception of the guests of honor, today consisting of the deputies and the ministers.)

In the past, at the time of the formal institution of the class, the two most beautiful women were chosen to be the ones charged with encouraging the warriors in preparing for the battle and welcoming them on their return. Today, this choreographic function of the Mbato female classes still survives (Paulme 1971c: 253–4).

In the end, in the context of our analysis, it cannot be said that the matrilineal nature of the Lagoon Peoples has any special effect on women's position. Women's age classes simply reflect the organization of the men's classes.

The ethnographic analysis of the Afikpo, the other West African people we

138

have considered, leads to the same conclusion. As has been noted, the Afikpo have a bilateral kinship system: patrilineal descent and matrilineal transmission of landed property. The age classes are decisively a male prerequisite and, through their organization, the responsibilities and administrative functions of the village and hamlets are regulated. Parallel to the men's age classes, there exist some forms of female organization having a loose structure whose public functions are subordinate to the control of the men's age classes.

Thus, within each hamlet the married women gather under the direction of one of the eldest women, but they lack any formal organization. The primary goal of these gatherings is the maintenance of peace among the women of the hamlet, and especially between co-wives. In particular, they were charged with responsibility for preventing "petty disputes between women in the compound, particularly cowives, from reaching the ears of the young men's age grade, *uke ekpe*. They fear this organization, and dislike its fines and its authority over them" (Ottenberg 1968: 74).

In the same way, within the hamlets the single girls are brought together in a class organization – *okpo Ntu* (literally, harvest of ashes) – which is given responsibility for the task of "maintaining the latrines and the garbage dump behind the compound." The class includes unmarried girls from the age of six or seven until the age of marriage. In addition to the tasks already mentioned, the class as a group must undertake various construction and other work arranged for them by the male class responsible for the labor. "The girls fine their own members for failure to take part in work activities." By tradition, the girls' class also served for dance instruction and performance and, though married women were expected to give advice and assistance, the girls' class clung onto its own organizational autonomy (Ottenberg 1968: 75–6).

Kertzer and Madison (1981: 123) quote a statement by Ottenberg that confirms that women in the Afikpo system occupy a similar, yet subordinate, position to that of the men. Indeed, Ottenberg (1971: 102) writes:

The fact that theirs [the women's class system] is not so actively or effectively organized as the male system reflects the females' lesser role in directing political and ritual affairs. It is also a result of their greater mobility . . . Nevertheless, the same forms of authority relationships are found between the elder and not-so-old females as in the case of males. But for females there is the ever-present possibility of male intrusion in their affairs; the reverse rarely occurs.

The Shavante case

Turning to the Americas, we are struck by the virtual absence of discussion in the ethnographic literature regarding women's participation in the North American age society systems. In the case of the Mandan and Hidatsa, women's participation is discussed explicitly, but only to say that there were age societies for the women that were parallel to, but "less elaborate" than, those of the men (see Stewart 1977: 257).

More insight is available into the South American Indian situation. In his monograph on the Akwẽ-Shavante of Brazil, Maybury-Lewis devotes a paragraph to women's position in the age class system. It is worth noting that this modest discussion represents a rare report on women in age class systems. Maybury-Lewis opens the description with a general observation, "A Shavante woman also belongs to an age-set" (1974: 149), but he then devotes an entire paragraph to various qualifications to this generalization.

In fact, the differences between the positions of women and men in the Shavante age classes are quite notable. Thus, the initiation rites, which are the central characteristic of the Shavante system, are essentially reserved for the men. There is no formal initiation for girls; indeed, they are explicitly excluded from participation in the *wai'a* ceremony, which, though it is considered the principal communal celebration, has an esoteric character. However, the women are distinguished collectively according to the grades into which the male age classes are divided, and it is only in this sense that it is correct to say that the Shavante women belong to an age class. Yet notwithstanding this parallel, the women remain excluded from participation in the class councils in which community affairs are decided.

Insofar as the women are divided into groups on the basis of age grade, they take part in certain initiation rites, which, however, involve the promotion of male youths. Thus, for example, the girls of the *tirowa* grade, in the initiation rites for the boys of that grade, take part as dance partners of the individual candidates, wearing decorations and ornaments distinctive of that grade. In the same way, the boys and the girls of *tirowa* together undertake the rite of the cutting of the hair of the candidates of the following class; this haircutting constitutes the formal element by which the class in the *tirowa* grade is promoted to the *nodzseu* grade.

With the exception of these occasions, women do not engage in any cooperative activity with the male members of the class occupying their grade. But even in their relations with their own female age mates, membership in the same grade does not bring with it any obligation to take common, cooperative action. The collective activities, such as gathering fruit or bathing and swimming in the river, are undertaken by groups formed not so much on the basis of age as on that of kinship and proximity of residence. Thus, as Maybury-Lewis (1974: 149) observes, it seems evident that women's position in the age classes is "comparatively meaningless." However, there remains the fact that women are provided with a class name and a gradation that corresponds to the men's: "The stages of a woman's life are referred to in terms which roughly correspond to men's age-grades." In this way, women's position in the age classes remains of nominal value. Nor does this value change when the assignment of the grade name seems to assume the meaning of a solemn social promotion, as in the case of first

140

menstruation, when the girls are publicly named *adaba*, the same term used with respect to the boys who are promoted and acquire the right to marriage.

The girls who experience this promotion are also juridically able to marry: In fact, however, they have already been promised to their husbands at a tender age and from that time have been required to participate in sexual games with their partners. Thus, at the moment when they are publicly declared to be *adaba*, "they are married and they are no longer virgins," and the public promotion to the grade consequently assumes simply a classificatory significance (1974: 152). In this way, we can well understand Maybury-Lewis's conclusion:

As far as women are concerned, then, the age-set system is solely a classificatory device. Its importance does not lie in the fact that it assigns them to corporate groups, for their membership in their age-sets is largely passive, but rather that it assigns them to arbitrary social categories which are independent of their bio-social status. (1974: 153)

Thus, the Shavante system also provides for groups of females parallel and similar to the male groups, but the women's groups are much less developed than the men's. This is even more notable if Maybury-Lewis's observation is kept in mind. He observed that the Shavante consciously "use" the age class system "as a model of their total society" (1974: 153).

Political control in age class systems

The ethnographic spectrum we have examined leads to two firm conclusions: First, age class systems have a decisively masculine character. Second, the positions of women are diversified in relation both to the structure and functioning of these systems. We have found forms of parallelism with corporate female groupings, which are distinct from male groupings and enjoy a certain functional autonomy, as is the case among the Lagoon Peoples of the Ivory Coast. We have also seen similar forms but where the female groupings lack autonomy or where they are entirely passive, as in the case of the Shavante. Finally, we have seen, especially in the case of the Boran, forms of female participation that lack any parallel to the male groupings and that in any case involve the complete subordination of women to men's classes.

One might think that the male prevalence derives from the patrilineal principle that characterizes almost all the societies having age class systems. In fact, the patrilineal structure constitutes a basic premise from which it is logical to expect a patrilineal or masculine slant for all forms that the social structure takes. Once the anthropemic principle of sex has lost its neutrality, with the choice being made in favor of the masculine element, the social structure based on that choice will develop accordingly, emphasizing the masculine bias.

Such an explanation may seem logical, but it is not exhaustive. It would be complete if the problem of the prevalently male nature of age classes did not extend beyond the patrilineal societies; there are, as we have seen, matrilineal societies, such as the Lagoon Peoples of the Ivory Coast, and bilineal societies, such as the Afikpo of Nigeria, where, in spite of their nonpatrilineal character, the structuring of the age classes shows a patrilineal bias.

This leads us to look further for an explanation of the problem of the essential nature of age class systems. Examination of the ethnographic models has been sufficient to bring to light the scope of age class systems. This scope is, above all else, that of establishing a political order that overcomes the divisions created by kinship and territory. For this reason, although age class systems may be viewed as cognitive and symbolic systems for the identification and social classification of individuals and groups, as Baxter and Almagor (1978: 5) assert, they also serve as mechanisms for the definition and distribution of the powers attached to these identities.

This does not necessarily lead to the emphasis on the male element, but the fact that this happens not only in patrilineal but also in matrilineal and bilineal societies is significant. Indeed, this impels us to recognize the existence of a direct link between age class systems and the political control exercised by men rather than women.

12

The ethnemic significance of the age class systems

We can now examine the relationship between the age class system and the other systems that, through their interaction, constitute the social structure. Such an examination should help us discover the ethnemic significance of the age class system. Indeed, I refer to every component element of the social structure as an ethneme, whereas by ethnemic significance I mean the relationship that binds the structural elements together within the confines of a particular cultural and social formation.

A few observations may be helpful here in developing a useful perspective on this problem. First, it must be noted that age class systems, regardless of the ethnographic model to which they correspond, cannot be dissociated from the other ethnemes, which through their joint action form the social structure.

Secondly, it should be recognized that the behavior of individuals and groups is predominantly oriented by the age class system only in those societies where this system constitutes the primary and characteristic element of the social structure. However, even in such cases, social behavior is also influenced by relationship to other ethnemes, such as kinship and territory. The way in which social behavior is influenced by the relationship to such different kinds of ethnemes, each of which interacts with each other, constitutes an important theoretical issue itself.

It must be emphasized that the relation among ethnemes is dynamic, not static, and hence subject to change and transformation. This means that the position and influence of the individual ethnemes in the formation of the social structure should never be considered crystallized, and the ethnographic descriptions that refer to them should not be read as if they expressed an eternal state of affairs: Rather, they actually described a changeable present. Now, whatever the reason that the significance of an ethneme changes, the change is reflected in and alters the configuration of the entire social structure. Such change is an intrinsic feature of culture, intimately connected to the flow of time. Thus, the dominant position of an ethneme – as for example, in our case, that of age class systems, is a historical situation that can and does change.

In other words, the ethnemic significance of the age class system varies in time: It may assume a predominant role in relation to all the other ethnemes constituting the social structure, but it may also lose this predominance or, indeed, never having attained it, play a secondary role in the social structure. (Such is the case of the primary polity described by Evans-Pritchard for the Nuer, among whom the role of the age class system is secondary to that played by the lineage system.) In the same way, it may happen that the age class system loses its significance entirely and is destined to disappear (as has already occurred among several East African societies, due to the cultural and social changes that have transpired throughout this century).

These considerations point out the necessity for a comparative and historical perspective in analyzing age class systems; I have tried to provide a conceptual framework for just this purpose in these pages. Thus, the question guiding this chapter – just what is the ethnemic significance of the age class system – cannot have a single answer. The multiplicity of forms found in the ethnographic and historical records permits no such simple generalization.

The age class system and the enculturation process

A characteristic of many ethnographic descriptions is that they identify the institution of age classes with the process of adolescent maturation and passage out of childhood. In this regard, it is worth recalling Prins's (1953: 123) admonition that we not confuse age classes with a species of the genus "organization of adolescence."

That the formation of age classes has an educational function and is an integral part of the enculturation process is evident. Through this process, each member of a society comes to know and absorb the cultural model that must orient his or her behavior and learns the proper social relations that will tie him or her to others in that society. Clearly, the various age class systems have such an educational and socializing function, in keeping with the model to which they correspond.

In the initiation model, the distinction between the initiate and noninitiate is basic. Those who are not yet initiated have no special personality, whereas, once postpubertal initiation has been undergone, youths obtain full social autonomy. This entails a social potential that is progressively actualized by passage through the grades of social promotion. The uniqueness of age class systems consists, as we have repeatedly stressed, in the placing of initiates together into a class and promoting them corporately – that is, as a class – through the grades of social power.

The condition of the noninitiates, though having social connotations, presents certain positive aspects for the enculturation of adolescents. In awaiting the time of their postpubertal initiation, their desire for the promotion grows greater; their imagination excites them and prepares them for the difficult ordeal of the initiation rites, which are often quite cruel. Their desire to obtain the rights associated

144

with being considered adult, to participate in community life, and to be promoted to all the social activities, makes them increasingly eager to undergo the initiation ceremonies.

In the initiation model, initiation also constitutes the form of recruitment into an age class, so that a kind of identification exists between being initiated and belonging to an age class. In this way, initiation and membership in an age class represent the basic premise for taking legitimate action in the social context. Having been initiated, the candidate acquires the personal autonomy associated with adults, and as a member of a class, he or she is provided with a precise social position.

The enculturation function of the classes lasts throughout the individual's life. In fact, class membership never ends, for together the age mates pass as a corporate group from grade to grade. The diversity of grades gives rise to a true social stratification, but mobility within this stratification system is regulated by the succession of classes through the grades. The passages from grade to grade take place in a continuum that constitutes the process of enculturation and socialization.

The situation is strikingly different in the generational model. The criteria of admission to and exclusion from social activities derives from the basic rule of structural distance between father and son within the age classes. As a result, initiation does not constitute the passage to social autonomy, and the processes of enculturation and socialization take place in a very different manner than in the initiation model. Thus, for example, young boys and adolescents are not excluded from the age class system; on the contrary, their placement in it can take place without delay, so that they are able to participate immediately in a social status having powers appropriate to the grade determined by their distance from their father's grade. They are limited only by their physiological condition in taking advantage of these powers.

Among the Boran, when observation of the generational norm entails it, infants are immediately placed in the first of the series of *gada* grades, *daballe*. Their membership has a symbolic value that gives them prestige, for they are considered virginal and pure and, for this reason, are thought to be mediators between God – *Waka* – and men, on the same level as the elders who have traversed the entire series of grades.

Among the enculturational effects found in all age class systems, the corporate sense binding together the members of a class should be emphasized. Membership in the same class makes of the age mates a distinct social body. All is based on the commonality of structural age, that is, on the simultaneous allocation of the same status to and the parallel exercise of the same powers by members of the class. Structural age and age class take on, in a certain way, a conceptual equivalency.

It is important to stress this equivalency because what makes a body out of a class is not the physical grouping of age mates, but rather their common structural

145

age. In other words, the corporate nature of the age classes is not a physical reality but essentially a juridical concept. The term corporate is appropriate in this context, for class members, in their local groups, share the same status and claim the same rights. Physically speaking, the class is almost never visible in its totality, but is found in local groupings where the resident age mates meet, hold assemblies, confirm the powers appropriate to their grade, and engage in pertinent activities. Whether the local groups come together for warfare, or for ritual, juridical, or political purposes, the placement of the participants in the meeting follows and reflects the order of their class membership according to the grade occupied by each. In cases where someone from outside the locality participates in such a grouping – far from simply a hypothetical occurrence – there are no doubts about his position because his placement is clearly regulated by his class membership.

The value of class equality

One of the inherent aspects of the corporate nature of the class is the equality of its members. This is an ideal that seems to be contradicted by the classificatory nature of the system and the chronological succession that governs both recruitment of the members of the class and the promotion of the individual classes along the series of grades.

Durkheim and Mauss (1903: 6) long ago observed that "every classification implies a hierarchy." Classifications based on age add a chronological factor to a purely classificatory one. Time is by its nature differentiating, even though some of its rhythms may appear to be repetitively identical, as for instance the rising and setting of the sun. Succession and differentiation are inevitably interconnected. The succession of births imposes the necessity of classifying people according to age and constitutes one of the differentiating elements of individual identity. It is in this way that time may affect the social structure. As a result, all age classifications are expressed in terms of the contrast between elders and youths, between those born earlier and those born later. Age and elderhood are basic concepts of all age class systems, yet their essential effect is to bring about differentiation, in contrast to the ideal of equality.

This conceptual opposition is inevitably reflected in social reality. Indeed, the very same concept of age commonality that makes the members of a class an essentially egalitarian body is itself a fiction, a *fictio juris*. It constitutes a true manipulative device whereby people of physiologically diverse ages come to be jointly characterized by the same structural age and placed at the same social level, determined by their class and the grade that their class occupies. The diversity of actual physiological ages is thus played down, even though it is a reality that cannot be entirely ignored.

Yet the differences reemerge within the class for various reasons. In the initiation model, for example, the open and closed times for initiation lead to

146

the formation of initiation units that serve to differentiate the members of the same class according to seniority. These units are almost always absorbed upon the closing of the period of recruitment, when the class emerges as a·unitary body; but they constitute a precedent just the same, and there are cases in which this distinction among initiation units persists.

In any case, within both the initiation units and the classes there is room for individual self-expression: Good fortune and success are not obtained by everyone. Individual differentiation within the class is thus another reality that contrasts with the ideal of equality. There are those who try to take advantage of their personal successes to gain influence over others, perhaps to the extent of telling others what to do. This question has been approached by Uri Almagor with regard to the age class system of the Dassanetch of southern Ethiopia. He concludes that "the ethos of equality is, in effect, one of 'pseudo-equality' " (1978a: 90). Appearances are always respected by Dassanetch age mates, but some may "accumulate more power" through their role in social mediation. However, despite this, it is significant that even among the Dassanetch equality remains an ideal of practical value, such that "the adherence to, and maintenance of, the ethos of equality supports the social process involved in the sequence of power transfer . . . " (Almagor 1978a: 90).

The problem of equality, as these last words of Almagor indicate, is intimately tied up with the problem of power and must be discussed in relation to this concept. We will return to this question later in this chapter. The structural tendency toward the ideal of equality should be seen as a basic trait of age class systems. Yet this is a tendency and not an established state of affairs. What makes reaching this ideal so difficult is the very chronological factor that lends to the concept of age the idea of succession and differentiation, with the effect of producing a social hierarchy in which individual rivalries and conflicting interests arise. But it is just the succession of classes through the grades that constitutes one of the correctives that serves to offset those possible abuses of power caused by the "particular" interest of the individual and by the lusting for power over others. Among the other corrective elements, we may list the exclusion of hereditary succession from the means by which people are allocated to grades, so that the accumulation of power by an individual does not pass to his sons, and also, the rejection of every attempt at the personal concentration of power, even to the extent that leaders or chiefs may be forced to resign.

Age class systems and kinship systems

The reference to kinship brings to mind Eisenstadt's hypothesis, according to which "age-homogeneous groups . . . tend to arise in societies in which the family or kinship unit cannot ensure, or even impedes, the attainment of full social status by its members" (Eisenstadt 1956: 54).

The meaning of this hypothesis is tied to the sociological context in which it

147

was formulated. Eisenstadt, in fact, refers to age groups in the generic sense, not in the specific sense of systems based on the interrelation of classes and grades. But age classes are not simple aggregations that facilitate social maturation; rather, together with age grades, they constitute one of the determining elements of a formally institutionalized system. Membership in a class should not be confused with the normal gatherings of age mates who get together for all sorts of purposes, whether recreational or economic, trying to obtain what they cannot get through their family. In his study of the Dassenetch, Almagor justly makes reference to Eisenstadt's hypothesis, but he does so to clarify the sense of equality that is produced among age mates from earliest childhood when they gather together for games or to lead animals to pasture. Gatherings of this kind, based on daily habits, have nothing to do with age classes, even if they may be considered a kind of preparation for class formation (cf. Almagor 1978a: 72).

The fullness of status is a result of the totality of the stages, which are separated in time and allocated in succession, one after the other. The systematic interrelation between classes and grades that constitutes the essential characteristic of age class systems responds precisely to this goal of ordering the allocation of statuses and the powers associated with them. In this process, the individual's relationship with his family or with other kinship units does not emerge as an obstacle to social promotion. Age class systems and kinship organization clearly represent two different ethnemes, or two distinct components of the social structure. This does not mean that the two are in conflict; indeed, they may interact in such a way as to complete each other.

In this regard, it is worth reporting Jacob's (1971: 19–20) observation on the *manyatta*:

The physical arrangement of houses in a warrior village is thus an expression of descent group and clan structure. Young warriors not only acquire knowledge of the structure of their local clansmen by living in the village, but they also learn and have opportunity to exercise the rights and obligations of close kinsmen which often leads to exchanges and gifts of livestock. Even sexual and marital rules are expressed in the physical arrangement of the village and the rules of exogamy enforced: age-mates not only learn who their clansmen's sisters are, but they are prohibited from courting or even sleeping in the same house with them.

To clarify more fully the relation between the kinship and age class systems, it is helpful to distinguish between the initiation and generational models. Jacobs's observations are on the Masai and thus relate to the initiation model. In this model, the effect of the age class system on kinship largely, if not exclusively, involves the norms of exogamy that regulate sexual relations and marriage.

In the generational model, the effect is greater and establishes the exact position that separates father and sons within the age class system, introducing a new type of generational relationship, different from the relation of descent. The novelty and uniqueness of such a relationship takes on a ritual connotation in the Boran concept of *gogessa*. As may be recalled, *gogessa* is the unit that includes both the living – father and sons – together with the dead – the fathers' fathers – all belonging to the same lineage. The *gogessa* concept does not represent the ancestry line as a whole, but rather that precise ancestral line formed by the members of the same lineage – fathers and sons – who entered, in regular succession at distances of forty years each, into the age class system. For this reason, Legesse translates the concept with the term patriclass, a composite that appropriately expresses the semantic combination joining the kinship system (patri-) with the age class sytem (-class).

The generational model also appears to be a reference point, though not expressly declared as such, in Bonte's analysis of the relation between age – expressed by systems of classes – and kinship. Bonte proposes that age, filiation, and sex be considered the categories of kinship having universal value:

The central function of the category of age in organizing the kinship systems in East Africa responds to the particular conditions of male dominance and the necessity of assigning "fathers" and "sons" to distinct categories according to a generational rule, conditions which are found in parallel form in the family organization of the same societies. (1983: 28)

The "particular conditions of the exercise of male domination" of which Bonte speaks clearly refer to the patrilineal system of family organization. Here we find a typical characteristic of East African societies that is not found in the matrilineal societies of West Africa.

Another aspect of the relations between age classes and kinship involves the terminology with which the class members address one another. The terminology is derived from the kinship system. The members of the same class normally call each other brothers, whereas the members of the father's class are considered part of the category of fathers. The terminology, as happens in the case of kinship, is not without social consequence; indeed, it is an index of behavior and reflects the matrimonial prescriptions that bind the members of the same class. Insofar as they call each other brothers, they should behave as if they truly were brothers; they cannot marry one another's sisters and daughters, whereas the exchange of wives is quite widely diffused as a mode of hospitality among members of the same class, a mode of emphasizing their equality of status.

Age class systems and marriage

Among the most notable functions of age class systems is the regulation of marriage. Scholars have been unanimous in recognizing this fact, but they have not always recognized it as an indication of the institutional uniqueness and multifunctional nature of age classes. The influence of age classes on the regulation of marriages is not of the same kind as that exercised by kinship systems. Kinship systems regulate matrimonial choices and alliances, whereas age class

systems regulate marital timing. Marriage rules based on kinship have endogamous or exogamous effects; marriage rules based on age classes have demographic effects.

If we exclude the choreographic model, which on the basis of the information
available in the literature does not seem to have had any connection with regulation of marital timing, all the other models imply such a function. And it is
difficult to see how age class systems could have functioned in this way without
having a clear effect on the demographic regulation of births.

The Masai's putting off marriage until the end of the first grade in their
initiation system delays the right of class members to have children. In the case
of the Samburu, described by Spencer, this delay was exacerbated by the arbitrary
actions of the elders, who had the decision-making power and were thus able
to hoard the women. It is worth noting that in the Samburu case it is certainly
not the family or kinsmen of the young men who were creating obstacles to their
attainment of full social status.

The demographic effects of the marriage rules associated with age class systems are easier to deduce intuitively than to demonstrate empirically. We need
detailed demographic data, which almost always are lacking. Legesse has attempted to estimate these effects for the Oromo Boran. On the basis of the 1962
and 1963 censuses of this Ethiopian population, he calculates the size of the
population back in the sixteenth century. He maintains that the marriage rules
of the *gada* system – delaying marriage and the right first to have male and then
female children – date back to that period and were desired by the Oromo to
contain the demographic explosion that had been taking place, for various historical and ecological reasons, in that epoch. Computer simulation techniques
provide confirmation of his estimate:

A most surprising and quite unexpected result of the experiment is the fact that *the
population declines by about 40 percent during the first eighty years* after the rules of
the Gada System are imposed on the normal age-graded population. The decline continues
until the end of the third eighty-year cycle. At this stage the population declines by a
total of 50 percent. This fact alone is a finding of considerable importance. It indicates
that the Gada System was a very powerful mechanism of population control. (Legesse
1973: 155; also see entire ch. 5; italics in original.)

The marriage rules of the *gada* system are a result of the central generational
norm that establishes the structural distance between father and sons. In addition
to its demographic impact, the rule and the rigidity with which it is applied are
the cause of great social conflict. The gravest of these is certainly the practice
of infanticide, but equally serious for its consequences is the exclusion from the
gada system of those who find themselves out of phase with the cycle of succession of grades due to their father's position in that system. Such exclusion leads,
among other things, to that form of pseudomarriage that Legesse terms cicisbean.
Although this represents a safety valve in an otherwise impossible situation, it

is a type of marriage considered illegitimate, deviating from the ideal norm, even though it must be tolerated and indeed is widely practiced.

The relation between age class systems and territory

In addition to the individual (*anthropos*), the collectivity (*ethnos*), and time (*chronos*), among the essential coordinates of human culture is the environment (*oikos*). These are anthropemic concepts of fundamental importance that, in the case of the environment, encompass the concepts of space and territory. Such concepts relate to all those aspects of human culture that develop around the exigencies of residence, production, and communication and include the theoretical and ideological implications deriving from them that more directly involve the fields of religion, magic, and, above all, science. In fact, all the cultural activity of human beings finds in the environment a field of limitless interest, curiosity, and interpretation.

Coming together in a society necessarily entails the ordering of space destined to define, even in its external structures, the residential forms and units. Even if such units can be closed off by hedges or protective walls, whether in urban agglomerates or simple isolated hamlets, they are always points of opening in the sense that they constitute centers for establishing a multiplicity of social relations. In the territory adjacent to the residential units, the cultivated fields or pastures are found, where rivers run, springs and wells are located, paths and roads radiate out, and bridges or places to ford the rivers are found. Even where the settlements are sedentary, as among the agriculturalists, the situation is not static, but rather dynamic with the rich variety of relationships characteristic of any form of human culture.

In other words, there is no social form of living together and of organization not found in an ethnemic relation with territory. What, then, is the relationship between age classes and territory?

Of all the models examined, the residential model would seem the most apt in highlighting the characteristics of the relation between age class systems and territory. The essential function of the systems that comprise the residential model is that of providing the organizational principle for the internal ordering of the villages and their administration, at least in the sense of maintaining order.

We can clarify the problem by asking why, in ordering residential units, preference is given to the principle of age and to age class systems instead of to other principles and systems, such as, for example, kinship, which seems at least as suitable to provide the basis for an orderly and rational residential system.

There is no simple answer to this question. Let us begin with the age village, which would seem to be the most pertinent case here. The reason age is employed as the ordering principle of the Nyakyusa villages is not as simple as it may seem, for the system is not simply based on the age of the candidates. It should here be recalled that the determining motivation for the residential segregation of pubertal adolescents is the great fear of incest. However, there remains the fact that the commonality of age of the inhabitants of the newly segregated residential unit furnishes the propellent that gives social cohesiveness to the unit and leads it to attain its own autonomy as a residential unit. In a certain sense, the concept of age class comes to be overwhelmed by and absorbed in the residential concept of the village.

In contrast, the systems of the Afikpo and the Lagoon Peoples appear to be of an entirely different kind. They seem to respond to the need for equality and to the distribution and regular rotation of the power that comes with the age class system. The validity of this interpretation is confirmed by the segmentary nature of the residential systems of the Afikpo and the Lagoon Peoples and by the autonomy enjoyed by every residential unit. Whether within the individual hamlets, or in the wards or villages, power is semantically complex, in keeping with the multiplicity of functions it entails, from the collective work of the youths to the elders' control over public order and decision-making power.

Each residential unit is aggregated with other units, and together they form a larger residential unit. This process involves ritual activity, as well as productive and commercial activity. At each level, councils are formed to discuss the normal affairs of the unit in question, to settle disputes and conflicts, and to deal with new situations and emergencies that require appropriate action in harmony with tradition and the established order.

In pastoral societies, nomadism and transhumance entail the continual movement of people. In such circumstances, meetings of individuals or groups usually take place by chance; in any case, they are temporary, and the only criterion common to everyone for social interaction, whether for ritual, political, or recreational purposes, is class membership. When it is maintained that, in societies of this kind (e.g., among the Nilo-Hamites; see Bernardi 1952), the categories of territorial organization and of the kinship system divide rather than unify, this does not mean that the kinship organization is weak or that the territorial organization is unimportant; rather, neither one offers a principle of aggregation, common to all, as the age class system does. It is in this sense that, in the acephalous nomadic societies, the age class system overcomes territorial limits and kinship division, providing a criterion for interaction on the basis of which operational groupings can be established.

Hierarchy and social stratification in age class systems

I have already noted the inherent conflict in age class systems due to the contradiction between the ideal of equality on the one hand and the hierarchical effect of the classificatory factor on the other. The most demanding issue in the analysis of age class systems is to explicate the relationship between classes and grades, which is, as I have already said, the essential and distinctive characteristic of these systems.

The ethnemic significance

We must begin by clarifying the meaning of the hierarchy concept in the systematic context of age classes. This is a concept that can only have a generic value, in the sense indicated by Durkheim and Mauss, according to whom "every classification implies a hierarchy." It would be out of place to assume an order in which some persons occupy a dominant position over a large mass of subordinates. Acephalous polities afford the normal context of age class systems. Within such polities, the efficiency of age class systems seems to be clear. The systems pursue the egalitarian ideal, the equality of the members of each class unit; in particular, they limit the individual power of those people who, in one way or another, are involved in leadership activity and have decision-making power, so that the rotation of power within the system is guaranteed.

Having said this, it should be recognized that the succession of classes entails both the placing of one class on top of the other and also class distinctions based on seniority. The result is the formation of a series of grades that generates true social stratification. I have already defined this as the constitutional plan of the age class system. The series of grades, in fact, establishes the framework of succession and the distribution of power within which the status of the individual classes is defined and the effective powers corresponding to the grade occupied by each class are specified.

The social stratification created by the age class system is neither static nor crystallized, but provides for the mobility of classes through the process of succession along the ladder of grades. The passages from grade to grade take place corporately; that is, within the age class system social mobility is class mobility, not individual mobility.

Although the hierarchical order is the inevitable product of the classificatory factor, the egalitarianism is a product of social mobility, guaranteeing the members of the society that they will have complete access to the same grades and will be able to move through the entire series of grades thanks to their class membership.

Mobility is an institutional element; the passage of the individual classes from one grade to another constitutes a right. This does not imply that the passages take place without tensions. People who occupy a coveted position do not give it up easily, even where they are supposed to do so.

Despite the egalitarian ideal, the classes are distinguished from one another because they follow one another in time and are differentiated in terms of seniority. Yet it would not be precise to translate the concept of seniority in terms of superiority: The classes are not superior and inferior except in terms of coming earlier or later. Similarly, not even the function undertaken by the different classes can be seen as making some classes superior to the others: One may be more envied, but among them is simply a relation of complementarity. The age classes are not castes, closed entities of inherited social condition, jealously guarding the privileged position they enjoy. Nor are they social classes in the normal sense of the term, for although they have a common social and economic

153

condition membership in the class is restricted to those age mates who are socially recognized as such through initiation rites.

The tensions that arise, especially during the period of promotional transitions, are real and strongly felt. But even though they lead to conflicts or episodes of arbitrary power wielding (as in the case of the Samburu elders), they show, by contrast, what the ultimate rights are to which all classes aspire. The allocation of such rights can be delayed, but in the end they cannot be denied.

The succession of the classes in the grades thus creates the social stratification of age class systems. But this same succession of the classes through the grades serves to correct the negative aspects – the inequality – built into the system by stratification and classification.

The allocation of power in age class systems

The nature of power in age class systems has been a recurring debate and the basis of lively theoretical discussions. The application of the concept of power to age classes requires, as has been indicated from the first chapters of this book, a careful evaluation that takes into account the uniqueness of age class systems.

By power I mean, first of all, the ability to take personal action. The noninitiate, in the initiation model, lacks this capacity. Once he has passed through the postpubertal initiation, he acquires the basic right to participate in social activities and, in the course of time, he acquires the executive rights that allow him to take part in specific military, social, economic, judicial, and ritual activities. The allocation of these rights takes place at intervals over time, for it is intimately bound up with the formation of the individual's own class and its subsequent promotion through the series of grades.

Every executive right is considered a power, in the sense that it recognizes the personal capacity of the members of a particular class to act with respect to the specific activity appropriate to the grade occupied by the class. In fact, the concept of power in age class systems should be seen as the synthesis of the basic right to participate personally in social activities and the executive rights attained through the promotion of the class through the grades.

In the context of age class systems, political power – the ability to make decisions and the possibility of bending the will of others to one's own wishes – constitutes one of the executive rights that in the course of time is allocated to each class.

To identify political power as *the* power, almost as if it were the key to the entire system (such as we find, for example, in state organizations, or in any case in centralized societies), would mean missing the unique nature of age class systems. This nature is represented by the articulation of the classes, each one of which, in succession through time, assures its members participation in all forms of social life.

Power, in this sense, must be seen as by nature distributive. While not ignoring the diversity of models and all the conflicts built into individual systems, we must recognize the distribution and rotation of power – involving the distinction of functions and the succession in the allocation of the rights pertaining to these – as the practical, or broadly speaking, the political aspect of the social order constructed by age class systems. It is hardly necessary to note that the regimental model differs from this picture because it is the product of an authoritarian, centrally propagated reform.

A typical illustration of what I have said can be found among the Latuka of southern Sudan. In the conclusion of their article on the age class system of the Latuka, Kertzer and Madison (1980: 101–2) note the following characteristics: Among the elements of the model to which the Latuka system conforms are:

a. An uncentralized polity lacking a powerful political officeholder either at the local or the tribal level.
b. A clan system which is separated from much of the political decision-making and executive process.
c. A territorial system in which strong allegiance to one's locality threatens the harmony of social relations among localities.
d. The age-set system provides a pan-tribal structure which promotes social integration through inter-village solidarity.
e. Differentiation of authority in 'practical matters' is largely based on age-set membership.
f. The judicial system is tied to the age-set system.
g. Political authority is vested in age-sets, distributed to different age-sets in different degrees and for different activities.

It is necessary, however, to reiterate the lack of identity between the age class system and the political system. The two concepts are not the same, nor are the structures behind them the same. As a system, age classes do not serve exclusively political ends, nor are they only involved in the control of decision-making power and executive force. Rather, they serve to insert political activity into the larger context of social activity, while fixing its limits and determining its timing. In the way that they arrange and order political activity in relation to all other aspects of social activity, the various age class systems differ profoundly among themselves, as we see from the distinctions made in our ethnographic models.

It seems improper to define the political aspect of age class systems in terms of government because this would contradict its distributive character. But if one wants to make use of a conceptualization of this type, the only adequate definition is provided by the concept of ''diffuse government'' (Mair 1962). In fact, age classes can be seen as so many political communities. As has already been noted, the classes are physically arranged in local groups where the members of the various classes identify themselves and are distinguished by the position their class occupies in the age grade structure. This structure is visibly reflected in the formation of local councils that, in discussing various issues, act in an entirely autonomous manner. It is in these councils that political communities can be recognized as examples of diffuse government.

There remains the question of the role played and the actual position of the individuals who, within the age class system, hold offices that permit the exercise of a particular authority. The presence of persons of this kind constitutes an aspect of a more general problem regarding the possibility that a single individual – a member of a class – has of expressing his own capabilities and emerging with full autonomy within an egalitarian system such as the age class system. Indeed, this is an issue that merits special attention.

The individual and the age class system

The ambivalence that characterizes the relations between the individual and the collectivity in every society is a fundamental problem in age class systems. Insofar as the class organization is truly in a position to assure equality of opportunity to class members, we may ask in what manner the emergence of leaders within the individual classes does not contradict the acephalous and egalitarian character of the classes.

In relation to the first aspect of the problem, it seems pertinent to recall the distinction between the initiation model and the initiation-transition model. The difference between the two models appears in the solidity of the age class structure. In the former case, the structure is permanent and solid, in the sense that it continues to bind members for the rest of their lives. In the latter case, the structure becomes attenuated because, although classes are not rejected or openly disbanded, class members may free themselves from their class ties and pursue their own individual ends through other channels, namely those provided by the bonds of kinship.

The difference between the two models is reflected in the position of particular individuals. In the initiation model, class members together traverse the entire series of grades, and each member undertakes his own activity with the assurance of enjoying all the executive rights pertaining to each grade. The tensions caused by the delays and abuses of power (as we see in the case of the Samburu elders) take place at the class level and affect the position of everyone.

In the Shavante case, which provides the typical example of the initiation-transition model, the class progressively loses its cohesion, while individual competition for success or power increases through entirely personal means.

Beyond these differences, there is a basic aspect common to both these models and, in the same way, characteristic of the other models as well. This is the personal condition of every individual within his own age class, which is not influenced by hereditary succession. This is true even for the generational model, where the structural position of every individual is determined by the position of his father. But this determination involves only the timing and placing of the son into the appropriate age class and the grade it occupies. The position of the individuals within their class is entirely independent of the father's prestige and success. It is not that the father does not aid his son; he does this, for example, by providing in whole or part the bridewealth necessary for his son's marriage,

The ethnemic significance

or by giving livestock for feasts for his son's age mates, or by giving his son a start toward economic autonomy. But all these are types of aid that, by their nature, are motivated by principles that do not directly pertain to age classes but are connected to kinship and family.

The nonhereditary nature of age class systems is a highly significant principle in evaluating the position of the individual in the context of these systems: Each person must be on his own; in this sense, he finds himself on an equal footing with his age mates and thus starts off in a position of equality.

The class becomes, in this way, the arena where its members take part in their appropriate activity and where they prove their capabilities, efficiency, and sense of personal responsibility. The individual's success reflects on the entire class. Every victory in combat and every good fortune in wealth, children, and force not only brings honor to the person who attains it but enhances the prestige of the entire class. The memory of a class is the memory of its great members, and the stories of the exploits of the class exalt this memory for the entire community.

It is through their display of effectiveness and sense of responsibility that the class leaders arise. In fact, each leader emerges as a result of the loyalty his mates show in spontaneously following his judgments and choices. This adherence is more in terms of recognition than election. In acephalous societies, there is no group that does not recognize some leader within it. The person who comes to be so recognized becomes a guide and spokesman of the group. But he is neither a head nor a chief. His recognition as leader does not alter his status, which remains basically the same as that of his fellows. Arrogant behavior, which might be tolerated or even required in dealings with members of other classes, would never be tolerated by one's age mates.

In the *gada* system, following the generational model, there are officials – the *Abba Gada* and his councillors – who are selected through an elective procedure that takes into account criteria connected with clan membership. In cases of this kind, we clearly cannot entirely exclude the influence of inheritance, but its importance is limited by the equality of status of the *Abba Gada* and his councillors in relation to their age mates and the temporary nature of their office, which is fixed by the eight-year period in which their class occupies the grade in question.

The temporary nature of these offices is indeed one aspect of the succession of the classes in the grades and represents a corrective against any potential deviations from egalitarianism, a corrective mechanism characteristic of age class systems. With the promotion of the class and its leaders to the next grade, the possibility for the individual's success and prestige to be transformed into the improper acquisition of personal, or even despotic, power is thwarted.

Among the Maa-speaking Parakuyo of Tanzania, the *aunoni* is addressed as *papa lainei* – "our father" – by his age mates (see Hurskainen 1984: 189). The analogy of such an address with the term *Abba Gada*, literally Father of *Gada*, is evident. Indeed, both figures have a common ritual character. But in spite of that, their structural position is very different. The *Abba Gada* is a full-blown leader, ritually, socially, and politically, inserted into his own age class structure. The *aunoni* is merely a ritual figure; as such, his position is marginal as far as it refers to his own class.

Though exclusively ritual, the *aunoni's* status and office are radically different from such other offices as the Masai *laibon* or the Oromo *kallu*, who are not directly tied to the structure of the age class system. Their function is tangential to this structure, even if their activities are utilized in the formative and functional processes of the classes.

Relations of age class systems with the economic system

We may now inquire into the relationship that age class systems have with the economic system. Some scholars treat such relations as irrelevant, or indeed, nonexistent, because they believe that the function of age class systems is of an entirely different kind. But despite such an extreme viewpoint, the question of these relationships must be asked, so that we can define their essential terms – even if these turn out to be negative – and determine what forms these relationships assume in the different ethnographic models.

It is appropriate here to take another look at the passage from Baxter and Almagor's (1978: 9) essay, already cited in Chapter 2, in which they state their thesis:

a striking feature of sets is that, though they may influence the use of resources and flow of labour, they neither own nor control stock nor any other means of material production. They do not have the vestigial or residual rights sometimes said to reside ultimately in clans or lineages. At the most sets, as sets, only own things which economically are trivia, such as smoking pipes or songs or drums and the rights in club houses or meeting places.

The extent of these claims is so broad and sweeping that they clearly require confirmation through comparative study. Their reference to the age class systems of the North American Prairie Indians, in particular, appears rather superficial and not really pertinent. In the systematic presentation I have attempted in the previous pages, these systems were assigned to the choreographic model: The dances, songs, and musical instruments, together with the sacred pipes, have a primary value and indeed are characteristic of this model. In such a model, age classes not only allocate the rights to carry out and control certain dances and songs, but they become the proprietors of them in the precise sense of "ownership," for they acquire rights to them from the preceding class that possessed them, paying the members of that class a true compensation, a payment involving the obligatory participation of all class members. To consider such a possession as having only insignificant economic value, a matter of "trivia," is to adopt

The ethnemic significance

an ethnocentric and erroneous perspective. It is demand that is responsible for producing an acute shortage of certain goods, regardless of their material value, and although it renders these things precious – that is, truly "goods" – it also spurs on economic activities through their production. It should hardly be necessary to note that the economy involves all aspects of production, not only material goods, but also more intangible goods, such as services.

To examine the relationship between age class systems and the economic system, we must clearly distinguish among the different modes of production connected with various age class systems. From the ethnographic models that I have described, two – the initiation and generational models – are embedded in a pastoral mode of production. Three are found in mixed modes of production, encompassing both cultivation and herding; these include the initiation-transition, residential, and regimental models. One, the choreographic model, is connected with the mode of production of big-game hunting. As we see, even in their relationship to mode of production, age class systems exhibit a multiplicity of functions.

What I have pointed out regarding the right of age classes in the choreographic model to own songs and dances suggests that we consider the relationship between age class systems and the economic system in terms of rights to economic activity. Here we are dealing with a right implicit in the basic power of participating in social life that is attained by every candidate at the moment of his recruitment to a class, and it is one of the many effective powers attained with the promotion of the class to the appropriate grade.

The basic power to participate in social activity is equivalent, as I have already indicated, to the attainment of social autonomy on the part of each class member. Social autonomy allows each individual to act with responsibility and legitimacy in relation to all other members and groups in society. At the appropriate moment, with promotion to the appropriate grade, the individual also obtains the effective power to start his own family and residence and to take part in the economic activity that permits him to maintain and expand his own family group.

We can also clarify the conceptual meaning of the corporate nature of age classes by utilizing this economic perspective. Whereas in the kinship system the corporate nature of lineal groups – the clan and lineage – is based on their common descent, with implicit common interests in inheritance and succession, in age class systems the only common element on which the corporate nature of the grouping of age mates is based is their contemporaneous and egalitarian attainment of certain powers – the fundamental power to participate in social life and various effective powers including the right to economic activity.

It is for this reason – because they define the fundamental power of participation and the resulting effective powers to which various duties correspond – that age classes "may influence the use of resources and flow of labour." It thus seems to me that a definite value must be attributed to age class systems in relation to

159

the economic system, and that this impact should be defined not so much in terms of the corporate ownership of goods, but rather in terms of the corporate allocation of rights that authorizes all legitimate economic activity.

The multifunctional nature of age class systems

From our previous discussions, we have seen the multifunctional nature of age class systems. This is a conclusion that contrasts with the once-prevalent tendency to give a unifunctional interpretation to such systems. They had often been explained as largely, if not exclusively, a type of military organization for the recruitment of youths, the conduct of military activities, and the eventual promotion of warriors to the status of elders. In this way, the objective differences among ethnographic situations was ignored. A similar oversight occurred when other analysts assigned a predominantly cognitive value and primarily ritual function to age class systems. It is not so much the emphasis placed on military or ritual function that makes these sorts of interpretations unacceptable; rather, it is the fact that they characterize age class systems in terms of a single function.

The uniqueness of these systems, in fact, consists in the comprehensiveness with which they include all social activities, divided up among the various classes. They bring together, through time, the acquisition of the status appropriate to the grades and the executive rights relative to each grade activity. Our task is, then, one of distinguishing the various functions of age classes rather than setting one against the other. The military, social, political, and ritual functions are not mutually exclusive; on the contrary, they articulate with one another according to an order of responsibility precisely determined by the succession of the classes through the grades.

Baxter and Almagor's interpretation of the primarily ritual function of age class systems has the merit of emphasizing the systems' cognitive character. Indeed, this character constitutes a significant value, for it is through class membership and promotion through the grades that the system provides the terms of reference to determine the social identity and the area of competence for each person in the general context of social activity.

The succession of the classes over time through the series of grades furnishes the mechanism for the distribution of power. The concept of distribution implies the fractioning of power, the division of different rights, and, as a consequence, distinctions of status. In age class systems, these are not simply theoretical or abstract distinctions; they are very much seen in the actual constitution of the classes and in their succession through the grades. It is in this sense that the totality of grades can be compared with a constitutional plan that distinguishes among different functions and determines executive rights.

The analogy of the constitutional plan should not be pushed so far as to consider the totality of the age grades a static and fixed structure. Like all other cultural phenomena, age class systems have a dynamic nature. Adjustment to the pres-

160

sures of the particular historical moment, and the succession of the classes itself – with new individuals continuously passing through – result in transformation and change.

What we know of the history of age class systems attests to this pattern of profound transformations. The most significant case is certainly that of the regimental model, the result of a reform perpetrated for purposes of military conquest. In more recent times, colonial occupation – both that of the Europeans and that of the Africans themselves (for example, the Ethiopian Amhara) – has had a profound effect on age class systems. In some cases, the effect has been limited to that of reducing some of the system's functions, especially in the area of military and political decision-making activities. Often, however, the result of the colonial incursion has been the decay and disappearance of the age class system as a whole. These phenomena raise historical problems and show that the multifunctional nature of age class systems is not separable from the historical context any more than it is from the ethnographic context.

13

History and changes in age class systems

Historical evaluation and processes of transformation

At the end of Chapter 2, I mentioned the possibility of using age class systems for historical research, particularly in the case of linear systems of class naming. In practice, despite the attraction of such an approach, the historical depth of age class systems is very limited. Rarely do the chronological indications connected with the lists of age class names provide sufficient bases for a precise historical tie-in. The further back in time we go, the vaguer our information becomes. The very dynamic of age class systems is not well reflected in the simple listing of class names; indeed, the linear series of names can lead to the erroneous impression that a fixed, static structure and functions must correspond to the fixed linearity of names. Only the fact that a class recruits new individuals and groups age mates on the basis of a common structural age differentiates the class from those that precede and follow it. But the temporal context in which the class is found differentiates it from the context of the other classes. Each class, in fact, must confront the situations and problems characteristic of its own time. This entails adapting to different circumstances, implying a structural and functional dynamism that the simple nominal lists fail to reflect. These same events and the stories connected to the classes are passed on to the point that the collective memory allows. They are then forgotten, so that the only memory of the class passed on is its name.

Yet despite serious efforts that have been made to judge the historical significance of age classes, the results must be described as unsatisfactory. The first attempt to provide a history of the Kikuyu people, who were among the main protagonists in the modern history of Kenya, is an instructive example. The ambitious task of historian Muriuki's (1975) work can be seen from the title of his book: *A History of the Kikuyu: 1500–1900*. Although the succession of Kikuyu classes serves the author well in his periodization of the nineteenth century, when he goes further back in time to the most remote point provided by the nominal lists, the year 1512, the dates merely correspond to the different class names. Moreover, each date is marked by a question mark, an indicator of approximation and uncertainty devoid of any other historical content (Muriuki 1975: 16, 21).

Unfortunately, despite more recent research, we know little about the transformations through which age class systems have passed in reaching our times. In some cases, the information we have shows that the adaptation of the system to the needs of the moment was not limited simply to action that was part of the internal dynamics of the system, but rather occasioned reflection, discussion, and direct interventions in the structure of the system itself. In the preceding chapters, I have often mentioned Shaka's reform, which transformed the age class system of the ancient Nguni into a regimental model. We also have reports of profound transformations in the *gada* system of the Oromo Boran. About three centuries ago, in Bahrey's history "of the Galla," circumcision is described as the rite of recruitment of young warriors into the *gada* system; currently, the same rite is practiced rather late in the context of the promotional cycle, and its significance remains obscure (cf. Legesse 1973: 90 n. 5). We do not know whether these and other changes in the *gada* system are the result of direct attempts at reform, but it is not implausible to suppose that this is the case when we think that "in the course of pre-ritual and intra-ritual crises the *gada* assembly may resolve any type of conflict be it ritual, political, moral, legal or economic in character" (Legesse 1973: 86). It is interesting, in this regard, to reread Legesse's description of such an assembly among the Boran. This is a gathering of the population and the leaders that, as an assembly of the multitudes – *gumi gayo* – is considered to have "the highest degree of political authority" (1973: 93). There they discuss cases of conflict, especially those that call for new behavioral norms. From this, Legesse (1973: 97) concludes that "we have evidence, perhaps for the first time in the study of preliterate societies, of a deliberate attempt to rethink and modify customary law."

Colonial impact

Intervention – both direct and indirect – designed to modify age class structures and functions was a normal part of colonial governments' political action, but the reactions of the various systems were quite different. Baxter and Almagor raise this issue, in the context of East Africa, asking: "Why have some age systems, or parts of age-systems continued to flourish even into the seventies, whereas others have collapsed at the first colonial puff, missionary whisper or clink of the first pice?" And they also ask: "What, then, are the social conditions in which age-systems seem to flourish or decay?"

Baxter and Almagor argue that an adequate response to this question is to be found in the "ritual benefits" that age class systems provide their members (1978: 25). But a response of this kind ignores the fact that the social context is not limited to simply the ritual aspect, but rather involves the entire spectrum of social activity. Nor does this view pay sufficient attention to the historical reality.

Limiting ourselves here to East Africa, what immediately leaps to mind is the contrast between pastoral societies, represented by the Masai and the Boran, and agricultural societies, represented by the Bantu-Hamites and in particular the Kikuyu. The former have preserved their traditional age class system almost intact, whereas the latter have entirely abandoned theirs. This difference in reaction might well lead us to seek the explanation in the nature of the two modes of production and in their efficacy in resisting foreign influences. Such an explanation, though suggestive, sounds partial because it relies only on one of the two sides in the relationship: Although it refers to the nature of the traditional societies, it does not consider the nature of colonial power. The different attitude of the colonial governments in dealing with pastoral populations, like the Masai as opposed to agricultural populations, like the Kikuyu, is well known.

The colonial attitude toward the Masai was one of special attention and at times leniency. At the beginning of the century, when the boundaries of the reserves were being drawn, the requirements of a pastoral-nomadic life were taken into consideration, making it possible for the Masai to continue their ancient way of life. Even when the Masai lands to the west of Mount Kenya were set aside for the Europeans, the Masai were compensated by the addition of a proportionately large amount of land to the southern reserve on the Tanzania border, which became the only Masai reserve of Kenya. The lands occupied by the Europeans had previously belonged to the Laikipia, a Masai ethnic group decimated by fratricidal warfare and cattle plague.

The colonial presence, however, drastically affected military activity with the requisitioning of shields and the ending of livestock raids. The consequences of this were seen in the old way of life of the warriors. Although the position of the *moran* was humbled, it was not eliminated. Their task and the duty of protecting the herds from animal predators could not be taken away from the young initiates, and although they were deprived of the shields that served in the battles between the various ethnic groups, they continued to be permitted the use of spears and clubs. Even today, the young Masai, whether he is taking the animals out to pasture or walking in the prairies or towns, always carries his spear and club. On the whole, the social formation of the Masai continued intact, and along with it the age class system continued to survive.

The Masai themselves, moreover, closed ranks, faithful to the old mode of pastoral production that made them self-sufficient; they offered amazing resistance to the consumerist attractions of colonial society. It is only by taking into account both the favorable attitude of the colonial governments and the desire of the Masai to keep to their traditions that it is possible to understand how, even today, the Masai have remained living testimony to a past otherwise practically gone in Kenya. It is only recently, a little more than a decade since the nation's independence, that the impact of the central government – no longer colonial but a modernizing influence just the same – is undermining the old structure, through both the capillary expansion of the educational system and the organization of local-level bureaucratic administration and participation of the people in parliamentary elections with their own deputies.

The history of the social and cultural change experienced by the Kikuyu is quite different. In modern Kenya, they have played a role as protagonists that in the past century and first phase of the present one was played by the Masai. In contrast to the latter, the Kikuyu saw a large part of their lands confiscated and set aside for European settlers. Despite an extraordinary openness toward the new way of life, especially in their eagerness for school education, they were deeply disturbed by land shortage. This led them into a growing conflict with the white rulers, whose domain they never entirely accepted. Their simmering dissatisfaction ultimately blew up in the Mau Mau rebellion. Finally, in 1963, through Kenyatta's leadership, they led Kenya to political independence.

In another heated conflict, the Kikuyu confronted the missionaries with regard to female initiation, in particular the performing of clitoridectomies on girls. The lethal consequences of the operation, resulting from the absence of hygenic protection of the candidates, were strongly condemned by the missionaries, whereas the Kikuyu were extremely sensitive about the traditional, symbolic, and social value of their custom.

They were quick to realize that, beyond the operation itself, what was at stake was the entire ancient initiation system. This conflict led to the secession of the most radical wing from the missionary church and the establishment of the Kikuyu Independent Church with its own educational system, similarly referred to as independent. It was, indeed, the acculturative influence of the schools that, more than any external interference, undermined the ancient system from within. Formal school gradually replaced the traditional enculturation process that had been tied to initiation, blocking at its source the channel of age class recruitment. At the same time, in response to the development of the conflict over land and the request for a greater expansion of the educational system, the colonial government reinforced its presence in the territory by taking almost all the power away from the traditional local councils. This was done not so much by abolishing the local councils as by tying them to the service of the local government functionaries. In this way, the age class system was sapped of its vitality and lost all its attraction for the younger generations. The age class system became for the Kikuyu a souvenir of the past. Its memory has assumed merely historical value, though at times it serves to inspire or sustain new forms of association based on the friendship of age mates or motivated by the desire for economic cooperation. In 1975, a socioanthropological study of the city of Nyeri, the principal urban center of the northern Kikuyu, concluded that "the *rika* [or age class] has lost most of its importance; and only 25 percent of the people could remember that they had attended any meeting of their *rika*. Among these are older people, 78 percent of all people over 50, and 50 percent of those between 40 and 50 years of age'' (Dutto 1975: 136).

If we turn to the situation of the Boran, we must observe, first of all, that they are the most marginal of all the Oromo with respect to the central governments. For this reason, both the Boran of southern Ethiopia and the Boran of northern Kenya have felt colonial impact – first of the Amhara and then of the Europeans – less than the other Oromo peoples. Likewise, the various minor ethnic groups – the Dassanetch, the Mursi, the Gabbra, and others – represent true cultural and social enclaves that have remained almost intact up to recent times due to their isolation. This is an isolation attributable mostly to the secluded ecological situation of their regions. A similar argument can be made for the Turkana, especially if we compare them to other Nilo-Hamites, such as the Kalenjin (Kipsigis and Nandi), among whom colonial impact, with the presence of government officials, missionaries, and white settlers, was great and led to radical social changes and the disappearance of age class systems.

"Unemployed warriors"

In her comparative analysis of the "age classes and associations" of West Africa, Paulme (1971c) notes the transformations undergone by age class systems. Almost all the analysts and ethnographers who describe the age class systems of West African societies assign a primary importance to their military function and see the age class system as having the task of providing for the recruitment and training of young warriors. This emphasis is certainly excessive. It relegates to secondary importance the socioeconomic function connected with the organization and the performance of collective communal works; it neglects the relationship between the age class system and the rotation of the classes in the exercise of decision-making power; and it fails to place the ritual aspect of the system in proper perspective. In any case, with the modification taking place in interethnic relations and the slackening of intertribal conflicts and tensions, the martial function of the age classes declined, and military activity was entirely absorbed in the organization of the colonial state and, subsequently, in the independent nation. The warriors, as Paulme (1971c: 212) puts it, are now unemployed.

Yet not only the military aspect of the system was affected by the phenomenon of transformation, but many other aspects of social life as well. In some cases, the results have been so radical as to overturn the most beloved ancient traditions. For example, among the Abé and the Gã, Paulme laments the disappearance of the ancient spirit of solidarity that once tied neighbors together in performing work in the fields. She attributes this to the rise of "unbridled individualism" caused by the introduction of the cultivation of coffee and coca: "Each is jealous that another may have greater success" (Paulme 1971c: 283). In a situation of this kind, "to say that the age classes are 'the force of the village' would sound ridiculous," for in fact they have entirely lost their value.

166

It is not that only the most general function of the institution has come to be ignored, that of providing constant mutual aid among the members of the same class. The age class survives in itself, but it no longer plays any role in social life; designed for skirmishes between tribes and villages, its *raison d'être* has disappeared. Many villages have already abandoned it. (Paulme 1971c: 283–4).

In other cases, however, the spirit of cooperation has not disappeared at all. But the terms of the relations among age mates do change. Just as among the Kikuyu of Kenya, where friendship and economic interests lead to the grouping and the cooperation of age mates, a similar pattern is found among the Lagoon Peoples of the Ivory Coast. Paulme provides some illustrations, such as the youth who proposes that his companions get together to acquire a vehicle to transport passengers, or a truck to transport supplies from the city to resell them at the local market. She also tells of the youth who, wanting to strike off on his own, asks a loan for initial financing from the common class fund.

At this point, the transformation of age class systems is total. We are no longer faced by a social and political order that, through the formation of age classes and their succession in the grades, sustains and regulates the entire range of social activities. The motives for grouping are no longer institutional ones: From public ends, they become private ones. The groupings founded on friendship and economic interest have a voluntary character, and their duration is entirely variable. Such associations can no longer be described as age classes in the unique and specific sense that typifies institutionalized age class systems; rather, they represent simple age groupings.

Global systems and alternative processes

The diverse ways in which age class systems have been modified, and indeed destroyed, raise again the question of how to explain the survival and disappearance of these systems. Among all the causes that may transform age classes, from cultural entropy to attempts at reform to the indirect effect of acculturation, undoubtedly the greatest influence is exercised by this latter force. The phenomenon is intimately bound to the dynamic of these colonial encounters and the cultural, social, and political clashes that occurred during the colonial period. But even after the end of this epoch, the acculturation process continued to transform traditional societies and, in particular, age class systems.

Colonial impact pitted two global social and political systems against each other. There is no doubt that age class systems constitute a global social system for those societies where they represent the major ethneme. In the one case, as in the other, that is, in the case of the colonial system and in the age class system, all social life is involved – from the cognitive and ideological to the political and economic aspects.

The encounter of the two systems did not take place in a uniform manner in the sense that not all aspects were affected to the same degree. As is well known, acculturation brings about the mutual penetration of the original culture's elements with the culture it encounters. Sometimes these elements interact to bring about new forms, whereas in other cases one element may take the place of another in performing a particular function. For example, in societies where the formal education of the youths was entrusted to so-called tribal initiations, introduction of school systems did not entail any fusion with traditional initiation, but rather its substitution. The methods and instruments for the school system do not correspond at all to the methods and instruments of the initiation system, even though both systems can be considered to share the goal of education.

The military function of age classes among the Masai and Boran, for example, was hindered and restricted and its area of action modified. But this function, insofar as it continued to be expressed in the defense of the herds, was not eliminated. This same function among the Kikuyu of Kenya and Lagoon Peoples of the Ivory Coast was not just impeded but entirely deprived of significance. In the end, it was abandoned by the people themselves.

The political functions of the traditional systems, including age class systems, were consciously and systematically replaced by the colonial governments in their quest for domination. The consequences of this action were not uniform, for the ways in which the social and political substitution was carried out and imposed on the local populations differed. Thus, in the marginal societies of pastoralists, such as the Masai and Boran, the weight and political presence of the colonial government was almost always limited to a necessary minimum, allowing the traditional system to continue to function through "indirect rule." In contrast, today the independent government has asserted itself in a decisive way as a substitute system, extending its presence and imposing its own forms of representation and participation. For this reason, as I have already noted, the inevitable disintegration of the traditional system is now evident.

Among the Kikuyu and related societies, the penetration of the new way of life has been widespread. The central colonial government quickly substituted for the traditional system. The first aspect to be substituted was the educational system through the school system set up by the pioneering work of the missionaries; soon thereafter, new administrative institutions paved the way for the replacement of the previous political system. No direct attack was waged on the age class systems; there was no need. But there was a logic to the process. As soon as it was put in motion by the introduction of the new political and educational systems, the change was ineluctable. The new systems proved to be the most efficient instrument, even though indirect, for the crippling and ultimately disappearance of the age class system.

It thus seems clear that, the more comprehensive the phenomenon of acculturational substitution, the faster the decline in the traditional age class system. If, instead, the acculturation process, whether simply involving the fusion of foreign elements or the radical substitution of elements, touches only some of its many functions, the age class system tends to adapt, adjusting itself in structure and function but retaining substantially intact its own nature as a global social and political system.

The further the new social and political system advances – based as it is on a different conception and distribution of power, a different mode of production, new ideologies and religious practices, and alien marital and social norms – the more profoundly will the age class system be modified and the more likely will it disappear entirely.

The nature of age class systems

Now that I have come to the end of my comparative analysis of age class systems, we can see that the picture drawn is a complex one. It may be useful here to synthesize briefly some of my findings to shed light on the underlying characteristics of these systems.

The interrelations between classes and grades is a characteristic specific to age class systems, but these relations are found in a great variety of forms. The type of organization generated by age class systems is distinct from all other types because it is founded on the principle of age. However, the individual systems, although having this element in common, certainly do not exhibit univocal organizational forms. The manipulation of the age concept clearly permits wide variation in its application. This is evident from the series of ethnographic models we have discussed.

That age class systems are a unique type of social organization and that they show great variety in the manipulation of the age concept are both claims of primary importance. The age in question is obviously not physiological age, but rather structural age. This is the conceptual key needed to understand the workings of age class systems.

Application of the structural-age concept to age class systems produces two contrasting effects, the one homogenizing and the other diversifying. The ambivalence between equality and inequality is, in fact, one of the fundamental problems that age class systems must confront and deal with. Manipulation of structural age is the instrument used to correct and contain the negative aspects of the differentiation built into the system.

Structural age is a fictitious age, and it is as a *fictio juris* that it comes to be applied to everyone in recruiting classes and defining the functional limits of the classes themselves. Classification reduces the differentiating effect of physiological age; in the process of classifying, all those individuals recruited in the same class are assigned an identical structural age. For this reason, they form a unitary body, a class. And because their structural age – the principle of class membership – is the same for all, their status is equal and they deal with one another as equals. Thus, within an individual age class, structural age generates equality.

However, each new class is differentiated from the existing classes because each is already characterized by its own structural age. In actual language, the class differentiation is indicated in terms of seniority. But in the age class systems, seniority – a concept that recurs wherever reference is made to age – is not that caused by physiological age, though it may coincide with it. Rather, seniority is determined by structural age. Thus, in relations between classes, structural age is the basis of differentiation and inequality.

It is up to the age grades to regulate the relations of class differentiation and limit the consequences of inequality. The series of grades represents the order of the classes, determined by the chronological order of their formation, or in other words by the specific structural age of each class. The succession of grades regulates the distribution of functions, and therefore of power, among the classes. In fact, along with their passage through the series of grades, the social status of the members of each class and the functions attributed to them change. Thus, in the same way that there are multiple grades, there are also multiple functions of age class systems. The multifunctionality or polivalence of the functions involved is another important characteristic of age class systems.

The uniqueness of age class systems not only results from the manipulation of structural age, but is also clear from the fact that the social orders established by the systems had a global extension in the sense that they affected all aspects of social life. To the question that has frequently stimulated scholars' discussions regarding the nature of age class systems, it is not legitimate to respond simply as if their functions were virtually limited to organizing military activity. In reality, the situation was complex. There is no doubt that certain functions were more visible than others, to the extent that they were taken to be the main characteristics of the system. But it is likewise clear that these same age class systems have, or had, at the same time, political, military, social, economic, and ritual functions, in addition to providing a cognitive basis for interpreting life and orienting action. In particular, it is worth emphasizing the regulation of the timing of marriage of the members of each class, and, in some cases, the regulation of the time at which it was legitimate to sire male and female children. From this observation, there emerges another characteristic, as noted by Legesse and Paulme: Age class systems have the effect of a birth-control plan.

In light of the multiple functions of age class systems, the meaning to assign the concept of power in this context seems clear. It should not be limited to, or identified with, the concept of political power; it involves the entirety of social activity. The concept of power thus assumes a global sense. At the same time, it is fractionalized as it is distributed to the classes as they move through the ladder of age grades. The succession of classes through grades, in fact, constitutes the mechanism for the distribution of power, for its abstract definition and practical limits.

The order created by age class systems represents an integrated and dynamic social and political order. Its integration results from the global interests regulated by these systems. Its dynamism derives from the physiological renewal occasioned by the continual birth of new individuals who are ultimately recruited into the system. Age class systems are also characterized by the fact that they continue to form new classes and to guarantee their succession through the grades that define the functions appropriate to each class during the period they are associated with the grade.

The typical characteristics of age class systems should be seen, first of all, from a synchronic perspective. However, this perspective should not mean seeing the systems as static. In fact, they are subject to change in terms of both development and entropy. Although it is useful to analyze individual systems synchronically and to compare them as such, it is evident that we can only attain an adequate understanding of them through a diachronic, historical perspective. Unfortunately, the possibility of acquiring such a perspective is limited by the lack of relevant documentation. But it should be clear that, in any case, we can only provide an adequate historical evaluation if we first have some preliminary understanding of the specific characteristics of these systems.

Contact with different sociopolitical systems, especially those of strong and dominant societies as occurred in the colonial period, not only exposed age class systems to change, but also made them vulnerable to extinction. New institutions were substituted for old ones connected to age class systems, and the past functions and activities of those systems diminished. The solidity of the systems eroded, and structural age lost its efficacy as the ordering principle. As a result, the value of age grades also diminished. There remained, however, some reference to informal grades. But these are the categories found everywhere: youths and elders. The kind of gradation such categories represent cannot be confused and identified with the age classes and age grades that form age class systems. In these systems, classes and grades are not informal groups, but rather institutionalized units. Institutionalization both of classes and grades through processes of formal structuring is the last of the characteristics that I emphasize. It is this fundamental characteristic that marks age class systems and differentiates them from every other kind of system involving the generic use of age.

Glossary

Italicized words are defined under their own entries.

age association: A spontaneously formed or noninstitutionalized grouping of age mates who have common interests in cooperation involving social, cultural, religious, political, economic, sports, or other activities.

age class: An institutionalized grouping, formally constituted according to different models. Members of a class form an egalitarian, corporate group that passes together through the progression of social grades. Class membership constitutes the jural basis for the acquisition of the executive right to engage in the social activities appropriate to each grade.

age class systems: Social formations founded on the classification of the society's members on the basis of structural age.

age grades, informal: The stages of physiological and social development commonly employed in distinguishing among the members of a society. Examples are childhood, adolescence, youth, adulthood, old age. The indication is always approximate.

age grades, institutionalized: The promotional stages traversed by age classes that determine people's status and their executive right to undertake social activities.

age groups: Generic groupings of age mates, either formal or informal. The term's meaning always depends on the situation and context. Despite its generic nature, the term can be used concretely to refer to all sorts of groupings. When used as a synonym for *age class*, without further specification, the term leads to confusion.

age set: Any institutionalized grouping of age mates.

age society: A generic term, used synonymously with both *age association* and *age class*. More specifically, it has been used to indicate the systems of the choreographic model found among the North American Prairie Indians.

age system: The way in which, in individual societies, age is socially employed.

anthropeme: Any basic element of meaning in a cultural system.

choreographic model: Those *age class systems* that are based on the right to perform certain songs and dances.

Glossary

ethneme: Any component element of the social structure (e.g., the kinship system, the territorial system).

ethnographic model: A description of the principles regulating the structure and functions of *age class systems*.

generational model: Those *age class systems* that are organized on the basis of the structural distance between a father and his sons.

initiation: The formal aspect of the enculturation process. It may take different forms but the intent is normally the promotion of youths to the grades of adults.

initiation model: Those *age class systems* that employ postpubertal *initiation* to recruit class members.

initiation-transition model: A variant of the *initiation model* in which at a certain point in the life course class membership is no longer the basis for the corporate transition of the class to a new grade.

initiation unit: Institutionalized grouping of age mates who go through *initiation* together. Such a unit normally blends into a class at the time in which class recruitment closes. It is sometimes referred to as a subclass.

promotion and promotional passages: The points that signal the passage of classes from grade to grade (the French term *promotion* can be used as a synonym for age class).

regimental model: Those *age class systems* in which the age classes are transformed into military regiments.

relative age: The use of social age to distinguish between different individuals or groups.

residential model: Those *age class systems* in which age classes serve to order residential distribution and social activities within the villages.

social age: Conceptualization of physiological age for purposes of social participation.

structural age: The elaboration of social age for purposes of social organization.

References

Abrahams, R. G.
  1978   "Aspects of Labwor Age and Generation Grouping and Related Systems," in Baxter and Almagor 1978: 37–67.
Almagor, Uri
  1978a   "The Ethos of Equality among the Dassenetch Age-Peers," in Baxter and Almagor 1978: 69–93.
  1978b   *Pastoral Partners. Affinity and Bond Partnership among the Dassanetch of South-West Ethiopia.* Manchester: Manchester University Press.
Augé, Marc
  1975   *Théorie des pouvoirs et idéologie. Etude de cas en Côte d'Ivoire.* Paris: Hermann.
Balandier, George
  1974   *Anthropo-logique.* Paris: Presses Universitaires de France.
Barth, Fredrick
  1966   *Models of Social Organization.* London: Royal Anthropological Institute Occasional paper no. 23.
Baumann, H., R. Thurnwald, and D. Westermann.
  1940   *Volkerkunde von Afrika.* Essen: Essener Verlaganstalt.
Bauman, H., and D. Westermann
  1948   *Les peuples et les civilisations de l'Afrique.* French trans. L. Homburger. Paris: Payot.
Baxter, Paul T.W.
  1954   "Social Organization of the Boran of Northern Kenya" University of Oxford (D. Phil. thesis).
  1977   "Boran Age-Sets and Warfare," in Fukui and Turton 1977:69–95.
  1978   "Boran Age-Sets and Generation-Sets: *Gada,* a Puzzle or a Maze?," in Baxter and Almagor 1978: 151–82.
Baxter, P.T.W., and Uri Almagor
  1978   *Age, Generation and Time. Some Features of East-African Age Organisations.* London: C. Hurst.
Beckingham, C.F., and G. W. B. Huntingford (eds. and trans.)
  1954   *Some Records of Ethiopia 1593–1646.* London: Hakluyt Society.
Bernardi, Bernardo
  1952   The Age Systems of the Nilo-Hamitic Peoples. *Africa* 22: 316–32.
  1955   The Age System of the Masai. *Annali Lateranensi* 18: 257–318.
  1959   *The Mugwe. A Failing Prophet.* London: Oxford University Press.
  1971   II Mugwe dei Meru, Kenya. *Africa* (Roma) 26: 427–42.

References

1973   Review of R. Buitenhuijs, *Le Mouvement 'Mau Mau': une Revolte Paysanne et Anti-Coloniale en Afrique Noire*. *Africa* 43: 374–5.
1983   *Il Mugwe. Un profeta che scompare*. Milano: Fr. Angeli.

Bernsten, John L.
1979   Maasai Age-Sets and Prophetic Leadership: 1850–1910. *Africa* 49: 134–46.

Bischofsberger, Otto
1972   *The Generation Classes of the Zanaki, Tanzania*. Fribourg, Switzerland: University Press of Fribourg.

Blackhurst, Hector
1978   "Continuity and change in the Shoa Galla *Gada* System," in Baxter and Almagor 1978: 245–67.

Bonte, Pierre
1974   *Organisation économique et sociale des pasteurs d'Afrique Orientale*. Paris: C.E.R.M.
1983   "Structures d'âge, organisation familiale et systèmes de parenté en Afrique de l'Est" (to be published in M. Abeles et C. Collard [eds.] *Age et Ainesse* (typewritten copy personally obtained from the author).

Bowers, A.W.
1959   *Mandan Social Ceremonial Organization*. Chicago: University of Chicago Press.
1965   Hidatsa Social and Ceremonial Organization. *Bulletin of the Bureau of American Ethnology*, 194.

Brantley, Cynthia
1978   Gerontocratic Government: Age-Sets in Pre-Colonial Giriama. *Africa* 48: 248–64.

Bryant, A.T.
1929   *Olden Times in Zululand and Natal*. London: Longmans.

Cagnolo, Carlo
1933   *The Akikuyu. Their Customs, Traditions and Folklore*. Nyeri: Mission Printing School.

Cecchi, Antonio
1886   *Da Zeila alle frontiere del Kaffa*. Roma: Società Geografica Italiana.

Cerulli, Enrico
1922   "The Folk Literature of the Galla of Southern Abyssinia," in E. A. Hooton (ed.), *Harvard African Studies*, vol. 3: 1–228. Cambridge, Mass.: Harvard University.
1923   I riti dell'iniziazione nella tribù Galla. *Rivista di Studi Orientali* 9: 480–95.
1933   *Etiopia Occidentale*.
         Roma: Sindacato Italiano di Arti Grafiche.

Cohen, Abner
1974   *Two-Dimensional Man. An Essay on the Anthropology of Power and Symbolism in Complex Society*. Berkeley: University of California Press.
1979   Political Symbolism. *Annual Review of Anthropology* 8: 87–113.

Cooper, John M.
1979   *The Gros Ventres of Montana. Part II. Religion and Ritual* (orig. ed. 1957) Regina Flannery. Catholic University of America anthropological series, 16. Washington, D.C.; Catholic University of America.

Douglas, Mary
1959   Age-Status among the Lele, *Zaire* 13: 386–413.
1963   *The Lele of the Kasai*. London: Oxford University Press.

Driberg, J.H.
1927   "*Age-Grades*," in *Encyclopedia Britannica*, 14th ed., vol. 1, 344–5.

References

Dundas, Charles
   1915   The Organization and Laws of Some Bantu Tribes in East Africa. *Journal of Royal Anthropological Institute* 45: 234–306.
Dundas, K.R.
   1908   Kikuyu Rika. *Man* 101: 180–2.
Durkheim, E., and M. Mauss
   1903   De quelques formes primitives de classification. *Année Sociologique* 1901–2: 1–72.
Dutto, Carl A.
   1975   *Nyeri Townsmen, Kenya.* Nairobi: E. A. Literature Bureau.
Dyson-Hudson, Neville
   1963   The Karimojong Age System. *Ethnology* 2: 353–401.
   1966   *Karimojong Politics.* Oxford: Clarendon Press.
Ehret, Christopher
   1974   "Cushites and the Highland and Plain Nilotes to A.D. 1800," in B.A. Ogot (ed.), *Zamani, a Survey of East African History*: 150–69. Nairobi: Longman Kenya (new edition).
Eisenstadt, S.N.
   1954   Plains Indian Age Groups: Some Comparative Notes. *Man* 44: 6–8.
   1956   *From Generation to Generation: Age Groups and Social Structure.* New York: Free Press.
Evans-Pritchard, E.E.
   1939   "Introduction," in Peristiany 1939: xix–xxxiv.
   1940a   *The Nuer. A Description of the Modes of Livelihood and Political Institutions of a Nilotic People.* Oxford: Clarendon Press.
   1940b   "The Nuer of Southern Sudan," in Fortes and Evans-Pritchard 1940: 272–96.
Flannery, Regina
   1953   *The Gros Ventres of Montana. Part I. Social Life.* Catholic University of America anthropological series, 15. Washington, D.C.: Catholic University of America.
Forde, Daryll, and G. I. Jones
   1950   *The Ibo and Ibibio-speaking peoples of south-eastern Nigeria.* London: International African Institute.
Fortes, Meyer, and E. E. Evans-Pritchard (eds.)
   1940   *African Political Systems.* London: Oxford University Press.
Fosbrooke, H. A.
   1948   An Administrative Survey of the Masai Social System. *Tanganyika Notes and Records* 26: 1–50.
   1956   The Masai Age-Group System as a Guide to Tribal Chronology. *African Studies* 15: 188–206.
Fratkin, Elliot
   1977   "A comparison of the role of prophets in Samburu and Maasai warfare", in Fukui and Turton 1977: 53–67.
Fukui, K., and David Turton (eds.)
   1979   *Warfare among East African Herders.* Osaka: National Museum of Ethnology.
Galaty, John G.
   1983   Ceremony and Society: The Poetics of Maasai Ritual. *Man* 18: 361–82.
Giaccaria, B. and A. Heide
   1971   *Auwe-uptabi. Uomini veri. Vita xavante.* Torino: Società Editrice Internazionale.

176

References

Glazier, Jack
  1976   Generation Classes among the Mbeere. *Africa* 46: 313–25.
Gluckman, Max
  1940   "The kingdom of the Zulu of South Africa," in Fortes and Evans-Pritchard 1940: 25–55.
  1962   *Essays on the Ritual of Social Relations.* Manchester: Manchester University Press.
Goody, Jack
  1976   "Aging in Nonindustrial Societies," in R. H. Binstock and E. Shanas (eds.), *Handbook of Aging and the Social Sciences*: 117–29. New York: Van Nostrand.
Guidi, I.
  1907   "Historia Gentis Galla," in K. Conti Rossini, *Historia Regis Sarsa Dengel (Malak Sagad)*, c.s.c., 1907, S.Ae. 3, pp. 221–32 (text), S.Ae. 4, pp. 195–208 (translation).
Gulliver, Philip H.
  1953   The Age Set Organization of the Jie Tribe. *Journal of Royal Anthropological Society* 83: 147–68.
  1958   The Turkana Age Organization. *American Anthropologist* 60: 900–22.
  1963   *Social Control in an African Society. A Study of the Arusha: Agricultural Masai of Northern Tanganyika.* London: Routledge & Kegan Paul.
  1968   "Age Differentiation," in *International Encyclopedia of the Social Sciences*, Vol. 1: 157–62. New York: Macmillan Free Press.
Haberland, Eike
  1963   *Galla Süd-Äthiopiens.* Stuttgart: W. Kohlhammer.
Hailey, Lord Malcolm
  1950   *Native Administration in the British African Territories Part 1—East Africa: Uganda, Kenya, Tanganyika.* London: Oxford University Press.
Hallpike, Christopher R.
  1972   *The Konso of Ethiopia. A Study of the Values of a Cushitic People.* Oxford: Clarendon Press.
Hamer, John H.
  1970   Sidamo Generational Class Cycles: Political Gerontocracy. *Africa* 40: 50–70.
Henige, David P.
  1974   *The Chronology of Oral Tradition. Quest for a Chimera.* London: Oxford University Press.
Hinnant, John
  1978   "The Guji; *Gada* as a Ritual System," in Baxter and Almagor 1978: 207–43.
Holding, E. Mary
  1942   Some Preliminary Notes on Meru Age Grades. *Man* 31: 58–65.
Hollis, A. C.
  1905   *The Masai: Their Language and Folklore.* London: Oxford University Press.
Huntingford, G. W. B.
  1951   The Social Institutions of the Dorobo. *Anthropos* 46: 30–5.
  1953   *The Nandi of Kenya: Tribal Control in a Pastoral Society.* London: Routledge & Kegan Paul.
Hurskainen, Arvi
  1984   *Cattle and Culture. The Structure of a Pastoral Parakuyo Society.* Helsinki: Finnish Oriental Society.

177

References

Jacobs, Alan H.
1965   "The Traditional Political Organization of the Pastoral Masai." University of Oxford (D. Phil. thesis).
1968   "A Chronology of the Pastoral Maasai," in B. A. Ogot, (ed.), *Hadith I*: 10–31. Nairobi: Historical Association of Kenya.
1971   The Warrior Village Ritual House of the Maasai. *Plan East Africa*, Journal of the Architectural Association of Kenya, 2: 17–21.
1979   "Maasai Inter-Tribal Relations: Belligerent Herdsmen or Peaceable Pastoralists," in Fukui and Turton 1979: 33–52.
Jeffreys, M. D. W.
1950   Age-group among the Ika and Kindred People. *African Studies* 9: 158–66.
Jensen, A. E.
1936   *Im Lamde der Gada*. Stuttgart: Strecker u. Schröder.
1954   Das Gada-System der Konso und die Altersklasses Systeme der Niloten. *Ethnos* 19: 1–23.
Johnston, H. H.
1902   *The Uganda Protectorate*. London: Hutchinson & Sons.
Jones, G. I.
1962   Ibo Age Organization with Special Reference to the Cross River and North Eastern Ibo. *Journal of the Royal Anthropological Institute* 92: 191–210.
Kenyatta, Jomo
1938   *Facing Mount Kenya*. London: Secker and Warburg.
Kertzer, David I.
1978   Theoretical Developments in the Study of Age-Group Systems. *American Ethnologist* 5: 368–74.
Kertzer, David I., and Oker B.B. Madison
1980   African Age-Set Systems and Political Organization: The Latuka of Southern Sudan. *L'Uomo* 4: 85–109.
1981   "Women's Age-Set Systems in Africa: the Latuka of Southern Sudan," in Christine L. Fry, (ed.), *Aging, Culture, and Health*: 109–13. New York: Praeger.
Krige, E. J.
1936   *The Social System of the Zulu*. London: Longmans.
Kuper, Hilda
1947   *An African Aristocracy: Rank among the Swazi*. London: Oxford University Press.
La Fontaine, J. S. (ed.)
1978   *Sex and Age as Principles of Social Differentiation*. London: Academic Press.
Lambert, H. E.
1947   *The Use of Indigenous Authorities in Tribal Administration. Studies of the Meru of Kenya Colony*. University of Cape Town: Communications of the School of African Studies, no. 16.
1956   *Kikuyu Social and Political Institutions*. London: Oxford University Press.
Legesse, Asmaron
1973   *Gada–Three Approaches to the Study of African Society*. New York: Free Press.
Levine, R. A., and W. H. Sangree
1962   The Diffusion of Age-Group Organization in East Africa; a Controlled Comparison. *Africa* 32: 97–110.

References

Lewis, Ioan
1961   *A Pastoral Democracy. A study of Pastoralism and Politics among the Norther Somali of the Horn of Africa*. London: Oxford University Press.
Lindig, Wolfgang
1970   *Geheimbünde und Männerbünde der Prärie – und der Waldlandindianer Nordamerikas – Untersucht am Beispiel der Omaha und Irokesen*. Wiesbaden: Fr. Steiner Verlag.
Lowie, Robert
1913   Societies of the Hidatsa and Mandan Indians. *Anthropological Papers of the American Museum of Natural History* 11: 219–358.
1916   Plains Indian Age-Societies: Historical and Comparative Summary. *Anthropological Papers of American Museum of Natural History* 11: 645–78.
1919   The Hidatsa Sun Dance. *Anthropological Papers of American Museum of Natural History* 16: 411–31.
1920   *Primitive Society*. New York: Liveright and Boni.
1948   "Age Societies," in *The Encyclopedia of the Social Sciences*, vol. 1: 482–3. New York: Macmillan.
McKenny, Michael G
1973   The Social Structure of the Nyakyusa. A re-evaluation. *Africa* 43: 91–107.
Mackenzie, W. J. M.
1967   *Politics and Social Sciences*. Harmondsworth. England: Penguin Books.
Maconi, Vittorio
1973   "L'iniziazione ai gruppi d'età femminili pressoi Karimojong." in Kurt Tauchmann (ed.). *Festschrift zum 65. Geburtstag von Helmut Petri*: 344–59. Köln: Böhlau Verlag.
Mahlobo, G. W. K., and E. J. Krige
1934   Transition from Childhood to Adulthood amongst the Zulu. *Bantu Studies* 8: 157–91.
Mair, Lucy
1964   *Primitive Government* (orig. ed. 1962). Harmondsworth, England: Penguin Books.
Maybury-Lewis, David
1974   *Akwe-Shavante Society* (orig. ed. 1967). London: Oxford University Press.
1984   "Age and kinship: A structural view," in David I. Kertzer and Jennie Keith (eds.), *Age and Anthropological Theory*: 123–40. Ithaca, N.Y.: Cornell University Press.
Merker, M.
1910   *Die Masai: ethnographisch Monographie eines ostafrikanischen Semitenvolkes*. 2d ed. Berlin: D. Reimer.
Middleton, John, and G. Kershaw
1965   *The Kikuyu and Kamba of Kenya*. London: International African Institute.
Middleton, John, and D. Tait
1958   *Tribes without Rulers*. London: Routledge & Kegan Paul.
Murdock, George P.
1959   *Africa: Its Peoples and their Culture History*. New York: McGraw-Hill.
1967   Ethnographic Atlas. *Ethnology* 6: 109–236; 481–7.
1968   Ethnographic Atlas. *Ethnology* 7: 106–12; 218–24.
Muriuki, Godfrey
1975   *A History of the Kikuyu: 1500–1900*. Nairobi: Oxford University Press.

References

Niangoran Bouah, G.
    1964   *La division du temps et le calendrier rituel des peuples lagunaires de Côte
            d'Ivoire*. Paris: Institut d'Ethnologie.
    1966   Les Abourés: une société lagunaire de Côte D'Ivoire. *Annales de l'Ecole
            de Lettres et Sciences Humaines de l'Université d'Abidjan* 1: 37–171.
Omer-Cooper, J.
    1976   "The Nguni outburst," in John E. Flint (ed.). *The Cambridge History of
            Africa*. Vol. 5: 319–52. Cambridge: Cambridge University Press.
Otite, Onigu
    1972   Continuance and Change in an Urhobo Age-Grade Organization. *Cahiers
            d'Etudes Africaines* 12–46: 302–15.
Ottenberg, Simon
    1968   *Double Descent in an African Society. The Afikpo Village-Group*. Seattle:
            University of Washington Press.
    1971   *Leadership and Authority in an African Society: The Afikpo Village-Group*.
            Seattle: University of Washington Press.
Parsons, Talcott
    1967   *Sociological Theory and Modern Society*. New York: Free Press.
Paulme, Denise (ed.)
    1966   Première approche des Aitié (Côte d'Ivoire). *Cahiers d'Etudes Africaines*
            6: 86–120.
    1971a   *Classes et associations d'âge en Afrique de l'ouest*. Paris: Plon.
    1971b   "Introduction," in Paulme (ed.) 1971a: 9–23.
    1971c   "Les classes d'âge dans le sud-est de la Côte d'Ivoire," in Paulme (ed.),
            1971a: 205–85.
Pecci, Domenico
    1941   Note sul sistema della gada e delle classi d'età presso le popolazioni Borana.
            Rassegna di Studi Etiopici 1: 305–21.
Peristiany, J. G.
    1939   *The Social Institutions of the Kipsigis*. London: G. Routledge & Sons.
    1951   The Age-Set System of the Pastoral Pokot. *Africa* 21: 188–206, 279–302.
    1975   "The Ideal and the Actual: The Role of Prophets in the Pokot Political
            System," in J. H. M. Beattie and R. G. Lienhardt, *Studies in Social An-
            thropology: Essays in Memory of E. E. Evans-Pritchard by His Former
            Oxford Colleagues*. Oxford: Clarendon Press.
Person, Yvonne M.
    1963   Classes d'âge et chronologie. *Latitudes*, n. spec.: 68–83.
    1964   "En quête d'une chronologie ivoirienne," in J. Vansina. R. Mauny, and
            L. V. Thomas (eds.), *The Historian in Tropical Africa*: 322–38. London:
            Oxford University Press.
Prins, A. H. J.
    1953   *East African Age-Class Systems. An Inquiry in the Social Order of Galla,
            Kipsigis and Kikuyu*. Groningen: J. B. Wolters.
Radcliffe-Brown, A. R.
    1929   Age-Organization–Terminology. *Man* 29: 21.
Ruel, M. J.
    1962   Kuria Generation Classes. *Africa* 32: 14–37.
    1969   *Leopards and Leaders. Constitutional Politics among a Cross River People*.
            London: Tavistock Publications.
Ritter, Madeline L.
    1980   The Conditions Favoring Age Set Organization. *Journal of Anthropological
            Research* 36: 87–104.

References

Schapera, Isaac
  1949   *Some Problems of Anthropological Research in Kenya Colony.* International
         African Institute memorandum 23. London: International African Institute.
Schurtz, H.
  1902   *Altersklasses und Männerbünde.* Berlin: D. Reimer.
Southall, Aldan
  1968   "Stateless Societies," in *International Encyclopedia of Social Sciences.* Vol.
         15: 157–68. New York: Macmillan and Free Press.
Spencer, Paul
  1965   *The Samburu, A Study of Gerontocracy in a Nomadic Tribe.* London: Rou-
         tledge & Kegan Paul.
  1973   *Nomads in Alliance. Symbiosis and Growth among the Rendille and Samburu
         of Kenya.* London: Oxford University Press.
  1976   Opposing Streams and the Gerontocratic Ladder: Two Models of Age Or-
         ganization in East Africa. *Man* 11: 153–74.
Sperber, Dan
  1974   La notion d'aînesse et ses paradoxes chez les Dorzé d'Ethiopie Meridionale.
         Cahiers International de Sociologie 56: 63–78.
Stanley, S., and D. Karsten
  1968   The Luwa System of the Garbiččo subtribe of the Sidama (Southern Ethiopia)
         as a Special Case of an Age Set System. *Paideuma* 14: 93–102.
Stewart, Frank H.
  1977   *Fundamentals of Age-Group Systems.* New York: Academic Press.
Thomson, J.
  1885   *Through Masai Land.* London: Sampson Low, Marston.
Tignor, Robert L.
  1972   The Maasai Warriors: Pattern Maintenance and Violence in Colonial Kenya.
         Journal of African History 13: 271–90.
Turner, Victor
  1955   The Spatial Separation of Generations in Ndembu Village Structure. *Africa*
         25: 121–37.
Uchendu, Victor C.
  1965   *The Igbo of Southern Nigeria.* New York: Holt, Rhinehart & Winston.
Von Wied-Neuwied, Maximilian
  1839   *Reise in das innere Nord-Amerika in den Jahren 1832 bis 1834.* Coblenz:
         J. Hoelscher (vol. 1; vol. 2–1841).
Webster, Hutton
  1932   *Primitive Secret Societies: a Study in Early Politics and Religion* (orig. ed.
         1908). New York: Macmillan.
Whyte, W. F.
  1944   Age-Grading of the Plains Indians. *Man* 56: 68–72.
Wilson, Monica
  1951   *Good Company. A Study of Nyakyusa Age-Villages.* London: Oxford Uni-
         versity Press.
  1959   *Communal Rituals of the Nyakyusa.* London: Oxford University Press.
Wissler, Clark
  1913   Societies and Dance Associations of the Blackfoot Indians. *Anthropological
         Papers of American Museum of Natural History* 11: 359–460.
  1918   The Sun Dance of the Blackfoot Indians. *Anthropological Papers of Amer-
         ican Museum of Natural History.* 16: 225–70.

Index

183

Index

Bamileké, 13
balli, 78, 85
   walirrafudu, 78, 85
Bantu-Cushites, Bantu-Cushitic, 12
Bantu-Hamites, Bantu-Hamitic, 12, 24
Bari, 12
Bassari, 13
BAXTER, P.T.W., 22, 23, 27, 29, 33, 35,
   36, 74, 75, 77, 78, 80, 81, 142, 158,
   160, 163
BECKINGHAM, C.F., 74
Bedik, 13
BERNARDI, B., 20, 21, 25, 45, 56, 86, 152
bilineal societies, 14, 41–2
birth – genealogical, physiological, 5, 9, 10,
   40, 77, 146
birth control, 80, 170
birthday, 9
Blackfoot, 14, 120, 126
BLACKHURST, H., 92, 93
Bobo, 13
BONTE, P., 23, 149
Boran, 10, 12, 32, 73–4, 75, 81, 84–6, 87,
   89, 92, 93, 137, 141, 145, 148, 150,
   163, 164, 166, 168
BOWER, A.V., 120, 125
breath of men, 110
Bwa Pesya, 13
Bushmen, 25
butta, 82
butwa, 116

Caraja (Karaja), 14
CECCHI, A., 78
celibacy, 41, 49
centralization, 29, 119
chief, chiefdom, 15, 24, 25, 71, 95, 106,
   108–9, 110, 116, 119
choreographic model (*see* model)
chronological factor, chronology, 6, 7, 33, 36,
   106, 146–7, 162
chronos, 151
cibra, 84
cicisbean union, 82, 150
circumcision, 18, 47, 48, 58, 59, 73, 78, 81,
   86, 96, 114, 133, 163
"class in power," 31–2
class d'âge, 17
Classe d'età, 17
climaterics, 1
clitoridectomy, 96, 165
coevals, coevality, 2, 5, 21, 47
cognatic kin, 25
COHEN, A., 33
colonial government, impact, 45, 163
comprehensive age-group system, 21
complementarity of age classes, 153

complementary opposition, 26
conflicts, 8, 29, 30, 70
conscripts, 1, 14, 31
contiguity (adjacent classes), 54, 89, 102
contradictions of age class systems, 71–2, 76,
   81–3
COOPER, J.M., 128
corporate groups, 5, 21, 27, 47, 123, 131,
   144, 159, 160
corrective measures, 76, 169
council, 28, 69, 98, 100, 121, 138
   of women, 133, 134
councillors, 77, 85, 106, 138
cuc (*see harriya*)
cusa, 75, 76–7, 79, 82 (*see kussa*)
Cushites, 76

Daarood, 12
daballe, 75, 76, 79, 89, 90, 92, 145
dances, 41, 67, 68, 112, 121–2, 123–5, 127,
   128–9, 130
dannisa, 82, 85
darara, 84
Dassanetch, 12, 148, 166
diachronic perspective, 48, 171
didica, 75
differentiation, 20, 30, 111, 146–7, 170
Digil, 12
Dinka, 12
disengagement, 70–1
disharmony, 72
distance, structural, 6, 39, 40, 73, 75, 77, 79,
   81, 144, 150
distribution, geographical, 11
distributive character, legitimacy, 26, 29, 30,
   94
Dodoth, 12
dori, 75, 90
doroma, 92
DOUGLAS, M., 94
DUNDAS, C., 24, 60
DUNDAS, K.R., 133
DURKHEIM, E., 146
DUTTO, C., 166
Dwala, 13
dwasama (*duassanowa*), 106

Ebrie, 13, 100, 103, 104, 106
economic activity, system, 49, 50–1, 158–60
EHRET, C., 12
EISENSTADT, S.N., 22, 147
embolosat, 46, 55, 56
Embu, 12, 20
emurata ekedyene, 47
emurata etatene, 47
enculturation, 1, 144–6
endungore engibata, 1, 144–6

184

Index

endungore ol piron, 58
equality, egalitarianism, 30, 53–5, 67, 97, 146–7, 152, 153, 156, 169–70
ethneme, ethnemic, 38, 143–4, 148
ethnos, 151
eunoto, 46, 47, 55, 56
EVANS-PRITCHARD, E.E., 9, 17, 18, 19, 20, 25, 26, 42
evolutionary theory, 15

faction, 60, 63, 66, 70
family activity, 50–1
farida, 135
female age classes, 21, 134
FLANNERY, R., 128
folkloric function, 117–9
folle, 92
FORDE, D., 94
FORTES, M., 18, 19, 25, 26
formal, formalization, 2, 3, 7, 16, 22, 33, 58, 83, 99, 148
FOSBROOKE, H.A., 52, 56, 60

Gã, 166
Gabbra, 12, 166
gada, 10, 11, 35, 40, 70, 73, 74–83, 84, 86, 87, 88, 90, 91, 92, 93, 144, 145, 150, 157, 163
GALATY, J.G., 47
Galla, 11, 12, 22, 73, 82, 133, 163
gamme, 75, 76, 79
gasapaneta, 21
gê speaking peoples, 14, 62
generation, 5, 6, 8, 32, 38, 44, 45, 73, 74, 110, 145
generational classes, 6
generational distance, 4
generational model (*see* model)
generational relationship, 101–2
generational rule, 79
generational system, 20
gerontocracy, 30, 59, 61, 95, 99
GIACCARIA, B., 62–6,
giefio, 105
global control, system, 43, 167, 170
GLUCKMAN, M., 114, 117, 118
gogessa (*see* patriclass)
Gona, 74, 85
government, diffused, 32, 77, 106, 155
Gros Ventres, 14, 120, 128–31
GUIDI, I., 74
GULLIVER, P.H., 20, 21, 45, 58–9, 137
Guji, 34, 86–93
gumi gayo, 78, 163
Gusii, 12

HABERLAND, E., 22
HAILEY, Lord, 57
HALLPIKE, C.R., 91, 135
harriya, 74, 77, 83–4, 91
harriya cuch (*cuc*), 83
HEIDE, A., (*see* GIACCARIA)
HENIGE, D.P., 37
Hidatsa, 120, 121–5, 139
hierarchy, 120–1
HINNANT, J., 34, 87, 88, 89, 90
ho, 67
HOLLIS, A.C., 3
hunting, 120, 125, 126, 153
HUNTINGFORD, G.W.B., 33, 74
HURKAINEN, A., 22, 47, 57, 157

Igbo, 25
ikpo, 96
il dasat, 48, 49
il moruak, 48, 49, 51
il murran, 48, 49 (*see* moran)
il oibonok, 45 (*see* laibon)
il oikop, 45
il piron, 48, 49, 51 (*see* piron)
incision, 18
Indians (*see* Prairie Indians)
individual, 7, 156–8
inequality, (*see* differentiation, equality)
infants, 70, 73, 79 (*see* daballe)
infanticide, 77, 82, 83, 90, 150
informal age grades, 2, 4, 14, 63–5
initiation, 5, 15, 38, 39, 44, 48, 62, 66–8, 73, 94, 101, 114, 115, 154
initiation model (*see* model)
initiation-transition model (*see* model)
initiation unit (*see* units)
institutionalization, 3, 4, 36, 63, 97
intal, 76
intangu, 116
interrelationship of age classes and age grades, 2, 3, 6, 28, 35, 36, 42, 91, 92, 169
intersecting kinship, 26
isogu, 96
itimaka, 92
iuba (*see* yuba)

JACOB, A., 22, 45, 148
jarsa, 76, 78, 79, 90
jarsa gudurru, 90
Jie, 12, 20, 123
JOHNSTON, H.H., 3
JONES, G.I., 96
jurisdictional hierarchy, 14
jutshwa, 116

Kalenjin, 12, 166
kallacha (*kallacia*), 87, 88

185

Index

Index

Nawdeba, 13
Ndebele, 13, 112
Ndembu, 12, 112
ndundu ya atumia, 133, 134
ngeherr, 46, 47, 55, 56
ngesher, 58
Ngoni, 13, 113
Nguni, 13, 31, 112–9
NIANGORAN, B.G., 100, 103
Nilo Hamites, Nilo-Hamitic, 12, 20, 21, 22, 152, 166
Nilotic, 12
nodzeu, 140
ntanga, 116
Nuer, 6, 12, 17, 18, 25, 42, 71, 133
Nyakyusa, 12, 40, 94, 95, 107–11, 133, 144, 151

odwo, 136
oikos, 151
ol aigwenani, 50, 55, 56, 57
ol aunoni, 50, 55, 57, 157, 158
ol oiboni, 45 (*see laibon*)
ol murrani, 45 (*see moran*)
officials, 56, 68
okpo ntu, 139
order – cognitive, social, 6, 26, 29, 33, 36, 37, 89
orkoyot, 33, 36
Oromo, 6, 9, 11, 12, 34, 35, 40, 70, 73–93, 150, 157, 163, 166
OTTENBERG, S., 95, 96, 97, 98, 99, 100, 139

pahiriwa, 68
papa lainei, 57, 157
Parakuyo, 12, 157–8
parallelism, women's, 134–7, 141
PARSONS, T., 26
patriclass, 77, 80–1, 90, 149
patrilineal, patrilineality, 5, 14, 46, 63, 66, 74, 95, 96, 97, 100, 102, 103, 107, 137–9, 141–2
PAULME, D., 22, 23, 99, 102, 104, 105, 106, 107, 138, 166, 167
PECCI, D., 74, 75, 76, 77, 81, 84, 85
PESRISTIANY, J.G., 19, 20
physiological age, 3
piron, 51, 58, 60
Pokomo, 12
Pokot (Suk), 12, 133
police, 98, 124, 125
political activity, 27
political authority, 86, 163
political control, 141–2
political function, 168
political order, 141–2

political power, 25, 26, 27, 28, 32, 106, 147, 154
political system, 14, 17, 18, 19, 24, 26, 27, 109, 119, 155, 168
polity, primary, 25, 26, 29, 35, 71, 84–6, 116
postpubertal initiation (*see* initiation)
power, 8, 9, 26, 27, 28, 142, 154
  allocation of, 154–6, 170
  attainment of, 71, 104, 105
  decision making, 32, 51–2, 98
  distribution, 21, 28, 29, 30, 154
  holding, 103
  legitimizing, 29
  personal, 57
  polivalent, 33
  potential, effective, 28, 30, 32, 33, 40, 47, 53, 69, 78, 89, 94, 153
  rotation, 152, 155
  supernatural, 34, 52, 53, 123–4, 129
Prairie Indians, 14, 15, 34, 120, 130, 158
prestige, 27, 35, 57, 97, 99, 125, 143
PRINS, A.H.J., 21, 22, 144
promotion, 3, 4, 29, 108–9, 122, 144
purchase, 121–2, 126, 127, 130
Pukapuka, 13

qumbhusa, 115

raba
  didica, dori, 75, 77–8, 79, 82, 83, 84
  mido, 90
RADCLIFFE-BROWN, A.R., 17
Rahawiin, 12
recruitment, 3, 5, 7, 10, 27, 28, 35, 36, 38, 39, 44, 48, 58, 66, 73, 83, 86, 94, 102, 115, 116, 121, 128, 144, 160, 163
reform, 31, 114, 119
regiment, 114, 116, 117
regimental model (*see* model)
religious conceptions, 6, 93, 124, 125, 129
Rendille, 12, 33
residence, 105, 106, 109, 125
residential model (*see* model)
retirement, 1, 29
rika, 165
ritai 'wa, 69
rites of passage, 4, 5, 33, 34, 46, 73
RITTER, M.L., 23
ritual, 38, 46, 47, 78, 81, 86
  observances, 87
  promotion, 4, 35, 108, 110
  recruitment, 34, 36
  superintegration, 26
ritualization, 33–6, 148
rivalry, 54

187

Index

CAMBRIDGE STUDIES IN SOCIAL ANTHROPOLOGY

Editor: Jack Goody

189

*Also available as a paperback